THE CULINARY INSTITUTE
OF AMERICA'S

Gourmet Meals in Minutes

ELEGANTLY SIMPLE MENUS AND RECIPES FROM
THE WORLD'S PREMIER CULINARY INSTITUTE

The Culinary Institute of America
HYDE PARK, NEW YORK

Photography by Ben Fink

LEBHAR-FRIEDMAN BOOKS
NEW YORK · CHICAGO · LOS ANGELES · LONDON · PARIS · TOKYO

THE CULINARY INSTITUTE OF AMERICA

Vice-President, Continuing Education	Mark Erickson
Director of Marketing and New Product Development	Sue Cussen
Editorial Project Managers	Lisa Lahey and Mary Donovan
Editorial Assistants	Margaret Otterstrom and Rachel Toomey
Marketing Project Assistant	Amy Townsend
Recipe Tester	Lynn Tonelli

The Culinary Institute of America would like to thank chefs Olivier Andreini, Bruce Mattel, and Michael Skibitcky
for their skilled execution and presentation of the recipes and methods for the photographs.

LEBHAR-FRIEDMAN BOOKS

A company of Lebhar-Friedman, Inc., 425 Park Avenue, New York, New York 10022

LIBRARY OF CONGRESS CATALOGING-IN-PUBLICATION DATA

Cataloging-in-publication data for this title is on file with the Library of Congress.

ISBN 0-86730-904-0

Designed and composed by Kevin Hanek
Set in Adobe Jenson

Photography by Ben Fink; photography appearing on pages 48, 58, 64,
67, 72, 78, 81, and 83,© 2004 by Louis Wallach

Manufactured in Singapore by Imago Worldwide Printing on acid-free paper

Contents

Introduction vii

CHAPTER ONE

Prior to Cooking

1

CHAPTER TWO

Appetizers

13

Tomatillo Salsa • Cannellini Bean Puree • Guacamole • Wonton Chips with Asian-Style Dipping Sauce • Hummus with Pita Chips • Fiery Fruit Salsa • Tapenade • Cucumber Raita • Papaya and Black Bean Salsa • Tomato Salsa • Salsa de Chipotle • Black Bean and Avocado Crostini • Prosciutto and Melon Canapé • Lobster and Prosciutto Crostini • Goat Cheese and Sweet Onion Crostini • Mussel Crostini • Shrimp Open-Faced Sandwich • Garlic and Parsley Butter • Marinated Goat Cheese with Fresh Herbs • Grilled Vegetable Appetizer • Prosciutto and Summer Melon Salad • Salad of Crab and Avocado • Shrimp Cocktail • Camembert Crisps • Spiced Mixed Nuts • Spicy Roasted Cashews • Chili-Roasted Peanuts with Dried Cherries

CHAPTER THREE

Soups

49

Vichyssoise • Thai Fresh Pea Soup • Curried Apple Squash Soup • Traditional Black Bean Soup • Chilled Cream of Avocado • Cream of Mushroom Soup • Cream of Tomato Soup with Rice and Basil • Corn Chowder with Chiles and Monterey Jack • Crab and Mushroom Chowder • Manhattan Clam Chowder • New England Clam Chowder • Shrimp Bisque with Fresh Tarragon • Double Chicken Broth with Shiitakes, Scallions, and Tofu • Egg Drop Soup • Stracciatella alla Romana • Amish-Style Chicken and Corn Soup • Chilled Gazpacho • Borscht • Chorizo and Vegetable Soup • Minestrone • Hlelm • Mussel Soup • Thai Hot and Sour Soup • Tortilla Soup

CHAPTER FOUR

Salads

85

French Lentil Salad • Panzanella • Soba Noodle Salad • Cucumber, Tomato, and Feta Salad • Mediterranean Salad • Spinach Salad with Tangerines and Mango • Orange and Fennel Salad • Mixed Bean and Grain Salad • Roasted Beet Salad • Fruit Salad with Orange-Blossom Syrup • Warm Salad of Hearty Greens and Blood Oranges with Tangerine-Pineapple Vinaigrette • Waldorf Salad •

Mixed Green Salad with Pears, Walnuts, and Blue Cheese • Frisée with Walnuts, Apples, Grapes, and Blue Cheese • Baked Goat Cheese with Mesclun, Pears, and Toasted Almonds • Lemon-Infused Greek Salad with Grape Leaves • Romaine and Grapefruit Salad with Walnuts and Stilton • Spring Herb Salad • Lobster and Red Pepper Salad • Grilled Steak Salad with Horseradish Dressing • Niçoise-Style Grilled Tuna • Grilled Tuna with Spring Herb Salad and Marinated Tomatoes • Spinach Salad with Marinated Shiitakes and Red Onions • Grilled Chicken Caesar Salad • Traditional Cobb Salad • Grilled Chicken and Pecan Salad • Lemon-Parsley Vinaigrette • Lime-Cilantro Vinaigrette • Port Wine Vinaigrette • Balsamic Vinaigrette

CHAPTER FIVE

Meat

129

Stir-Fry Citrus Beef • Reuben Sandwich • Grilled Flank Steak • Satay of Beef with Peanut Sauce • Tenderloin of Beef with Blue Cheese and Herb Crust • Beef Tenderloin with Southwestern-Style Sauce • Veal Scallopine with Lemon and Capers • Pan-Fried Veal Cutlets • Veal Saltimbocca with Fettuccine • Cider-Braised Pork Medallions • Jerk Pork Kebabs • Roasted Pork Tenderloin with Honey-Mustard Sauce • Sautéed Pork Medallions with Southwestern-Style Sauce • Sautéed Pork Medallions with Apple Chutney • Fennel and Chorizo Strudels • Roasted Pork Loin with Apricot-Armagnac Compote • Thai-Spiced Loin Chops with Hot-Sweet Mustard • Eggplant and Prosciutto Panini • Broiled Lamb Chops with White Bean and Rosemary Ragout

CHAPTER SIX

Poultry

167

Chicken Breast with Artichokes and Mustard Sauce • Grilled Chicken Sandwich with Pancetta, Arugula, and Aïoli • Moroccan Lemon Chicken with Mango Chutney • Grilled Chicken Burritos • Jerk Chicken • Whole Wheat Quesadillas with Chicken, Jalapeño Jack, and Mango Salsa • Lemon-Ginger Grilled Chicken • Herb-Breaded Chicken with Creamy Mustard Sauce • Chicken Curry with Almonds • Pesto-Stuffed Chicken Breasts with Tomato Relish • Walnut Chicken • Spicy Szechuan Chicken Stir-Fry • Smoked Turkey and Roasted Red Pepper Sandwich • Turkey Burger • Duck, Shrimp, and Andouille Gumbo • Sautéed Duck Breast with Pinot Noir Sauce • Turkey Club Sandwich

CHAPTER SEVEN

Seafood

199

Flounder Sauté à la Meunière • Sea Bass with Gingered Broth • Spicy Asian Grilled Shrimp • Seared Salmon with a Moroccan Spice Crust • Scallop and Mushroom Gratin • Sautéed Shrimp with Penne Pasta and Puttanesca Sauce • Peanut-Crusted Catfish with Creole Rémoulade Sauce • Seared Tuna with Salsa Verde • Seared Scallops with Fiery Fruit Salsa • Salmon en Papillote • Oyster Po' Boy with Rémoulade • Mussels in Saffron and White Wine Broth • Grilled Swordfish with Lentil Ragout • Risotto with Scallops and Asparagus • Grilled Herbed Salmon with Southwest White Bean Stew • Bass and Scallops en Papillote • Grilled Halibut with Roasted Red and Yellow Pepper Salad • Crabmeat and Shrimp Sandwich • Seared Cod in a Rich Broth with Fall Vegetables • Classic Boiled Lobster • Broiled Swordfish with Tomatoes, Anchovies, and Garlic • Grilled Swordfish with Peppered Pasta

CHAPTER EIGHT

Vegetarian

235

Vegetable Stew • Tofu with Red Curry Paste, Pease, Scallions, and Cilantro • Goat Cheese and Red Onion Quesadilla • Vegetarian Refried Bean Quesadilla • Vegetable Fajitas • Vegetable Burgers • Stir-Fried Garden Vegetables with Marinated Tofu • Risotto with Peas and Scallions • Tempeh Club Sandwich • Spicy Vegetable Sauté • Moo Shu Vegetables • Chickpea and Vegetable Tagine • Pasta Quattro Formaggi • Asparagus with Shiitakes, Bowtie Pasta, and Spring Peas • Capellini with Grilled Vegetables • Eggplant and Havarti Sandwiches • Madeira-Glazed Portobello Sandwiches • Orechiette with Cannellini Beans & Spinach • Fettuccine with Corn, Squash, Chiles, Crème Fraîche, and Cilantro

CHAPTER NINE

Side Dishes

267

Roasted Carrots and Parsnips with Herbs • Tarragon Green Beans • Coleslaw • Warm Vegetable Slaw • Ratatouille • Sautéed Broccoli Rabe with Toasted Pine Nuts • Sautéed Swiss Chard • Summer Squash Sauté • Pan-Steamed Lemon Asparagus • Pan-Steamed Zucchini and Yellow Squash Noodles • Black Bean Salad with Lime-Cilantro Vinaigrette • Grilled Vegetables • Vegetarian Refried Beans • Sweet and Sour Green Beans • Haricots Verts with Walnuts • Haricots Verts with Prosciutto and Gruyère • Braised Belgian Endive • Sautéed Apples • Broccoli with Orange-Sesame Sauce • Sautéed Brussels Sprouts with Pancetta • Stewed Chickpeas with Tomato, Zucchini, and Cilantro • Artichokes and Mushrooms in White Wine Sauce • Asparagus with Morels • Asian Vegetable Slaw • Tabbouleh Salad • Bulgur and Lentil Pilaf with Carmelized Onions • Potato Gratin • Oven-Roasted Potatoes • Potato Puree • Mediterranean Potato Salad • Warm Potato Salad • Sweet Potato Cakes • Steak Fries • German Potato Salad • Boiled Potatoes with Saffron and Parsley • Jalapeño Jack Polenta • Corn, Pepper, and Jicama Salad • Lima Bean and Roasted Corn Succotash • Cornbread • Vegetarian Dirty Rice • Basic Rice Pilaf • Wild Rice Pilaf • Spicy Dill Rice • Rice Salad • Coconut Rice with Ginger • Curried Rice Salad • Herbed Basmati Rice • Quick Couscous • Herbed Israeli Couscous • Red Pepper Orzo

CHAPTER TEN

Desserts

331

Classic Caramel Sauce • Cider and Raisin Sauce • Vanilla Sauce • Hot Fudge Sauce • Raspberry Coulis • Vol au Vents with Fresh Berries and Whipped Cream • Tiramisu • Swedish Oatmeal Cookies • Chocolate Chunk Cookies • Sand Cookies • Grand Marnier-Honey Chocolate Fondue • Apple Strudel • Baklava • Fresh Fruit Galette • Fresh Berry Napoleon • Molten Chocolate Cake • Individual Pecan Pies • Cheesecake • Rice Pudding • Bread Pudding • Fresh Fruit Sabayon • Broiled Pineapple with Coconut • Clafouti • Tart Dough • Chocolate Crèpes with Brandied Cherry Filling • Chocolate Mousse • Espresso-Hazelnut Brittle

Index 365

Introduction

COOKING IS A DYNAMIC PROFESSION, ONE THAT PRESENTS SOME OF THE GREATEST CHALLENGES, AS WELL AS SOME OF THE GREATEST REWARDS. SINCE 1946, THE CULINARY INSTITUTE OF AMERICA HAS PROVIDED ASPIRING AND SEASONED FOODSERVICE professionals with the knowledge and skills needed to become premier advocates within this industry.

Here at the CIA, we teach our students the fundamental culinary techniques they need to build a sound foundation for their foodservice careers. There will always be another level of perfection to achieve and another skill to master, through our rigorous curriculum we provide the springboard for growth and success.

Home cooks and the most accomplished of professional chefs share a common purpose. There is no difference in the care and attention that goes into selecting the freshest ingredients, and preparing them to perfection. Training alone does not make a great chef; the most vital component, passion, is the one thing that cannot be taught. Whether in a professional kitchen preparing items from a menu for paying customers, or your own home kitchen preparing a meal for family and friends, the food you prepare illustrates your passion, enthusiasm and individuality, and this you alone can bring to the table.

Food is far more than sustenance and energy fueling you and your family through your hectic lives. It can conjure memories, through smell, taste, and flavor, of simpler times. Cooking is not only an art and a science; it also represents history.

Food prepared with care epitomizes the love, appreciation, and sensory fulfillment that you bring to your friends and family.

The motivation for this new book was to cultivate a passion for cooking and the simple pleasures associated with a "home-cooked" meal while keeping in mind the hectic pace and intensity of everyday life.

After culling through literally thousands of recipes, developed in our professional kitchens over the past fifty-five years, we believe we have created a "quick meal" cookbook that meets the quality standards of the CIA. The 200-plus recipes selected will help the home cook to get in and out of the kitchen expeditiously, without sacrificing quality of ingredients, nutrition, or most importantly, flavor.

Each chapter centers on one particular ingredient or menu category and focuses on the selection of ingredients, flavors, and/or preparation techniques; giving you "tricks-of–the–trade" insights that professional chefs use that will help you work efficiently, so you can quickly prepare exciting and flavorful meals. Every chapter contains a step-by-step illustration of one culinary foundation technique, that will help enhance your culinary knowledge and hone your culinary skills, which is then followed by an array of recipes that can be prepared with a limited investment of time.

We hope our new book inspires you to get out of the fast-food drive-thru lane, avoid the world of pre-packaged foods and ignites your passion for preparing home-cooked meals served in your own dining room, surrounded by family and friends.

CHAPTER ONE

Prior to Cooking

*MISE EN PLACE (Fr.): Literally, "put in place." The preparation
and assembly of ingredients, pans, utensils, and plates or serving pieces
needed for a particular dish or service period.*

PREPARATION PRIOR TO THE ULTIMATE STAGE OF COOKING IS
THE MOST IMPORTANT STEP THAT ANY HOME COOK MUST
EMBRACE, ESPECIALLY WHEN YOU ARE TRYING TO PUT A MEAL ON
THE TABLE WITHIN AN ALLOTTED AMOUNT OF TIME.

Good cooking is the result of carefully developing the best possible flavor and
most perfect texture in any dish. Basic flavoring and aromatic combinations con-
stitute the flavor base, and effective preparation prior to cooking is essential
whether you are an aspiring home cook or a seasoned professional.

With some advance planning, smart shopping, an organized kitchen and
time-saving techniques, healthy, exciting meals can become the norm rather than
the exception in your household. You may also grow to enjoy the creative outlet it
provides as well as the satisfaction of a delicious, home-cooked meal spent with
your family.

To expedite your cooking time, build up a supply of products that are easy to access and easy to use. Quick meals generally have fewer ingredients; for this reason, you should use quality products that will most efficiently enhance meal flavor. Using inexpensive components of lesser quality in a meal inevitably leads to unsatisfactory results. A well-stocked pantry also provides a springboard to go beyond a given recipe, substituting ingredients and creating exciting variations.

DAIRY

Butter

Eggs

Milk

Sour cream

Parmesan cheese

Ricotta cheese

Variety of cheeses, shredded or whole

MEAT/POULTRY/SEAFOOD

Beef chuck, lean, or turkey, ground

Chicken breasts, boneless, skinless

Italian sausage, Bratwurst/Kielbasa

White fish fillets

Frozen shrimp, shelled, deveined

FRESH HERBS/VEGETABLES/FRUITS

Chives, scallions

Parsley

Basil

Ginger

Broccoli florets

Cabbage

Carrots, peeled, baby

Celery

Onions, yellow

Potatoes, Red Bliss

Salad greens

Tomatoes

Yellow squash or zucchini

White mushrooms

Apples

Pears

Lemons, limes

Tropical fruit (mangoes, papayas, etc.)

FROZEN VEGETABLES/FRUITS

Bell peppers

Green beans

Corn kernels

Green peas, petite

Blueberries, strawberries

Orange juice concentrate

Spinach

Vegetable blends

French fries, hash browns

OTHER

Frozen pie crusts

Frozen pizza dough or base

Frozen puff pastry

BASICS

All-purpose unbleached flour

Cornstarch

Baking powder

Baking soda

Sugar

Confectioners' sugar

Brown sugar

Salt

Black peppercorns

PASTA, GRAINS, AND LEGUMES

Capellini (angel hair pasta)

Egg noodles, medium

Fettuccine

Linguine

Penne

Basmati/Texmati rice

Arborio rice (risotto)

Couscous

Lentils

BROTHS AND STOCKS

Beef broth or stock

Chicken broth or stock

Vegetable broth or stock

CONDIMENTS AND SEASONINGS

Mustard (Dijon, whole-grain, honey)

Hot pepper sauce

Soy sauce

Worcestershire sauce

Wine (sherry, dry red/white)

OILS AND DRESSINGS

Extra-virgin olive oil

Vegetable oil

Nonstick cooking spray

Mayonnaise

VINEGARS

Balsamic vinegar

Red wine vinegar

White wine vinegar

HERBS AND SPICES

Bay leaf

Basil

Chili powder

Dill

Oregano

Rosemary

Sage

Thyme

DRIED FRUITS AND VEGETABLES

Raisins

Dried mushrooms

CANNED AND BOTTLED ITEMS

Tuna (chunk light/white, in water)

Peanut butter

Tomatoes, crushed

Tomato paste

Beans, black and red kidney

Artichoke hearts

With the availability of international ingredients, it is easy to create meal variations with a particular ethnic flavor. Use some of these items as recipe substitutions.

MEXICAN

Barbecue sauce

Cilantro

Cumin

Jalapeño or chipotle peppers

Monterey Jack cheese

Refried beans

Salsa

Tortillas

CARIBBEAN/SOUTH AMERICAN

Avocados

Bananas

Coconuts

Collard greens

Hearts of palm

ASIAN

Coconut milk

Green and red curry pastes

Hoisin sauce

Mirin

Nori

Oyster sauce

Rice and soba noodles

Rice vinegar

Sesame oil

Soy sauce

Wasabi

MEDITERRANEAN/MIDDLE EASTERN

Anchovy paste

Chickpeas

Cornmeal

Dried apricots and dates

Eggplant

Goat cheese

Mint

Olives

Pesto

Pine nuts

Sun-dried tomatoes

Yogurt

FRENCH

Brie

Capers

Green peppercorns

Herbes de Provençe

Tarragon

INDIAN

Cardamom

Chutney

Curry paste/powder

Fennel seeds

Turmeric

Yogurt

EQUIPMENT

The right cooking equipment simplifies and speeds up meal preparation. Setting up a kitchen, however, reflects personal preference and depends on the amount of people typically fed as well as the types of food prepared. Expensive or fancy equipment is not essential, however, quality equipment will last a lifetime and is worth the investment.

KNIVES/CUTTING BOARDS

8-inch chef's knife

Paring knife

Serrated knife

Knife sharpener

2–3 wood or plastic cutting boards, different sizes

POTS/PANS

Made of hard anodized aluminum, enameled cast-iron or heavy stainless steel with copper or aluminum-enforced bottoms and tight-fitting lids.

1–2-quart saucepan

3–4-quart saucepan

6–8-quart saucepan

5–7-inch skillet (nonstick is helpful)

9–12-inch skillet (nonstick is helpful)

Wok

OVENPROOF BAKING DISHES

If pots and pans are not ovenproof, use glass, stainless steel or enamel-lined baking dishes with reinforced bottoms.

UTENSILS

Wire whisk

Wooden spoons

Metal and rubber spatulas

Tongs

Vegetable peeler

Measuring spoons

OTHER

Bowls

Colander, strainers

Measuring cups

Pepper mill

Hand grater

Salad spinner

Food processor

Can opener

Timer

Electric mixer

Microwave oven

Toaster oven

Blender, handheld

Time-Saving Tips

Efficiently using the little time you have for cooking is essential. The following suggestions will hopefully become second nature and your meal preparation a pleasurable experience.

Shopping

- Become familiar with a favorite market or two. Try to do all the shopping for staples only once a month or every few weeks, with fresh items purchased as needed.
- List some meals you will prepare, in advance. Use this to help plan your shopping trips.
- Keep a running shopping list in your kitchen, jotting down items when you are low (see pages 2–4).

Freezing

- Freeze what you can so items are readily available, using the microwave to defrost items or thaw them in the refrigerator overnight.
- Make extra servings of meals and freeze for a later date. Freeze in usable sizes and in appropriate storage containers (rigid plastic with tight lids or heavy zipper-lock bags). Label and date the items.
- Freeze small amounts of broth or stock in nonstick muffin tins. Once frozen, twist as you would an ice cube tray, then place in a plastic bag. Or freeze directly in quart-sized, zipper-lock bags. Place in a mug for support as you fill the bags.
- Fresh herbs can be chopped, placed in ice cube trays with a bit of water, then frozen. Once frozen, the cubes can be placed in freezer bags, then easily added as you cook.
- Fresh herbs, garlic or shallots can also be pureed, mixed with some vegetable or olive oil and refrigerated or frozen in small portions.
- Freeze a stick of butter and use a vegetable peeler to shave bits onto food or grate the butter to mix in for baked items or mashed potatoes.
- If you don't use a pound of bacon quickly, roll the bacon up in groups of 2–4 slices. Store flat in the freezer in a zipper-lock bag. Once frozen, store as preferred.
- Partially frozen meat or poultry is easier to cut for sauces, soups, stir-fries and scaloppine.
- To save overripe fruit, such as bananas for bread, freeze in zipper-lock bags and thaw when needed.
- Peel raw ginger with a teaspoon. Freeze in a plastic bag, grating as needed.
- Open both ends of a tomato paste can, pushing one end with the lid to remove the paste onto some plastic wrap. Wrap and freeze. Slice off pieces as needed.

Fresh and Refrigerated Goods

- Store fresh asparagus upright in an inch or so of water and cover loosely with plastic.
- Avocados and pears will ripen more quickly in a brown paper bag.
- To use avocados, slice around the pit through both ends. Twist and separate the two halves. Using the blade of a chef's knife, lodge the knife into the pit, twist slightly and lift the pit out with the knife. Pry the pit off with another utensil. Use a paring knife to make slices inside the avocado, but not through the skin. With a spoon or spatula, loosen the slices just inside the skin and pop out.
- Blueberries can be refrigerated longer than strawberries or raspberries. Do not wash berries until just before

needed, although raspberries should not be washed at all. Any berry can be easily frozen and used as needed.

- To seed a cucumber or zucchini, slice it in half lengthwise, then slide a small spoon down the centers to scoop out the seeds. Use an ice cream scoop to remove seeds from winter squashes.
- If cheese sticks to your grater or dried fruit sticks to your knife, spray the grater or knife first with nonstick vegetable spray. Cleanly slice goat cheese or other soft cheeses with dental floss.
- To more quickly peel hard-boiled eggs, tap and roll the eggs until cracked all over. Peel from the flatter end with the air pocket, moving around the eggs in a spiral. To crumble the eggs for a salad or garnish, press the eggs through a mesh sieve or grate on a box grater.
- Keep fresh herbs stored in a tall container of water in the refrigerator. Use a container with a tight-fitting lid. Trim the ends as you would flowers and add water to the bottoms of the stems (about 1 inch).
- Lemons or limes are more easily juiced by first rolling them firmly on a hard surface, which loosens the membranes inside. The spent lemons and limes can be kept frozen in a zipper lock bag to use later for flavoring dishes or to add to water to prevent the browning of cut apples, potatoes or artichokes.
- When selecting melons, check for a sweet aroma at the stem end. It should yield slightly to pressure. Honeydews are more difficult to assess. The rind should be creamy white without any green. Avoid any fruit with bruises or soft spots. To remove rinds quickly, slice off the ends, then place on end, slicing strips of rind off with a serrated knife. Cut in half, remove seeds, then cut as desired.

- Store fresh mushrooms in a paper bag, so they can breathe.
- Besides slicing hard-boiled eggs, an egg slicer quickly cuts mushrooms and mozzarella cheese.
- Buy partially prepared fresh items such as shredded carrots or cheese, florets of broccoli and cauliflower, pre-sliced mushrooms, washed spinach and salad mixes.
- To chop a bell pepper quickly, slice the top off first, then stand the pepper up, slicing down the sides. This easily separates the core and seeds from the sides.
- When selecting chili peppers, generally red ones are sweeter than green as they have had more time to ripen. Usually, the larger the chili, the less hot it is.
- If needing a certain weight of potatoes to peel or cut, get the largest size you can so there are less potatoes to prepare.
- Scissors are an easy way to cut scallions or chives into precise pieces.
- To easily shock blanched vegetables, fill a bowl with ice water, drain the vegetables through a strainer, then place the strainer into the ice water. The vegetables can easily be retrieved out of the strainer.

Dry Goods

- Storing flour, sugar, grains, legumes and pasta in capped, half-gallon, wide-mouth preserving jars allows you to easily reach a measuring cup inside.
- Starting with hot tap water quickens boiling time for pasta water. Using two pots initially, then combining into one of them also hastens boiling time. Use thin dried pasta, such as angel hair, for quicker cooking. Fresh pasta cooks very quickly but the consistency is quite different from dried. Drain the pasta in a colander, holding it in the sink while you use the pasta pot to make the sauce.

- When using herbs and spices which are to be removed before serving, put them in a mesh tea ball. Close the ball and hang by the chain over the pot's side into the cooked item.
- Apply barbecue or other sauces to grilled items with a squeeze bottle.

Equipment

- Keep often-used utensils such as whisks, wooden spoons and spatulas in open containers that are easy to reach.
- Use the same cutting board for different ingredients, especially if used in the same recipe (this is not safe, however, with raw meat, poultry, fish or seafood). Place a damp paper towel under the cutting board to keep it secure, then use the paper towel to clean up scraps when done.
- A bench scraper or Chinese cleaver easily removes cut items from a cutting board.
- To spray pans or tins with nonstick spray and avoid covering your workspace as well, spray the item on the flat, open door of the dishwasher. The excess spray will be washed off when the dishwasher is run again.
- When using a standing mixer, place ingredients in the mixing bowl, then cover the front of the mixer and around the bowl with a piece of plastic or a damp towel. This will prevent ingredients from splattering out.
- Measure all dry ingredients with the same utensil first, then measure the liquid ingredients so you can avoid washing between measurements. Follow the same procedure with your food processor as well.
- Use pans with ovenproof handles so the same pan may be used for sautéing on the stove and finishing in the oven.
- Clean hands are often the quickest and most thorough tool for mixing some foods such as salads or other cold preparations.
- Anticipate cleanup while preparing and cooking items. Use as few dishes as possible, line pans with foil or use nonstick sprays and soak baked-on dishes as soon as possible. Paper towels or wax paper can be used instead of dishes to hold recipe ingredients such as grated cheese or minced garlic.
- Prepare food, as much as possible, in the same dish that it will be served in. For example, blend salad dressings in the bottom of the bowl before adding the rest of the ingredients.

FOCUS ON | Salt and Pepper

Salt and pepper should be added before cooking to bring out the inherent flavors in food: if these seasonings are added only after the cooking is complete, the salt and pepper may take on too much significance in the finished dish's flavor. Generally, it is better to add salt and pepper separately; using your fingertips is a good way to control the amount of salt added and results in a more even coating.

If you want to add some bold new flavors to your dishes, you can further intensify the taste of seeds or spices through toasting.

Oven Method: Spread the seeds out on a dry baking sheet and place in a moderate oven just until a pleasant aroma is apparent. Stir often to ensure even browning. Remove immediately and transfer to a fresh pan or plate to cool.

Stovetop Method: Spread the seeds in a shallow layer in a preheated, dry sauté pan and toss, shake, or swirl the pan until a rich, penetrating aroma arises. Transfer them to a cool pan to avoid scorching.

NOTE: Be sure to pay close attention when toasting; the spices can go from perfectly toasted to scorched very quickly.

- Remove meats and vegetables from the refrigerator as you begin preparation. Room temperature food cooks faster than cold.
- Begin boiling water for pasta as soon as possible. Once boiling, the pot can be kept covered at a simmer and brought back up to a boil when needed.
- Read through the entire recipe first before beginning preparation, then assemble all the ingredients needed. For soups or stews, layer ingredients in a bowl divided by plastic wrap or wax paper, based on the cooking times. For stir-frying, ingredients may be placed on a cutting board or plate, in order of use.

General Cooking Techniques

- Sautéing, stir-frying, poaching, steaming, broiling and grilling are the best methods for quick cooking.
- Always preheat stovetop pans, the oven or grill.
- Sauté in nonstick or seasoned pans so less fat is needed.
- Butter has a low burning point so it may start smoking and burning before the item is cooked. Oils have higher smoking points, so adding oil to butter makes sautéing and pan frying easier while retaining a butter flavor in the dish.

Flavoring

Bringing out the best flavor in ingredients is a skill that seems to come naturally to a professional chef. A home cook can realize these talents through proper cooking techniques, seasonings, and a thorough understanding of how to achieve the point of perfection within a dish.

Seasonings

Adding seasonings at the proper point in the cooking process is one of the keys to giving a finished dish the fullest possible flavor.

The array of seasonings added to a dish can run from the ordinary salt and pepper, to the more complex array of herb and spice blends, or marinades with oils, acids, or other aromatics. In every case, though, seasonings are meant to enhance flavor, not to detract from or overwhelm the dish.

Experimenting with different flavors allows for creativity, but don't forget the basics. With the abundance of fresh herbs, spices, and aromatics now available to the home cook, the flavor rewards of salt and pepper have been somewhat forgotten. Many beginning cooks sometimes fail to use these two essential seasonings early enough during cooking, or in a quantity large enough, to bring out the best flavor of the food.

Dry Rubs

Fresh herbs and other ingredients such as garlic, fresh or dry breadcrumbs, or grated cheeses can be blended into a paste or coating to add additional flavor to dishes. The ingredients can be moistened with oil, prepared mustard, or similar ingredients to create a texture than can easily adhere to a food, or make it easier to blend it into a dish as a final seasoning.

When a spice blend is used as a dry rub to coat food, the food is left to stand after application, under refrigeration, to absorb the flavors. Very often, these rubs contain some salt to help intensify the flavors in the dish.

Dry rubs may be left on the food during cooking or they may be scraped away first. Barbecued beef and Jamaican jerked pork are examples of dishes that may be prepared using a dry rub.

Marinades

Marinades generally contain one or more of the following: oil, acid, and aromatics (spices, herbs, and vegetables).

Oils protect food from intense heat during cooking and help hold other flavorful ingredients in contact with the food.

Acids, such as vinegar, wine, yogurt, and citrus juices, flavor the food and change its texture. In some cases, acids firm or stiffen foods; in others, it breaks down connective fibers to make tough cuts of meat more tender while aromatics provide specific flavors.

Marinades can be used to flavor or as a dipping sauce. Any marinade which has held raw meat or poultry and is to be used as a dipping sauce must be cooked first. Marinating times vary according to the food's texture. Tender or delicate foods such as fish or poultry breast require less time, while a tougher cut of meat may be marinated for days.

FOCUS ON | Marinades

To use a liquid marinade, add it to the ingredient and turn the ingredient to coat evenly.

Cover and marinate, under refrigeration, for the length of time indicated by the recipe, the type of meat, poultry, or fish, and the desired result.

Brush or scrape off excess marinade before cooking and pat dry, particularly if the marinade contains herbs or other aromatics that burn easily.

An egg wash is made by blending eggs (whole, yolks, or whites) and water or milk; a general guideline calls for about 2 ounces of milk for every 2 whole eggs.

Items can be dipped into milk or buttermilk before applying breading, rather than using an egg wash. Or for some dishes, this step is not necessary; the natural moisture of the food holds the breadcrumb coating in place without requiring an egg wash.

It is very important to season the food before applying any coating. Flour and similar meals or powders, such as cornstarch, are used to lightly dredge or dust foods before they are dipped in an egg wash.

Standard Breading

The "standard" breading procedure is the most efficient way to coat a number of items, using a consistent sequence, and is done to create a crisp crust on fried foods. It is prepared by coating foods with flour, egg wash, and/or breadcrumbs.

Breadcrumbs are usually the standard for most coated items; however, other ingredients may be used in place of or in addition to breadcrumbs. Options include nuts, seeds, shredded coconut, corn flakes, potato flakes, shredded potatoes, grated cheese, ground spices, or chopped herbs.

Blot the food dry with absorbent toweling and season as desired.

Hold it in one hand and dip it in flour.

Shake off any excess flour and transfer the food to the container of egg wash.

Switch hands, pick up the food, and turn it if necessary to coat it on all sides, and transfer it to the container of breadcrumbs.

Use your dry hand to pack breadcrumbs evenly around the food and then shake off any excess and transfer to a plate or platter (keep breaded food in single layers, but if you must stack the pieces, use parchment or wax paper to separate the layers).

Discard any unused flour, egg wash or breadcrumbs, to prevent cross-contamination and eliminate the potential for food poisoning.

CHAPTER TWO

Appetizers

*E*VERY CULTURE AND CUISINE HAS ITS OWN TRADITION OF "LIT-
TLE FOODS," ENJOYED BEFORE A MEAL OR EVEN ON THEIR OWN.
POPULAR THROUGHOUT THE MEDITERRANEAN ARE MEZES SUCH AS
STUFFED GRAPE LEAVES, OLIVES, AND LUSCIOUS GARLICKY BEAN OR
vegetable spreads. In Spain, the tradition of tapas runs a gamut from seafood to
eggs to savory pastries. Throughout Mexico and South America, antojitos (or "little whims") are enjoyed in a wide range of forms, from tostadas to tacos. Dim sum,
Cantonese for "heart's delight," includes steamed dumplings and pot stickers. The
Russians enjoy a zakuski table, laden with preserved and pickled foods; while in
Scandinavia, it is the smörgåsbord, with fabulous open-faced sandwiches and
gravlax, that fills this culinary slot. Classic French hors d'oeuvre encompass a vast
array of dishes, featuring a range of specialties from foie gras and oysters to marinated salads of lentils and celeriac. While these examples of "little foods" may seem
daunting, the recipes included in this chapter are quick and easy to prepare.

A meal that includes an appetizer course is perceived as extraordinary; however, you need not reserve appetizers for special occasions or holidays. There are
quite a number of simple foods that are quick to prepare and don't demand a lot of
effort in the kitchen. With the addition of an appetizer, you can enhance ordinary
meals, even on a workday evening.

Typically, appetizers are small portions of intensely flavored items. Sometimes, they are meant to be eaten with the fingers and are only a bite or two; in this case, the term hors d'oeuvre is often used instead of appetizer. These tidbits are often served with drinks before dinner. In other cases, the appetizer is served as part of the meal itself, as the first course. In both situations, appetizers are meant to take the edge off your appetite so that you can thoroughly enjoy the rest of the meal. A well-chosen appetizer plays an extremely important role in the dining experience.

A prelude to the courses that follow, an appetizer should be of a reasonable portion size, and it should have a direct relationship to the main course; for instance, you might choose a Mexican antojito, like Black Bean and Avocado Crostini (page 27), as the perfect opener for a Southwestern or Mexican inspired dinner.

Appetizers play yet another important role—they are a great way to introduce your friends and family to new and exciting dishes. The appetizer course allows your guests to discover a rich array of hot and cold starters, with both tremendous flavor impact and visual appeal. Moreover, they expand your culinary repertoire, while satisfying your guests' palates.

Serving salad as a first course is an a effortless way to create an appetizer. Top a simple green salad with Marinated Goat Cheese with Fresh Herbs (page 37), or serve a small salad alongside the Camembert Crisps (page 44). Highlight a wonderful regional specialty, such as a locally made cheese, or pick up some vegetables from your local farm stand. Vegeta-bles play an important role in our meals, and they can really shine as appetizers. Present them very simply; for example, serve a plate of mixed Grilled Vegetables with a Balsamic Vinaigrette (page 39). Similarly, by serving smaller portions, you can turn a pasta entrée, such as Pasta Quattro Formaggi, (page 257), into an appetizer.

Use a marinade or dressing, such as Lime-Cilantro Vinaigrette (page 127), that features flavors from a less familiar cuisine to change the flavor profile of a dish into something new and exotic. Broiled or grilled fish, shellfish, and poultry may be featured as an appetizer, especially when cut into strips and threaded on skewers, as in Satay of Beef with Peanut Sauce (page 141). Look through the chapters in this book for more inspiration.

Serving foods at the optimal temperature is important. Some foods are best when they are perfectly chilled (Shrimp Cocktail, page 44), while others are best served sizzling hot. There are also those dishes that come into their own when served warm, or at room temperature. You can achieve interesting effects by contrasting temperatures, as you might when you serve a hot dish with a cool sauce or salsa. An example of this would be accompanying Seared Scallops (page 214) with Papaya and Black Bean Salsa (page 24).

Since the appetizer is the first course of the meal, it comes with a specific obligation-it must advance the meal from the first course to the main course. To do this effectively, the appetizer should have some logical connection-whether it is a flavor, an ingredient, or a technique-that makes a flavor bridge. Good choices include dishes selected from the same cuisine, or featuring a series of seasonal favorites.

| # Making Crostini or Canapés

Crostini and canapés are both bite-sized open-faced sandwiches. Simple and quick to make, they offer the busy cook a wide range of flavors, textures, and colors. All canapés have a base of bread, a spread, a main item, and a garnish. Crostini, meaning "little toasts" in Italian, are not held to the same rigid guidelines of a canapé. Crostini refers both to a toasted piece of Italian or French bread, and the hors d'oeuvre that is created when a savory item is placed on top of the toast. Crostini and canapés should be easy to pick up, and small enough to eat in one or two bites. For the most appealing crostini and canapés, choose your ingredients with attention to color, shape, and texture. In the following recipes, the term crostini and canapé can be used interchangeably.

➡ PREPARE THE CROSTINI OR CANAPÉ BASE

Select the bread for your crostini or canapé base and cut it into shapes, if necessary. Cocktail rye or pumpernickel bread is easy to use for canapés, but you can use other breads as well. Trim away the crust, and cut the cocktail bread in half on the diagonal to make triangles. For an elegant affair, use small round cutters to create a more uniform and finished-looking base.

Make crostini, as done in the recipes on pages 27–33, by thinly slicing baguettes in rounds, or on the bias. You can then toast, grill, or broil them for more flavor and texture.

➡ ADD A FLAVORFUL SPREAD TO THE BASE

A spread adds immeasurably to the success of every crostini or canapé. It acts as a moisture barrier between the main item and the bread as well as to hold the topping in place. It also adds mouthfeel and flavor. Spread a thin layer of softened butter, cream cheese, mustard, a bean spread, or mayonnaise from edge to edge. Add flavoring ingredients to the spread if you like: minced garlic, shallots, or scallions; purees of roasted peppers or chilies, Parmesan cheese, or olives can all be blended into the spread.

➡ GARNISH THE CROSTINI OR CANAPÉ WITH THE TOPPING

Sliced toppings should be very thin and cut or trimmed so that they won't hang over the edge of the base. Another option is to dice or mince the main item and fold it into the spread to make a flavorful salad topping for the base. Take the time to trim the meat or poultry of any fat or sinew so that it is easy to bite into them without separating them from the base.

When you plan on making larger numbers of crostini or canapés for a party or reception, you can add the spread and topping to an entire slice of bread, then use cutters to trim or cut them into shape.

Garnishes can add more than just color to a crostini or canapé. You can use a variety of techniques and ingredients. A bit of a fresh fruit, vegetable, or herb adds texture and flavor. Make the garnish small enough so that it won't overwhelm the entire canapé. Small sprigs of fresh herbs, especially if they have been used to flavor the spread or main item, a tiny dollop of caviar or sour cream, chopped or sliced eggs, or a topping of avocado or salsa are just a few of the options you can explore.

See the step-by-step photographs accompanying the recipes for Black Bean and Avocado Crostini (page 27) and Prosciutto and Melon Canapés (page 28).

Tomatillo Salsa

MAKES 2 CUPS | PREPARATION TIME: 25 MINUTES

A tomatillo is a fruit that looks like a small, unripe tomato with a papery husk. Tomatillos have a tart and lemony flavor and are commonly used in Southwestern and Mexican cuisines. This easy salsa is an excellent complement to grilled meats.

10 tomatillos

1 jalapeño

2 garlic cloves

1 teaspoon salt, or to taste

1 bunch cilantro

Remove the husks from the tomatillos.

Place the tomatillos and the jalapeño in a pot and cover them with water. Boil until the tomatillos are fully cooked and have become a dull olive green color, about 10 minutes.

Remove the stem, seeds, and veins from the jalapeño.

Strain the tomatillos from the water and place them directly into a food processor fitted with a metal chopping blade. Add the flesh from the jalapeño, the garlic cloves and the salt. Process the mixture until completely smooth.

Add the cilantro to the food processor and pulse to chop and incorporate.

Serve warm or chilled.

NOTE: To make a hotter salsa, do not remove the seeds and veins from the jalapeño.

Cannellini Bean Puree

MAKES 2 CUPS | PREPARATION TIME: 40 MINUTES

*C*annellini are large, flesh-colored, kidney-shaped beans grown in Italy. You can find them dry or canned. This easy puree is an excellent alternative to chickpeas or black beans and provides a healthy backdrop for a wide variety of garnishes.

²/₃ cup onion, roughly chopped

¹/₄ cup carrot, roughly chopped

¹/₂ cup celery, roughly chopped

1 teaspoon black peppercorns

6 garlic cloves, crushed

2 rosemary sprigs

2 thyme sprigs

2 bay leaves

1 pound canned cannellini beans

2 garlic cloves, roughly chopped

1¹/₂ tablespoons lemon juice

1 teaspoon salt, or to taste

¹/₂ teaspoon hot pepper sauce

¹/₂ teaspoon ground white pepper

¹/₄ cup extra-virgin olive oil

1 tablespoon parsley, chopped

Tie the onion, carrot, celery, whole peppercorns, garlic cloves, rosemary, thyme, and bay leaf in a cheesecloth pouch, and combine with the canned beans in their liquid in a medium saucepan. Simmer for 15 minutes.

Discard the cheesecloth bag and drain the beans, reserving the cooking liquid. Cool the mixture to room temperature.

Puree the beans in a food processor, using the reserved cooking liquid to adjust the texture to a spreadable consistency. Season with chopped garlic, lemon juice, salt, hot sauce, and pepper.

Garnish the puree with a sprinkle of oil and parsley.

NOTE: This would be a very good spread for the base of a vegetarian canapé, or it could be used as a vegetable dip.

Guacamole

MAKES 8 SERVINGS | PREPARATION TIME: 30 MINUTES

Shown with Aïoli (page 172) and Tapenade (page 22)

Guacamole is a Mexican condiment made from mashed avocados, lemon or lime juice, and chili peppers. Variations can include tomatoes, cilantro, garlic, and scallion. It is important to remember that avocado begins to oxidize as soon as its flesh is exposed to air. Remember to work efficiently and before refrigerating, cover your guacamole with a layer of plastic wrap pressed directly onto the surface of the mixture.

4 avocados, halved, pitted, and peeled

3 tablespoons lime juice

2 plum tomatoes, diced (optional)

1 jalapeño (optional), seeded and minced

1 bunch scallions, sliced

1/2 cup cilantro, chopped

1 teaspoon Tabasco sauce, or to taste

Salt, to taste

Freshly ground black pepper, to taste

Mash the avocados with a fork.

Add the remaining ingredients and adjust seasoning with lime juice, salt, and spices.

Hold the guacamole under refrigeration in a tightly covered storage container. It is best to make guacamole the same day it is to be served.

Wonton Chips
with Asian-Style Dipping Sauce

MAKES 8 SERVINGS | PREPARATION TIME: 45 MINUTES

*P*repared, pre-cut wonton skins are available in the refrigerator aisle of most supermarkets. They are light, crispy, and delicious with this Asian-Style Dipping Sauce.

DIPPING SAUCE

1 cup soy sauce

1/2 cup white vinegar

1/2 cup water

4 garlic cloves, minced

4 scallions, minced

1 tablespoon ginger, minced

1 teaspoon dry mustard

1 teaspoon hot bean paste

2 tablespoons honey

WONTON CHIPS

32 wonton skins

3 cups peanut oil

Salt, to taste (optional)

Combine all of the ingredients for the dipping sauce and mix thoroughly.

Use the dipping sauce immediately or hold it under refrigeration. After storage, stir the dipping sauce and adjust seasoning, if necessary, before serving.

Pour the peanut oil into a large skillet. Heat oil to 350°F. Cut the wonton squares in half diagonally and fry the pieces in the oil for approximately 1 minute, or until golden brown. Only put one layer of wonton triangles at a time in the pan and do not overcrowd. Remove the chips from oil with a slotted spoon and drain on paper towels. Sprinkle with salt, if desired, and serve with the dipping sauce.

Hummus
with Pita Chips

See photograph on page 301.

A Middle Eastern spread made from cooked, mashed chickpeas, seasoned with olive oil, tahini, lemon juice, salt, and garlic. This version can be made in a snap from canned chickpeas, and can also be used as a delicious condiment or spread on vegetarian sandwiches.

2 cups canned chickpeas, drained and rinsed

3 tablespoons tahini (sesame paste)

$^1/_2$ cup olive oil (or sesame oil)

2 tablespoons lemon juice, or as needed

2 garlic cloves, or as needed

Salt, to taste

Freshly ground black pepper, to taste

6 pieces pita bread, cut into 6 pieces each

Puree the chickpeas, tahini, 2 tablespoons olive oil, lemon juice, and garlic in a food processor, adding water to thin the mixture as necessary.

Adjust the seasoning with lemon juice and garlic, as needed. Refrigerate the hummus until needed.

Heat 1 tablespoon of olive oil in a sauté pan over medium heat. Sauté 6 pita wedges for 2 minutes on each side or until light golden brown at the edges and crisp.

Repeat with remaining olive oil and pita wedges. Serve warm with the hummus.

Fiery Fruit Salsa

MAKES 8 SERVINGS | PREPARATION TIME: 45 MINUTES

See photograph on page 215.

A perfect combination of spicy and sweet flavors, this salsa is an excellent accompaniment for seared seafood, grilled poultry, or simply served with tortilla chips as a snack.

$^2/_3$ cup mango, peeled, diced

$^1/_2$ cup papaya, peeled, diced

$^1/_4$ cup pineapple, canned or fresh, cored, peeled, diced

$^1/_4$ cup red bell pepper, diced

$^1/_3$ cup red onion, diced

1 tablespoon cilantro, chopped

$^1/_2$ tablespoon lime juice

$^1/_2$ tablespoon white wine vinegar

1 teaspoon jalapeño, seeded, minced

$^1/_2$ teaspoon extra-virgin olive oil

$^1/_8$ teaspoon salt, or to taste

Freshly ground black pepper, to taste

Combine all of the ingredients in a bowl.

Allow the salsa to sit for 15 minutes before serving.

NOTE: Be sure to wear gloves when mincing the jalapeño to prevent irritation.

VARIATION: This salsa can be turned from savory to sweet by changing just a few ingredients. Substitute mint for the cilantro, strawberries for the red pepper, honey for the olive oil, and leave out the vinegar, salt, and pepper. Serve the sweet-style salsa as dessert, for brunch with muffins, pancakes, French toast, or as a filling for crêpes.

Tapenade

MAKES 8 SERVINGS | PREPARATION TIME: 15 MINUTES

See photograph on page 19.

T apenade originated in France's Provençe region. It is a thick, pungent paste used as a condiment for hors d'oeuvre and as an alternative condiment on rustic sandwiches.

2 cups pitted kalamata or other cured black olives

3 anchovy fillets, drained

2 tablespoons capers, rinsed

2 garlic cloves, minced

2 tablespoons lemon juice

$^1/_4$ cup extra-virgin olive oil

1 tablespoon chopped parsley, rosemary, or basil

Put the olives, anchovy fillets, capers, and garlic in the bowl of a food processor fitted with a steel blade. Pulse the machine on and off in short blasts until a coarse paste forms. There should still be distinct pieces of olive in the mixture.

With the machine running, drizzle in the olive oil until the paste is smooth enough to spread, though it should be slightly chunky.

Transfer the mixture to a bowl and stir in the lemon juice and fresh herbs. Serve at room temperature. Will keep for up to 1 week in the refrigerator

Cucumber Raita

MAKES 8 SERVINGS | PREPARATION TIME: 45 MINUTES

See photograph on page 252.

*R*aita is an East Indian yogurt-based salad that commonly features cucumber, eggplant, potatoes, or spinach. These salads are typically flavored with cumin or garam masala, an Indian spice mixture that includes fenugreek, ginger and garlic, among other spices.

2 cups plain yogurt

$^1/_2$ cup seedless cucumbers, peeled and diced small

2 garlic cloves, minced

1 tablespoon mint, chopped

$^1/_2$ teaspoon ground cumin

$^1/_4$ teaspoon salt, or to taste

$^1/_4$ teaspoon freshly ground black pepper, or to taste

Dash cayenne pepper

Drain the yogurt through a cheesecloth-lined colander for 30 minutes. Transfer to a bowl.

Mix in the ingredients and serve.

NOTE: For a thicker, creamier result, drain the yogurt in the refrigerator overnight.

A quick and easy way to prepare the cucumbers is to peel them and chop them in the food processor. Excess water may be drained before the cucumbers are added to the yogurt.

To remove the sharp garlic "bite" and impart a more subtle garlic flavor, toss the garlic cloves in a small pot of boiling water for a minute, drain them and repeat the process. The garlic may then be chopped in the food processor with the cucumber, or minced separately.

Papaya and Black Bean Salsa

MAKES 8 SERVINGS | PREPARATION TIME: 25 MINUTES

Canned black beans make this sweet, hearty salsa a cinch to make. Papayas are readily available in the tropical fruit section of most supermarkets. They have flesh that is bright orange and are very juicy when fully ripe.

1 cup canned black beans, drained and rinsed

1 papaya, ripe, small dice

2 red peppers, small dice

1 red onion, small dice

1 jalapeño, minced

1/4 cup cilantro, chopped

1/4 cup olive oil

3 tablespoons lime juice

2 teaspoons salt, or to taste

Combine all of the ingredients and adjust the seasoning with salt and pepper.

Hold the salsa under refrigeration.
Serve with tortilla chips.

Tomato Salsa

MAKES 8 SERVINGS | PREPARATION TIME: 35 MINUTES

Common to the cuisines of the Southwest and Mexico, the variations of tomato salsa are endless. Serve Tomato Salsa with tortilla chips as an appetizer, or as an accompaniment to a variety of Southwestern and Tex-Mex dishes such as fajitas, burritos, and enchiladas; or enjoy it with grilled meats, fish, and poultry.

4 plum tomatoes, chopped

4 scallions, sliced thin

1/2 onion, medium-sized, minced

1 garlic clove, minced

2 tablespoons cilantro, chopped

1 jalapeño, seeded, chopped fine

1 1/2 tablespoons lemon juice

Salt and freshly ground black pepper, to taste

Combine all of the ingredients.

Let the salsa rest for 15 minutes before serving in order to develop the flavor. Adjust the seasoning with salt and pepper.

VARIATIONS: Add additional jalapeño peppers, Tabasco sauce, or cayenne pepper for a hotter salsa. A small amount of white wine or sherry vinegar may be added to adjust the flavor. Other ingredients, such as parsley, chopped celery, jicama, celeriac, and sweet bell peppers may also be added.

Salsa de Chipotle

MAKES 8 SERVINGS | PREPARATION TIME: 30 MINUTES (WITH COOLING)

*C*hipotles are dried, smoked jalapeño peppers that are commonly canned and packed in adobo sauce—a mixture of ground chiles, herbs and vinegar. Usually found in the Mexican specialty food section of supermarkets, they are strong in flavor and should be added in small increments until the desired flavor is achieved.

2 tablespoons peanut oil

1 cup onion, chopped

2 garlic cloves, minced

28 ounces canned plum tomatoes, drained

1½ teaspoons dried oregano

Pinch sugar

2–3 chipotles in adobo, including a little of the sauce from the can

Heat the oil in a medium sauce pan until it is almost smoking. Add the onion and garlic and sauté over medium-high heat, stirring often, until the onion is translucent, about 2–3 minutes.

Add the tomatoes, chipotles, oregano, sugar, and salt.

Stir thoroughly to combine and simmer uncovered over low heat for 10–15 minutes, stirring often.

Cool the salsa to room temperature and puree the sauce in a blender.

NOTE: If you want a milder sauce, remove all or some of chipotle chiles before pureeing. Keeps up to three days tightly covered in the refrigerator, or 2–3 months in the freezer.

FOCUS ON | ## Principles for Presenting Appetizers

Use the following basic principles to help you select, prepare, and plate appetizers like the pros:

Serve appetizers at the proper temperature.

Season all appetizer items with care. Appetizers are meant to stimulate your taste buds, so proper seasoning is of the utmost importance.

Slice, shape, and portion appetizers carefully. There should be just enough of every element to make the appetizer interesting and appealing from the first bite to the last.

Presentation counts. Take the time to choose attractive plates, platters, serving utensils, and cups for dipping sauces. A beautifully presented item can excite the palate before the first bite.

Black Bean and Avocado Crostini

MAKES 8 SERVINGS | PREPARATION TIME: 45 MINUTES

A finished platter of Black Bean and Avocado Crostini alongside Prosciutto and Melon Canapés (page 28).

Crostini is a general term that refers to "little toasts" which are usually topped with one or more garnish items. This Southwestern version combines the creaminess of black beans with the heat from the guacamole for a terrific hors d'oeuvre or snack idea.

24 baguette slices, 1/4-inch thick

1/4 cup Garlic and Parsley Butter (page 36)

1/2 cup Vidalia onion, small dice

2 plum tomatoes, small dice

3/4 cup cooked or canned black beans, drained and rinsed

1 1/2 tablespoons cilantro, chopped

1 teaspoon white wine vinegar

1 teaspoon salt, or to taste

1/2 teaspoon freshly ground black pepper, or to taste

2 avocados

2 tablespoons lime juice

1 garlic clove, minced

1/4 teaspoon chili powder

1/8 teaspoon ground cumin

24 cilantro or parsley leaves, washed

Preheat the oven to 400°F.

Toast the baguette slices in the oven for 5–7 minutes, or until the outside edges are golden brown. Spread each baguette slice with approximately ½ teaspoon of the garlic butter. Reserve the toasts until needed.

Combine the onion, tomato, black beans, cilantro, and vinegar. Season with salt and pepper.

Peel and core one of the avocados and dice into ¼-inch pieces.

Combine the avocado with 1 tablespoon of the lime juice, garlic, chili powder, and cumin. Season with salt and pepper.

Peel and core the remaining avocado. Slice each half across the meridian into 8 slices. Sprinkle the avocado with the rest of the lime juice to prevent oxidation.

Spread 1 heaping teaspoon of the avocado mixture on each crostini. Top with 1 tablespoon of the black bean mixture.

Garnish with an avocado slice and a cilantro or parsley leaf.

ABOVE, LEFT TO RIGHT: A base is selected for the crostini or canapé, commonly a small piece of toasted bread, cut into triangles, circles, or squares. The spread is added to the base as a moisture barrier.

The filling or topping, cut to fit the base without overhang, is placed on top of the spread. A topping can also be spooned on top of the spread. Lastly, a garnish is added to give the canapé a fresh and appealing look.

Prosciutto and Melon Canapé

MAKES 8 SERVINGS | PREPARATION TIME: 25 MINUTES

*T*he best time to serve this delicate, sweet and savory hors d'oeuvre is when melon varieties are in peak season, allowing you to achieve the fullest contrast between juicy cantaloupe and lightly salty, paper-thin slices of prosciutto.

8 slices white bread

Olive oil, as needed

MASCARPONE CHEESE SPREAD

5 ounces mascarpone cheese

$^1/_4$ teaspoon Tabasco sauce

$^1/_4$ teaspoon Dijon mustard

Dash salt, or to taste

Dash freshly ground black pepper,
 or to taste

1 cantaloupe, scooped into 24 small balls

8 slices prosciutto, thinly sliced
 (about $^1/_4$ pound)

1 bunch mint leaves, chiffonade

Preheat the broiler.

Brush the bread slices lightly with olive oil and broil for 30 seconds per side until crisp.

Combine the mascarpone cheese, Tabasco, Dijon mustard, salt, and pepper. Mix well.

Using the small side of a melon baller, scoop approximately 24 balls out of the cantaloupe.

Spread the mascarpone mixture on the toasted bread slices.

Lay a slice of prosciutto on each slice of bread, then cut canapés out of the bread using a round cutter.

Top each canapé with a cantaloupe melon ball. Garnish with mint chiffonade.

CROSTINI VARIATION: Spread the mascarpone cheese mixture onto toasted $^1/_4$-inch-thick baguette slices. Cut each prosciutto slice into thirds; top each crostini with a folded piece of prosciutto and a cantaloupe melon ball. Garnish with mint chiffonade.

RIGHT: Using a round cutter to more efficiently assemble the canapés.

OPPOSITE: The finished platter of Prosciutto and Melon Canapés.

Lobster and Prosciutto Crostini

MAKES 8 SERVINGS | PREPARATION TIME: 20 MINUTES

See photograph on page 32.

*T*his very elegant hors d'oeuvre is so simple that even on a tight schedule you can achieve impressive results. Frozen lobster meat is generally of excellent quality and it is already cooked, so it only requires thawing time.

24 baguette slices, 1/4-inch thick

1/4 cup Garlic and Parsley Butter (page 36)

6 tablespoons olive oil, for frying

24 large fresh sage leaves

1/2 cup goat cheese, soft

8 slices prosciutto, thinly sliced
(about 1/4 pound)

1 cup cooked lobster meat
(thawed if frozen)

Preheat the oven to 400°F.

Toast the baguette slices in the oven for 5–7 minutes, or until the outside edges are golden brown. Spread each baguette slice with approximately ½ teaspoon of the garlic butter. Reserve the toasts until needed.

Heat the olive oil in a small sauté pan over medium-high heat. Gently place the sage leaves in the oil and lightly fry for 2–3 minutes. Remove and drain on absorbent paper. Hold at room temperature until needed.

Spread each of the toasted baguette slices with 1 teaspoon of the goat cheese. Cut each prosciutto slice into thirds; top each crostini with a folded piece of prosciutto.

Place 2 teaspoons of the lobster meat on top of the prosciutto. Garnish each crostini with a fried sage leaf.

NOTE: It is possible to substitute fresh lobster in this recipe; however, the recipe time will increase to 40–45 minutes. See page 230 for tips on fabricating lobster.

Goat Cheese and Sweet Onion Crostini

MAKES 8 SERVINGS | PREPARATION TIME: 45 MINUTES

See photograph on page 32.

*G*oat cheese provides a creamy backdrop for this delicious topping of oven-roasted onions and sun-dried tomatoes. Though it takes just a bit of time, the flavor developed by caramelizing onions in the oven is well worth the effort.

24 baguette slices, 1/4-inch thick

1/4 cup Garlic and Parsley Butter (page 36)

3/4 cup Vidalia onions, medium dice

3 tablespoons olive oil

1 1/2 teaspoons salt, or to taste

3/4 teaspoons freshly ground black pepper, or to taste

2 tablespoons sun-dried tomatoes, steeped in oil, chopped

1 teaspoon garlic, chopped

2 teaspoons sugar

1 1/2 teaspoons red wine vinegar

1/2 cup goat cheese

Preheat the oven to 400°F.

Toast the baguette slices in the oven for 5–7 minutes, or until the outside edges are golden brown. Spread each baguette slice with approximately ½ teaspoon of the garlic butter. Reserve the toasts until needed. Turn the oven down to 350°F.

Toss the chopped onions in 2 tablespoons of the olive oil and season with salt and pepper.

Roast the onions in a 350°F oven for 25 minutes, or until soft and fork tender, stirring occasionally.

Sauté the sun-dried tomatoes in the remaining olive oil over medium heat for about 3 minutes, until slightly tender. Stir the mixture with a wooden spoon. Add the garlic and onions and continue to cook over low heat for 7–10 minutes, or until the ingredients are warm and the flavors have blended together.

Add the sugar and red wine vinegar and season to taste with salt and pepper.

Spread 1 heaping teaspoon of goat cheese on each slice of baguette, and top with 1 tablespoon of the onion and sun-dried tomato mixture.

Mussel Crostini

MAKES 8 SERVINGS | PREPARATION TIME: 40 MINUTES

Mussel Crostini are shown here with Goat Cheese and Sweet Onion Crostini (page 31)

and Lobster and Prosciutto Crostini (page 30).

*T*his seafood lover's hors d'oeuvre is an elegant alternative to standard party fare. Garlic, white wine, and tomatoes provide an excellent complement to this mussel mixture made-easy.

24 baguette slices, $^1/_4$-inch thick

$^1/_4$ cup Garlic and Parsley Butter (page 36)

$^1/_2$ cup white wine

$^1/_2$ cup water

3 garlic cloves, minced

1 bay leaf

3 to 4 pounds mussels, cleaned and de-bearded (6 dozen)

$^1/_4$ cup shallots, minced

$2^1/_4$ teaspoons olive oil

2 plum tomatoes, peeled, seeded, and chopped

$^1/_2$ teaspoon red wine vinegar

$^1/_4$ teaspoon salt, or to taste

Pinch freshly ground black pepper, or to taste

1 tablespoon parsley, chopped

Preheat the oven to 400°F.

Toast the baguette slices in the oven for 5–7 minutes, or until the outside edges are golden brown. Spread each baguette slice with approximately ½ teaspoon of the garlic butter. Reserve the toasts until needed.

Combine the wine, water, garlic, and bay leaf in a large pot and bring to a simmer. This should take about 2–3 minutes.

Add the mussels, cover, and cook over high heat for 5 minutes, or just until the mussels open.

Remove the mussels and cool. While the mussels are cooling, return the cooking liquid to a simmer for about 15 minutes,

or until reduced by three-quarters. Reserve the liquid. Sauté the shallots in the olive oil over medium heat, stirring frequently, for 3–4 minutes, or until translucent. Add the tomatoes and the reduced liquid, and cook for 3 minutes, or until the mixture reaches a simmer. Allow to cool completely.

Remove the mussels from their shells and, just before serving, toss them together with the vinegar and parsley. Season to taste with salt and pepper.

Place 3 mussels on each crostini. Garnish each crostini with 1 teaspoon of the tomato mixture.

Shrimp Open-Faced Sandwich

MAKES 8 SERVINGS | PREPARATION TIME: 30 MINUTES

The Shrimp Open-Faced Sandwich is shown here with Red Pepper Orzo (page 329).

Shrimp can be served in a variety of ways, but here, these simple toasts make a unique presentation. Green mayonnaise is easy to make and your favorite herbs can be substituted as desired. Mâche is the ideal garnish, and is most often sold in small quantities in the fresh herb section of the produce aisle.

24 baguette slices, ¼-inch thick
½ cup butter
4 garlic cloves
1½ pounds shrimp (26/30 count), peeled and deveined (48 shrimp)

1 cup white wine
2½ tablespoons parsley, chopped

GREEN MAYONNAISE

½ cup mayonnaise
1 tablespoon dill, chopped

1 tablespoon chives, chopped
1 tablespoon parsley, chopped

48 radish slices (very thinly sliced)
48 mâche leaves

Preheat the oven to 400°F.

Toast the baguette slices in the oven for 5–7 minutes, or until the outside edges are golden brown. Reserve the toasts until needed.

Heat the butter in a large sauté pan until bubbly. Add the garlic and shrimp and sauté 2 minutes on each side. Transfer to a bowl and reserve. Add the white wine to the pan and simmer until it has reduced. Add the chopped parsley to the pan, then pour the reduced wine over the shrimp.

Combine the ingredients for the green mayonnaise in a bowl and mix thoroughly.

Spread 1 teaspoon of the green mayonnaise on each toast. Top each slice with 2 whole cooked shrimp and 2 radish slices. Garnish with mâche leaves.

Garlic and Parsley Butter

MAKES 2 CUPS | PREPARATION TIME: 10 MINUTES

*V*ersatile and delicious, this is a compound butter used in classical French cuisine. The butter holds well, so make enough to enjoy with crostini, or simply on toasted bread as an accompaniment to pasta dishes.

1½ bunches parsley, stems removed

4 garlic cloves, roughly chopped

1 teaspoon salt, or to taste

1 pound butter, diced into small cubes, cold

Place the parsley, garlic, and salt in a food processor fitted with a metal chopping blade and pulse until evenly minced and well blended.

Add the cubed butter to the parsley-garlic mixture. Process, scraping down the sides as needed, until butter is softened and mixture is well blended. The butter should be light green in color.

The butter may be placed into a ramekin, or shaped into a log and rolled in plastic wrap. Refrigerate until ready for use. The butter be can be held for at least a week in the refrigerator, or frozen for several weeks.

Marinated Goat Cheese
with Fresh Herbs

MAKES 8 SERVINGS | PREPARATION TIME: 45 MINUTES

*L*ightly marinated goat cheese serves as a wonderful filling inside of grape leaves. This recipe works best on the grill, but a broiler will do just fine in the off-season.

24 baguette slices, $^1/_4$-inch thick

1 pound fresh goat cheese

$^1/_4$ cup fresh herbs, minced (combination of parsley, tarragon, chives, chervil, tarragon, and a bit of fresh lavender)

1 teaspoon salt, or to taste

$^1/_2$ teaspoon freshly ground black pepper, or to taste

$1^1/_4$ cups extra-virgin olive oil

16 grape leaves, or as needed

Slice the cheese into equal size pieces and place in a small baking dish.

Press the minced herbs evenly over the entire surface of the cheese and season with salt and pepper. Drizzle the cheese with olive oil and let marinate for at least 20 minutes.

While the cheese is marinating, preheat the grill.

Rinse the grape leaves, blot dry, and lay flat on a work surface. Center a portion of the cheese on each grape leaf and fold the edges around the cheese, making sure it is completely en-closed. Continue with the remainder of the cheese. Brush the packets and the slices of bread lightly with olive oil.

Grill the grape leaves and bread until slightly charred, about 2–3 minutes total grilling time. Place the grape leaves on the grilled bread and serve.

NOTE: The size of jarred grape leaves can vary quite a bit, so you may need to overlap a couple of them to get the correct amount of area to wrap around the cheese. If the stems are very coarse, cut them out before wrapping the cheese.

Grilled Vegetable Appetizer

MAKES 6 SERVINGS | PREPARATION TIME: 30 MINUTES

*T*his appetizer would be lovely to serve with French bread which has been sliced on the bias, brushed with the same olive oil mixture used on the vegetables, and grilled. As an alternative, the grilled vegetables could easily be transformed into a vegetarian entrée; look at the similarly prepared Capellini with Grilled Vegetables recipe found on page 260.

1 cup olive oil

$^1/_2$ bunch basil leaves

Salt, to taste

Freshly ground black pepper,
    to taste

1 pound eggplant, sliced into $^1/_2$ -inch thick
    rounds

1 pound zucchini, sliced on the bias into
    $^1/_2$-inch thick slices

1 pound yellow squash, sliced on the bias
    into $^1/_2$-inch thick slices

$1^1/_2$ pounds red peppers, cut into eighths

$^3/_4$ pound yellow peppers, cut into eighths

1 pound portobello mushrooms, stems and
    gills removed, cut into 4 slices each

3 red tomatoes, halved

3 yellow tomatoes, halved

6 scallions, trimmed

6 tablespoons Balsamic Vinaigrette
    (page 128)

Combine the olive oil with the basil, salt, and pepper. Brush the vegetables with this mixture.

Grill the vegetables until they are tender and very hot, about 5 minutes per side. For the tomatoes, grill them just until they are warm, about 1 minute per side.

For each serving, arrange 2–3 slices of eggplant, zucchini, and yellow squash on each plate. Add 2 strips of red pepper, 1 strip of yellow pepper, a half each of grilled red and yellow tomato, and a scallion. Drizzle with the balsamic vinaigrette.

Serve warm or at room temperature.

Prosciutto and Summer Melon Salad

MAKES 8 SERVINGS | PREPARATION TIME: 15 MINUTES

*L*ate summer, when melon is at its peak season, is the best time to enjoy this easy-to-make salad. For the most delicate flavor, make certain that the prosciutto is sliced paper-thin.

2 pounds melon, sliced or diced, mixed (cantaloupe, honeydew, casaba, etc)

8 ounces prosciutto, thinly sliced

4 teaspoons cracked black pepper

16 grissini or breadsticks

3 tablespoons aged balsamic vinegar

For each serving, arrange ¾ cup melon on the plate. Fold in 1 ounce prosciutto or arrange it next to the diced melon.

Drizzle a few drops of aged balsamic vinegar on the melon just before serving. Scatter ½ teaspoon pepper on the plate and serve with two grissini.

NOTE: This simple appetizer can be prepared as a platter for a buffet or individual cubes or spears of melon may be wrapped with a bit of prosciutto and skewered as an hors d'oeuvre.

Salad of Crab and Avocado

MAKES 8 SERVINGS | PREPARATION TIME: 35 MINUTES

*T*his salad is substantial enough to serve as a summertime entrée when accompanied by cornbread (page 316) to accent the salad's Southwestern flavor profile.

$\frac{1}{2}$ cup red pepper, small dice

2 plum tomatoes, cored and chopped

2 scallions, thinly sliced on the bias

1 clove garlic, minced

2 tablespoons cilantro, coarsely chopped

2 teaspoons jalapeño, minced, seeds and veins removed

1 teaspoon salt, or to taste

$\frac{1}{4}$ teaspoon freshly ground black pepper, or to taste

$2\frac{1}{2}$ cups lump crabmeat, pasteurized, picked over to remove cartilage and shell

2 avocados, ripe, small dice

3 tablespoons lime juice

$\frac{1}{4}$ cup sour cream

Toss together the red pepper, tomato, scallions, garlic, cilantro, and jalapeño to form a salsa. Season with $\frac{1}{4}$ teaspoon salt and a pinch of black pepper and let the mixture sit at room temperature while working on the rest of the appetizer (about 20 minutes). Combine the avocado, lime juice, $\frac{1}{2}$ teaspoon salt, and a pinch of black pepper.

In a 6-fluid-ounce glass, layer $\frac{1}{4}$ cup of the tomato salsa, about 5 tablespoons of crab and 2 tablespoons of the avocado mixture. Spoon approximately 1 teaspoon of sour cream on top of the avocado layer. Garnish with a little bit of the salsa.

NOTE: Be sure to wear gloves while mincing the jalapeño to prevent irritation.

RIGHT: After assembling the layers of ingredients in all the glasses, top each with a teaspoon of sour cream and garnish with the salsa.

OPPOSITE: The completed salad.

Shrimp Cocktail

MAKES 6 SERVINGS | PREPARATION TIME: 30 MINUTES

The seasoning for the shrimp pairs well with the Southwestern cocktail sauce. This recipe is nice because it allows you to prepare other dishes while waiting for the shrimp to cool.

1 pound shrimp (26/30 count), peeled and deveined

$1/2$ teaspoon salt, or to taste

$1/4$ teaspoon freshly ground black pepper, or to taste

$1/4$ teaspoon ground cumin

1 tablespoon vegetable oil

1 cup prepared cocktail sauce

1 tablespoon cilantro, minced

2 teaspoons lime juice

1 jalapeño, seeded and minced

Season the shrimp with the salt, pepper, and cumin.

Heat the oil in a sauté pan over medium-high heat. Sauté the shrimp for 2 minutes on each side, or until cooked.

Chill the shrimp for 20 minutes.

While the shrimp are cooling, combine the cocktail sauce, cilantro, lime juice, and jalapeño in a small serving bowl.

Arrange the shrimp around the cocktail sauce and serve.

Camembert Crisps

MAKES 6 SERVINGS | PREPARATION TIME: 35 MINUTES

Timing is important when preparing these delicious treats. For the Camembert to be warm and creamy, the crisps should be served immediately. These crisps pair well with crusty bread, fresh and dried fruits, or a simple green salad.

2 eggs

1 tablespoon milk

3 small Camembert wheels

6 sheets phyllo dough

$1/2$ cup butter, melted

1 cup vegetable oil, or as needed

Whisk together the eggs and milk to make egg wash.

Cut the Camembert wheels in half. Layer three sheets of phyllo, brushing in between each layer with melted butter.

Repeat with remaining sheets, for a total of two stacks of phyllo dough.

Cut each layered phyllo stack lengthwise into three equal strips. Wrap one strip around each piece of cheese. Secure the seam by brushing it with a bit of egg wash. Repeat this procedure until all of the cheese is wrapped in phyllo.

Heat about ¼-inch of oil in a large skillet. Pan fry the wrapped Camembert over high heat until well-browned and crisp on all sides.

Drain on absorbent paper and serve immediately.

Spiced Mixed Nuts

MAKES 1 POUND | PREPARATION TIME: 25 MINUTES

Good for cool autumn afternoons, or just about any time, this delicious nut mixture is great to have on hand for unexpected guests.

¹/₂ teaspoon celery seed

¹/₂ teaspoon garlic powder

¹/₂ teaspoon chili powder

¹/₄ teaspoon ground cumin

¹/₈ teaspoon cayenne pepper

1 teaspoon salt, or to taste

3 tablespoons butter

1 tablespoon Worcestershire sauce

1 pound unsalted raw whole mixed nuts

Preheat the oven to 375°F.

Combine the celery seed, garlic powder, chili powder, cumin, cayenne, and salt.

Melt the butter in a saucepan over medium heat. Add the Worcestershire sauce and bring to a simmer. Add the nuts and mix until evenly coated.

Sprinkle the combined spices over the nuts and stir. Place the nuts on a nonstick or well-greased baking sheet and bake, stirring occasionally, for 15–17 minutes, or until evenly browned.

Cool completely before serving. Store in an airtight container for up to 2 weeks.

NOTE: If saltier nuts are desired, sprinkle with kosher salt while still warm.

Spicy Roasted Cashews

MAKES 1 POUND | PREPARATION TIME: 25 MINUTES

Special enough for the holiday season, these cashews, whether served as a snack or given as a small gift, can be made just as spicy as you like.

1 pound whole raw cashews

2 tablespoons butter, melted

1 teaspoon salt, or to taste

¹/₄ teaspoon garlic powder

¹/₄ teaspoon onion powder

¹/₈ teaspoon cayenne pepper

Preheat the oven to 375°F.

Toss the cashews and melted butter together until evenly coated. Place on a baking sheet and bake until golden brown, about 15–17 minutes.

While the cashews are in the oven, combine the salt and spices; reserve.

Remove the cashews from the oven and toss with the combined spices while still warm. Allow to cool before serving.

The cashews may be stored in an airtight container for up to 2 weeks.

VARIATION: For Spicy Curried Cashews, follow the same procedure, but simply add 1 tablespoon of curry powder to the spice mixture.

Chili-Roasted Peanuts
with Dried Cherries

MAKES 1 POUND | PREPARATION TIME: 25 MINUTES

*S*weet and tart dried cherries add a delicious twist to freshly oven-roasted peanuts, spiked with a light and spicy mixture of cumin, chili powder, cayenne pepper, and oregano.

2 tablespoons butter

1 pound peanuts, raw

1 tablespoon chili powder

2 teaspoons ground cumin

2 teaspoons ground white pepper

1 tablespoon salt, or to taste

$1/2$ teaspoon dried oregano

$1/2$ teaspoon cayenne pepper

$1/2$ pound dried cherries (or raisins)

Preheat the oven to 325°F.

Melt the butter in a small sauce pan.

Coat the raw peanuts with the melted butter.

Spread the peanuts on a large baking sheet and lightly toast for about 10 minutes, shaking the pan occasionally.

Mix together the remaining ingredients, except the cherries, in a large bowl. Transfer the toasted peanuts to the bowl and coat with the dry ingredients. Mix in the cherries.

Cool completely before serving. Store in an airtight container for up to 2 weeks.

CHAPTER THREE

Soups

$\mathcal{F}$ROM THE MOST DELICATE BROTH, TO LIGHT, COOL FRUIT SOUPS, AND ON TO HEARTY PUREES, IT IS POSSIBLE TO FIND A SOUP TO SUIT NEARLY ANY MENU. SOUPS MAY SERVE AS A SINGLE COURSE OF A MEAL, OR THEY MAY BE ITS CENTERPIECE.

Soups can be among the best teachers of important culinary lessons. They fill your mouth completely and instantly, giving you a simultaneous experience of aroma, texture, taste, and temperature. You can taste and evaluate soups at virtually any stage of preparation: if something goes awry, you can usually fix it as you go.

Soups are a good practice ground, for they rely on the most basic skills to prepare something truly delicious. Most soup recipes are extremely adaptable, and can be easily adjusted to meet the needs of the moment, especially when you want to add or substitute ingredients or flavorings. And, when you need a head start on a satisfying meal for busy days, soups are a convenient answer. Most soup recipes are easy to double for a big batch, so you can make them when time permits, then refrigerate or freeze whatever you aren't serving right away to keep for another meal.

Ingredients

Preparing soup within a time constraint can sometimes be a challenge; however, there are many ways you can adapt a soup recipe to meet your schedule by choosing and preparing ingredients wisely.

A variety of broths and other liquids, including water, vegetable essences, milk, or juices can be used as the base for soup. Choose a good quality canned broth; look for brands that are low in sodium with a neutral flavor, so that the broth does not overpower your soup. You can personalize and adjust the taste of prepared broths by adding a few more aromatic vegetables or seasoning ingredients while the soup simmers.

If you are in a pinch, and don't have canned or prepared broth at the ready, don't be afraid to use water and an array of flavorings. A pinch of parsley or other herbs, a splash of lemon juice, dried or fresh mushrooms, a dash of salt and pepper, chiles, fortified wines, vinegar, or a bit of hot sauce are all excellent choices for a flavor adjustment; they can intensify the taste, complement the recipe, and add a whole new flavor dimension to your soup.

Some soups contain an array of aromatic vegetables for a flavor boost. Others are based primarily upon one or two vegetables. Fresh vegetables are the best choice for a full-bodied soup, but at certain times of the year, you may prefer to substitute good quality frozen vegetables. Trim and cut the vegetables properly. The smaller you cut them, the more quickly the soup will cook. If you are going to puree the soup before serving it, neatness isn't extremely important, but a relatively consistent size is, to permit the vegetables to cook evenly. If you are making a soup that is not strained or pureed, pay a bit more attention to the appearance of the cuts for a more attractive finished dish.

If your soup is to be thickened, as you would a cream soup or bisque, be sure to add any additional thickeners, like flour or potatoes, at the point suggested in the recipe. If these ingredients don't have enough time to cook thoroughly, the soup might end up tasting and feeling starchy or pasty.

Heavy cream, sour cream, crème fraîche, or yogurt can be stirred into the soup, or simply added as a dollop right before you serve the soup. Chopped fresh herbs, herb pastes, olive oil, fragrant vinegar, or a few drops of lemon juice are all good ways to make your soup special.

Preparing and Serving Soups

Cook soups at a gentle simmer until they are flavorful, stirring them as often as necessary to keep them from scorching, especially soups made with beans or potatoes or thickened with flour. Taste the soup as it simmers and season it throughout the cooking time.

Serve hot soups very hot and cold soups very cold. Try heating the bowls for hot soups, or chilling the bowls for cold soups; this allows the soup to remain at its optimum temperature for a longer period of time. If you are reheating a soup, be sure to bring it to a simmer. Broth-style soups can be heated over high heat, but start puree or cream soups over low heat until they soften, and stir them frequently as they heat. Taste the soup when it is the right temperature for serving and adjust the seasoning with salt and pepper.

Cream soups are made by simmering a flavorful ingredient such as tomatoes, broccoli, or chicken in a liquid-most often broth, but sometimes milk or cream, and occasionally, water. The soup should be pleasantly thick, an effect achieved by adding flour, potatoes, or rice, or by pureeing the main flavoring ingredient.

➡ PREPARE THE AROMATIC INGREDIENTS

Onions and garlic are two of the most popular aromatics in any soup; you'll find them in most soups, along with additions like carrots, celery, mushrooms, tomatoes, leeks, herbs, or spices. Cook this flavor base gently in a little oil or butter over low to medium heat until they are tender, but without any noticeable browning to keep the soup's color light and appealing. Some recipes call for the main flavoring ingredient to be added at this stage to start developing the flavor. Others call for the main ingredients to be added along with the liquid.

➡ ADD THE LIQUID AND THE ADDITIONAL INGREDIENTS AND SIMMER

When you are preparing large quantities of soup, it can be helpful to bring the liquid to a simmer over low heat while preparing the other ingredients. This will help reduce overall cooking time, since the soup will come to the correct cooking speed more quickly. Simmer the soup, stirring frequently and tasting as you go, until everything is tender enough to puree.

➡ STRAIN THE LIQUID AND PUREE THE SOLIDS

Strain the soup through a colander or wire-mesh sieve, catching the liquid in a bowl or a clean pot. Remove and discard any bay leaves or cheesecloth pouches. Puree the solids in a food processor or blender, adding just enough of the liquid so they puree easily. Then, put the puree in a clean pot and add the liquid until you achieve a good texture and flavor.

➡ FINISHING

Hot cream soups are finished by adding a good quality cream; for the best results, bring the cream to a simmer before you add it to the hot soup. For a cold cream soup, let the hot soup cool completely before stirring in cold cream. Use enough cream to mellow and enrich the soup, but not so much that the taste of the cream overpowers the main ingredient. Adjust the final consistency of the soup with the reserved liquid, if necessary.

See the step-by-step photographs accompanying the recipe for Cream of Tomato Soup with Rice and Basil (page 60).

Vichyssoise

MAKES 2 QUARTS | PREPARATION TIME: 45 MINUTES

*T*his is The Culinary Institute of America's recipe for the classic warm-weather soup. First prepared by French chef Louis Diat at New York City's Ritz-Carlton Hotel in 1917, the chilled potato and leek soup sprinkled with chives was inspired by a favorite hot soup made by Diat's mother.

2 cups leeks, white part only, finely chopped

1/2 onion, minced

2 tablespoons vegetable oil

1 1/4 pounds potatoes, small dice

3 1/2 cups chicken broth

1 cheesecloth pouch containing 2 whole cloves, 2 parsley stems, 2 peppercorns, 1/2 bay leaf

1 1/2 cups half-and-half, chilled

1/2 bunch chives, snipped

1 teaspoon salt, or to taste

1/8 teaspoon ground white pepper

Sweat the leeks and onion in the oil until tender and translucent, about 5 minutes.

Add the potatoes, broth, and cheesecloth pouch. Bring the mixture to a full boil, then reduce the heat and simmer until the potatoes begin to fall apart, about 15 minutes.

Remove and discard the cheesecloth pouch. Use a handheld blender to puree the soup. Transfer to a wide, shallow vessel and place in the freezer for 20 minutes, stirring occasionally.

To finish the soup, add the cold half-and-half to the soup, fold in the chives, and season to taste with salt and pepper.

Thai Fresh Pea Soup

MAKES 2 QUARTS | PREPARATION TIME: 30 MINUTES

*T*his soup adds a subtle twist to the delicate taste of peas. It is a great recipe if you have a bumper crop of fresh peas (though frozen peas will work equally well), or if you are looking for an easy starter course for an evening of Thai cuisine.

1 cup onions, diced

4 garlic cloves, finely minced

2 teaspoons green curry paste

1½ quarts vegetable broth

2½ pounds shelled peas (thawed if frozen)

1 teaspoon salt, or to taste

½ teaspoon freshly ground black pepper, or to taste

1 teaspoon mustard seeds, lightly toasted

¼ cup mint, chopped

Sweat the onions, garlic, curry paste, and a small amount of the broth in a soup pot over medium heat, about 2–3 minutes.

Add the remaining broth to the pot and bring to a boil. Add the peas, cover the soup, and simmer for 10 minutes. Remove the soup from the heat and allow to cool for 5 to 10 minutes.

Puree the soup with a handheld blender, or in batches in a food processor or countertop blender. Season to taste with salt and pepper and reheat the soup, if necessary.

Sprinkle the toasted mustard seeds over the finished soup before serving, and garnish with chopped mint.

Curried Apple Squash Soup
with Lime Gremolata

MAKES 2 QUARTS | PREPARATION TIME: 45 MINUTES

*T*his mildly spicy soup is perfect for an early fall lunch. Choose tart, full-flavored apples that are in season for best results.

This soup is easy to make and benefits from being prepared up to a day ahead.

2 stalks celery, diced

2 leeks, diced

2 tablespoons garlic, minced

9 cups vegetable broth, divided use

2 teaspoons curry powder

$1/4$ teaspoon ground cinnamon

$1/2$ teaspoon ground nutmeg

18 ounces butternut squash, peeled, seeded, chopped

$2^1/4$ pounds apples, peeled, chopped

1 teaspoon salt, or to taste

LIME GREMOLATA

1 tablespoon garlic, minced

$2^1/4$ teaspoons lime zest

$1/2$ teaspoon thyme, minced

In a soup pot, sweat the celery, leeks, and garlic in a small amount of the broth until the onions are translucent, about 5–7 minutes.

Add 7 cups of the broth along with the curry powder, cinnamon, and nutmeg. Bring to a boil.

Add the squash and simmer for 8 minutes.

Add the apples and continue to simmer until all of the ingredients are tender, about 5 minutes. Remove the soup from the heat and allow to cool for 5 to 10 minutes.

Puree the soup with a handheld blender, or in batches in a food processor or countertop blender. Add in just enough of the remaining 2 cups of broth to thin the soup to the desired consistency, and season with salt to taste. Chill the finished soup thoroughly.

Combine the gremolata ingredients.

Garnish each serving of soup with a rounded ½ teaspoon of the gremolata.

Traditional Black Bean Soup

MAKES 2 QUARTS | PREPARATION TIME: 40 MINUTES

*T*his version of a traditional Mexican favorite removes the time-consuming steps required in preparing dried black beans. This vegetarian rendition develops excellent flavor using garlic, dried herbs, peppers and sun-dried tomatoes.

¹/₄ pound onion, diced

2 tablespoons garlic, minced

2 tablespoons olive oil

¹/₂ teaspoon cumin, ground

1 lemon, thickly sliced

1 ounce sun-dried tomatoes, chopped

1 teaspoon jalapeños, minced

1 teaspoon dried oregano

¹/₂ teaspoon salt, or to taste

3 pounds canned black beans, drained and rinsed

2 quarts vegetable broth

1¹/₂ tablespoons sherry vinegar

In a 3 quart pot, sauté the onions and garlic in the oil until translucent. Add the ground cumin and continue to sauté until fragrant, about 1 minute.

Add the lemon slices, tomatoes, jalapeños, oregano, salt, beans, and vegetable broth. Simmer for 15 minutes.

Remove and discard the lemon slices. Use a handheld blender, or a food processor or countertop blender, to partially puree 3 cups of the soup (it should be thick and chunky), and add it back to the pot. Cook for an additional 10 minutes.

Finish the soup by adding the vinegar.

FOCUS ON | Evaluating the Quality of Puree and Cream Soups

Cream soups and purees are best when they are intensely flavored and lightly thickened with a good color and an appealing aroma.

Soups should be made with quality ingredients, from the aromatics through to the main ingredient, and on to the finishing ingredients. Be sure that the vegetables, meats, and cream are fresh and flavorful. Trimming and cutting them properly before you add them to the soup pot allows them to release their flavors quickly, without overcooking or turning a muddy or grayish color.

TOO THICK: These soups should pour easily from the ladle or spoon; a soup thick enough to hold the spoon upright is too thick. And because they contain starchy ingredients, these soups may keep getting thicker as they simmer, or during storage. If your soup is too thick, use additional broth or water to thin it and adjust the seasoning again once the texture is right.

BURNT OR SCORCHED FLAVOR OR AROMA: Stir soups as they simmer so that they don't scorch. As you stir, check the way the spoon feels against the bottom of the pot. If the soup has started to thicken and stick, transfer it to a clean pot to prevent it from burning.

HARSH FLAVOR: If the flavor is too harsh, the ratio of ingredients used was incorrect. The vegetables may not have been properly sweated or the soup might not have been cooked long enough. Taste the soup as it simmers to determine when the flavor is best.

Chilled Cream of Avocado

MAKES 2 QUARTS | PREPARATION TIME: 40 MINUTES

*T*his soup, one of the easiest in this book, manages to preserve the elusive flavor of the avocado. Use only very ripe avocados for this soup. If you buy avocados that aren't ripe, you can speed the ripening process by placing them in a closed paper bag with an apple. The apple will give off ethylene gas, which accelerates ripening. You can garnish this soup with the suggested tomato and tortilla strips, or for a more elegant (albeit expensive) touch, garnish with lump crabmeat, cooked fresh corn kernels, and a touch of finely diced red pepper tossed with a dash of lemon or lime juice.

4 avocados	$^1/_2$ teaspoon ground coriander	Salt, to taste
4 to 5 cups vegetable broth	$2^1/_2$ tablespoons lime juice	Ground white pepper, to taste
1 teaspoon chili powder	2 cups plain yogurt	1 red pepper, diced

Cut each avocado in half from top to bottom, following the contour of the pit in the center. Remove the pit and scoop out the avocado.

Puree the avocado in a food processor or blender with 4 cups of the broth, the chili powder, coriander, lime juice, and yogurt until very smooth. If the soup is too thick, add more broth to correct the consistency. Transfer to a bowl, cover, and chill in the freezer for 30 minutes.

Adjust the seasoning to taste with salt and white pepper. Garnish the soup with the red pepper.

Cream of Mushroom Soup

MAKES 2 QUARTS | PREPARATION TIME: 45 MINUTES

So-called exotic varieties of mushrooms, such as cremini and oyster, work well in this soup, as do regular white mushrooms. Use a combination or a single variety, depending on your taste and what's available.

2 tablespoons butter	2 quarts mushrooms, sliced	3/4 cup heavy cream
2 garlic cloves, chopped	1/4 cup all-purpose flour	Chives, sliced, as needed
1 cup onions, chopped	1/4 cup sherry wine	1/8 teaspoon nutmeg (optional)
1/2 cup celeriac, chopped	6 cups vegetable broth	

In a large soup pot, melt the butter and sweat the garlic, onions and celeriac until translucent, about 5–7 minutes.

Add the mushrooms and cook until tender, about 5 minutes.

Sprinkle the mixture with flour and mix well.

Add the sherry wine and vegetable broth and simmer everything until the mushrooms are completely tender, approximately 25 minutes. Allow the soup to cool slightly before pureeing.

Puree the soup with a handheld blender, or in batches in a food processor or countertop blender. Strain the pureed soup through a colander or sieve, then return it to a simmer.

Gently simmer the heavy cream before adding it to the soup. Adjust the consistency of the soup with a little more broth, if needed. Season to taste with salt and pepper.

Pour into warmed soup cups or bowls and garnish with sliced chives and the nutmeg, if using.

Cream of Tomato Soup
with Rice and Basil

MAKES 2 QUARTS | PREPARATION TIME: 35 MINUTES

*T*his delicious version of an old favorite is full of tomato flavor and is sure to bring back memories of home. If you have really flavorful, ripe tomatoes, use them in place of canned tomatoes. Otherwise, canned tomatoes offer the best flavor and consistency.

2 tablespoons olive oil	¼ cup basil, chopped	1 cup heavy cream
1½ cups onions, chopped	28 ounces canned plum tomatoes	2 cups rice, cooked
1 tablespoon garlic, chopped	1 quart vegetable broth	1 tablespoons basil, chiffonade

Sweat the onions and garlic in a little olive oil until translucent, about 5–7 minutes. Add the broth, fresh basil, and tomatoes, reserving some of the juice from the tomatoes. Simmer until everything is tender, about 20 minutes.

Puree the soup with a handheld blender, or in batches in a food processor or countertop blender.

Return the pureed soup to a low simmer. Gently simmer the heavy cream before adding it to the soup, then use the reserved tomato juice to adjust the final consistency. Add the rice just before serving.

Serve the soup in preheated soup cups or bowls and garnish with the chiffonade of basil.

ABOVE, LEFT TO RIGHT: Aromatics are cooked to the desired stage before the liquid is added; cream is added to the soup before adjusting the final consistency; the final consistency of the cream soup. The soup is garnished before being brought to the table.

Corn Chowder
with Chiles and Monterey Jack

MAKES 2 QUARTS | PREPARATION TIME: 45 MINUTES

This chowder is best made with fresh corn on the cob, but if corn is out of season and you are desperate for corn chowder, you may substitute frozen corn that has been thawed. To avoid this situation altogether, make an extra batch or two at the height of corn season, and freeze to enjoy in the dead of winter, when fresh corn is but a distant memory.

4 cups corn kernels, fresh or frozen

1 cup heavy cream

2 slices bacon, minced

1 onion, medium, finely diced

1 red bell pepper, finely diced

1 celery stalk, finely diced

1 garlic clove, minced

1½ quarts chicken broth

3 yellow potatoes, peeled and diced

3 tomatoes, peeled, seeded, chopped, juices reserved

4 ounces canned green chiles, drained and chopped

1 cup Monterey Jack cheese, shredded

1 tablespoon salt, or to taste

Freshly ground black pepper, to taste

Tabasco sauce, to taste

Cut the corn kernels from the cobs with a sharp knife, capturing as much of the juice as possible. Reserve ¾ cup of the corn kernels and puree the rest with the heavy cream in a food processor or blender. Reserve until needed.

Cook the bacon in a soup pot over medium heat until crisp, about 8 minutes. Add the onion, pepper, celery, and garlic. Cover and reduce the heat to low. Cook, stirring occasionally, until the vegetables are tender, about 8–10 minutes.

Add the broth, potatoes, and tomatoes, including their juices. Bring the soup to a simmer and cook, covered, until the potatoes are tender, about 15 minutes. Skim any fat from the surface of the soup and discard.

Add the pureed corn and cream, the reserved corn kernels, the chiles, and the cheese. Warm the soup and season to taste with salt, pepper, and Tabasco.

Crab and Mushroom Chowder

MAKES 8 SERVINGS | PREPARATION TIME: 45 MINUTES

*M*any supermarkets now carry a wide selection of more unusual mushroom varieties, such as shiitake, oyster, and enoki. You can make this delicious chowder using a single variety or a combination.

1 pound assorted mushrooms (oyster, shiitake, cremini, white)

6 tablespoons butter

$^1/_2$ onion, diced

$^1/_2$ celery stalk, diced

$^1/_2$ leek, white and light green part, diced

4 garlic cloves, minced

$^1/_2$ cup all-purpose flour

1 quart chicken broth

1 pound russet potatoes, peeled, diced

$^3/_4$ cup milk

1 tablespoon dry sherry

2 tablespoons heavy cream

1 teaspoon salt, or to taste

1 teaspoon freshly ground black pepper, or to taste

3 tablespoons sherry

10 ounces crabmeat, picked over for shells

Cut the stems from the mushrooms and slice the mushroom caps into ¼-inch thick slices. Set the caps aside. Simmer the stems in ¾ cup water for 15 minutes to make a mushroom broth. Strain the broth and set aside.

While the broth is simmering, heat 5 tablespoons of the butter in a large soup pot. Add the onion, celery, leek, and garlic. Cook, stirring occasionally, until tender, 8–10 minutes.

Add the flour and cook, stirring, for 3–4 minutes. Gradually whisk in the chicken broth and bring to a simmer. Cook for 15 minutes. Strain through a sieve, pressing hard on the solids to recover as much thickened broth as possible. Return the broth to a simmer and discard the solids.

Add the potatoes to the broth and simmer until tender, about 15 minutes. Remove the pot from the heat and add the milk, sherry, and heavy cream. Season to taste with salt and pepper.

Meanwhile, melt the remaining tablespoon of butter in a skillet over medium heat. Add the sliced mushroom caps and sauté until tender, 7–10 minutes. Deglaze the pan with the sherry, stirring and scraping the bottom of the pan with a wooden spoon to loosen any particles of mushroom stuck to the pan. Season to taste with salt and pepper.

Stir the crabmeat, along with the mushrooms and their reserved broth, into the chowder. Check the seasoning and adjust with additional salt or pepper if needed.

Manhattan Clam Chowder

MAKES 2 QUARTS | PREPARATION TIME: 45 MINUTES

*T*his is the classic mid-Atlantic clam chowder, not to be confused with New England's version. So controversial was the inclusion of tomatoes to New Englanders that a piece of legislation attempting to ban tomatoes from any true chowder was once introduced in Maine. Fresh clams taste great in the chowder, and leaving them in the shell provides a dramatic presentation. In the interest of time, you can substitute 1 cup canned clam meat and an additional ¾ cup bottled clam juice for the fresh clams and juice.

1 tablespoon canola oil

2 leeks, white and green parts, diced

1 onion, diced

1 carrot, diced

1 celery stalk, diced

1 red bell pepper, seeds and ribs removed, diced

2 garlic cloves, minced

2 plum tomatoes, canned, coarsely chopped

2 white or yellow potatoes, peeled and diced

3 cups clam juice

1 cup tomato juice

1 bay leaf

Pinch dried thyme leaves

3 dozen chowder clams, shucked, chopped, juices reserved

Salt, to taste

Freshly ground black pepper, to taste

Tabasco, to taste

Heat the oil in a large soup pot over medium-high heat. Add the leek, onion, carrot, celery, pepper, and garlic. Cover the pot and cook over medium-low heat, stirring occasionally, until the vegetables are soft and translucent, about 8–10 minutes.

Add the tomatoes, potatoes, clam juice, tomato juice, bay leaf, and thyme. Bring to a simmer and cook until the potatoes are tender, about 15 minutes.

Add the clams with their juices and simmer until the clams are cooked, about 1–2 minutes more. Using a shallow, flat spoon, remove any surface fat and discard. Remove the bay leaf and season to taste with salt, pepper, and Tabasco.

VARIATION: Replace the clams with one pound of lean boneless fish such as fresh cod, Pollock or haddock, cut into a 1-inch dice. Use fish broth instead of the clam juice.

New England Clam Chowder

MAKES 2 QUARTS | PREPARATION TIME: 45 MINUTES

*T*his is the Culinary Institute of America's version of the American classic, rich and creamy. Paired with a salad and bread, it becomes a hearty meal.

1¼ pound canned clams, minced, juices reserved

2–3 cups bottled clam juice

2 bacon slices, minced

1 onion, diced

2 tablespoons all-purpose flour

1 bay leaf

½ teaspoon thyme leaves, chopped

1 pound potatoes, peeled, diced

3 cups heavy cream or half and half

6 tablespoons dry sherry, or to taste

Salt, to taste

Freshly ground black pepper, to taste

Tabasco sauce, to taste

Worcestershire sauce, to taste

Oyster or saltine crackers, as needed

Drain the clam juice from the minced clams and combine with enough bottled juice to equal 3 cups of liquid.

Cook the bacon slowly in a soup pot over medium heat until lightly crisp, about 8 minutes.

Add the onion and cook, stirring occasionally, until the onion is translucent, about 5–7 minutes. Add the flour and cook over low heat, stirring with a wooden spoon, for 2–3 minutes.

Whisk in the clam juice, bring to a simmer, and cook for 5 minutes, stirring occasionally. The liquid should be the consistency of heavy cream. If it is too thick, add more clam juice to adjust the consistency. Add the bay leaf and fresh thyme.

Add the potatoes and simmer until tender, about 15 minutes.

Meanwhile, place the clams and cream in a saucepan and simmer together until the clams are cooked, about 5–8 minutes.

When the potatoes are tender, add the clams and cream to the soup base. Simmer for 1–2 minutes.

Stir in the sherry. Season to taste with salt, pepper, Tabasco, and Worcestershire sauce. Serve in bowls with the crackers on the side.

Shrimp Bisque
with Fresh Tarragon

MAKES 2 QUARTS | PREPARATION TIME: 45 MINUTES

Much of the flavor of this soup comes from the shrimp shells, but don't think that you have to buy pounds of expensive shrimp just to make good bisque. Instead, every time you purchase shrimp, save the shells in the freezer. Also consider checking with your local fishmonger, who will most likely just sell you what you need.

1/2–1 pound shrimp shells

2 tablespoons vegetable oil

1 cup onions, large dice

1 cup leeks, large dice

2 celery stalks, diced

3 garlic cloves, crushed

1 bay leaf

4 tarragon sprigs

10 black peppercorns

1/4 cup tomato paste

1/4 cup all-purpose flour

3/4 cup sherry wine, plus as needed to taste

1 quart vegetable or chicken broth

1 cup heavy cream

Salt, to taste

Ground white pepper, to taste

Tabasco sauce, to taste

Worcestershire sauce, to taste

1 pound shrimp, peeled and deveined

2 tablespoons tarragon leaves, chopped

In a large soup pot, sauté the shrimp shells in the vegetable oil until bright pink or red, about 2–3 minutes.

Add the onions, leeks, and celery, and cook over medium-high heat until they develop a light brown color, 10–12 minutes.

Add the garlic cloves, bay leaf, tarragon sprigs, and peppercorns; continue to cook for 3–4 minutes.

Add the tomato paste and cook until it becomes slightly reddish brown, about 2 minutes.

Add the flour and cook, stirring frequently, until the raw smell is gone, 3–4 minutes.

Add the sherry wine and stir to work out any lumps. Add the broth and bring to a simmer for about 10–15 minutes.

Strain the soup through a fine sieve into a clean pot. Gently heat the cream and add it to the soup. Season to taste with salt, pepper, Tabasco, and Worcestershire. Finish with additional sherry wine, to taste, if desired.

Dice the shrimp meat and add it to the bisque. Return to a simmer until the shrimp is just cooked, 3–4 minutes. Garnish with chopped tarragon leaves.

Double Chicken Broth
with Shiitakes, Scallions, and Tofu

Double chicken broth means simply that chicken broth is used to poach more chicken, creating a richer and more intensely flavorful broth.

6 ounces tofu, firm, diced

$^1/_2$ pound chicken breast, boneless, skinless

2 quarts chicken broth

8 shiitake mushrooms, woody part of the stem removed, sliced

6 scallions, sliced thinly on the bias

2 tablespoons cilantro, chopped

2 teaspoons ginger, minced

2 tablespoons soy or tamari sauce

$^1/_2$ teaspoon freshly ground black pepper, or to taste

Lime juice, to taste

Place the tofu on absorbent paper and allow it to drain while the soup is simmering.

Trim any visible fat from the chicken breast and discard. Cut the breast meat into strips.

Bring the broth to a simmer in a soup pot over high heat. Add the chicken, reduce the heat to low, and simmer for 10 minutes. Skim away any foam that rises to the surface.

Add the tofu, shiitakes, scallions, cilantro, and ginger. Simmer until all of the ingredients are heated through and the flavors are blended, 5–10 minutes.

Season with soy sauce, pepper, and lime juice to taste.

Egg Drop Soup

*T*his homemade version of the Chinese restaurant favorite, with its subtle ginger and scallion flavor, is quick and easy to make.

3 teaspoons vegetable oil

5 tablespoons scallions, thinly sliced

1¹/₂ teaspoons grated ginger

2 quarts chicken broth

1 teaspoon salt, or to taste

3 eggs, large

Heat the oil in a large wok or a soup pot over medium-high heat. Add 1 tablespoon of the scallions and the grated ginger. Stir-fry until softened, about 1 minute.

Add the broth and bring to a boil. Season to taste with the salt.

Beat the eggs gently in a bowl. Pour them into the soup while slowly stirring with a spoon, breaking the eggs into pieces.

Serve in heated bowls and garnish with the remaining scallion greens.

Stracciatella alla Romana
(Roman Egg Drop Soup)

*T*his simple soup is traditionally made with either beef or chicken broth as its base. Essentially an Italian "egg drop" soup, this version is easy to make and shows off a delicate garnish of baby spinach.

8 cups chicken or beef broth

10 ounces spinach, stems removed, or whole baby spinach leaves

4 eggs, large

1 cup Parmesan cheese, grated

¹/₂ teaspoon salt, or to taste

¹/₂ teaspoon freshly ground black pepper, or to taste

Bring the broth to a full rolling boil.

Combine the eggs, spinach, and cheese together.

Pour the egg mixture into the broth and give the pot one stir. An egg "raft" will form; allow the raft to cook for five minutes or until solid.

Break the raft apart with a spoon or by pouring the soup into another container; season with salt and black pepper.

Amish-Style Chicken and Corn Soup

MAKES 2 QUARTS | PREPARATION TIME: 35 MINUTES

*T*he Amish are famous for their use of herbs and spices. The use of saffron in this soup lends it a deep, golden color as well as a subtle flavor. The delicate threads should be crushed just before they are added to the dish.

6 cups chicken broth

2 chicken breasts, boneless, skinless

1 onion, chopped

1 carrot, peeled, chopped

1 celery stalk, chopped

$^1/_2$ teaspoon saffron threads, crushed (optional)

1 cup corn kernels, fresh or frozen

1 cup egg noodles, cooked

$^1/_2$ teaspoon salt, or to taste

$^1/_2$ teaspoon freshly ground black pepper, or to taste

2 tablespoons parsley, chopped

1 tablespoon dill, chopped (optional)

2 teaspoons tarragon, chopped (optional)

Bring the broth to a simmer in a large soup pot.

While the broth heats, dice the chicken breast and reserve it in the refrigerator. Add the onion, carrot, and celery to the simmering broth along with the saffron, if using.

If using fresh corn, remove the husk and cut the kernels from the cob. If using frozen corn, remove the corn from the freezer and let it thaw while preparing the soup; it does not have to be fully thawed.

Bring the mixture to a boil, reduce the heat and simmer, covered, for 15 minutes, or until the carrots and celery are tender to the bite. Occasionally skim off any scum that accumulates on the surface.

Add the chicken, corn, and noodles to the broth and continue to simmer until the chicken and noodles are fully cooked, another 10 minutes. Season with salt and pepper to taste.

Add the parsley, and optional dill and tarragon, to the soup. Simmer for another 2–3 minutes and adjust the seasoning with salt and pepper.

Chilled Gazpacho

MAKES 2 QUARTS | PREPARATION TIME: 40 MINUTES

*T*his tangy marriage of fresh tomato, cucumber, pepper, and onion is a summer favorite. The flavor of gazpacho improves if allowed to chill overnight, but thereafter this soup has a short shelf life. It is best prepared no more than a day or two before it will be eaten.

1 quart chicken or vegetable broth

28 ounces canned plum tomatoes, with liquid

1 green pepper, sliced in eighths

6 scallions, roughly chopped

1 cucumber, peeled, seeded, and sliced

1 jalapeño, diced

3 tablespoons basil, chopped

1½ tablespoons extra-virgin olive oil

1½ tablespoons balsamic vinegar

1 tablespoon tarragon

2 teaspoons Worcestershire sauce

1 tablespoon lime juice

½ teaspoon salt, or to taste

½ teaspoon Tabasco sauce

¼ teaspoon ground white pepper

GARNISH

1 garlic clove

2 teaspoons extra-virgin olive oil

2 bread slices, cut into ¼-inch cubes

Combine all of the ingredients (except for the garnish) and puree until smooth in a food processor or blender. Chill in the freezer for 30 minutes, stirring occasionally.

To make the garnish, sauté the garlic clove in the olive oil until aromatic, 1 minute.

Remove the garlic clove from the oil and add the bread cubes. Sauté over medium-high heat, turning frequently, until crisp and lightly browned, 3–4 minutes.

Garnish each serving of soup with a small amount of the croutons.

Borscht

MAKES 2 QUARTS | PREPARATION TIME: 45 MINUTES

*B*orscht is one of those soups that has dozens of variations. This version of the classic Russian beet soup uses lots of vegetables and a touch of bacon for extra flavor. You can leave the bacon out and use vegetable broth if you prefer a vegetarian soup. Grating the beets into the soup releases maximum beet flavor. Though this recipe calls for the borscht to be served hot, it is also delicious when served cold.

2 quarts beef, chicken, or vegetable broth

1 tablespoon vegetable oil

2 onions, diced

2 garlic cloves, minced

1 teaspoon dried marjoram

2 celery stalks, trimmed, thinly sliced

2 parsnips, peeled, thinly sliced

1 carrot, peeled, thinly sliced

1 leek, white and light green parts, thinly sliced

1/2 head savoy cabbage, shredded

1 bay leaf

1 teaspoon salt, or to taste

1/2 teaspoon freshly ground black pepper, or to taste

2 beets, peeled, grated

1/4 cup dill, minced

2–3 tablespoons red wine vinegar, or as needed

1/2 cup sour cream

Bring the broth to a simmer while you peel and prepare the vegetables.

Heat a large soup pot over medium heat with the oil. Add the onions and garlic. Cook, stirring frequently, until the onions are tender and golden, about 5 minutes. Stir in the marjoram.

Add the celery, parsnips, carrot, leek, and cabbage. Cover and cook over low heat, stirring occasionally, until the vegetables are slightly tender, about 8 minutes

Add the broth and the bay leaf. Season to taste with salt and pepper. Bring the soup to a simmer and cook, partially covered, for 10 minutes before grating the beets directly into the soup. Simmer, partially covered, until the soup is flavorful and the vegetables are completely tender, about 15 minutes. Stir in the dill. Add the red wine vinegar, salt, and pepper to taste.

Garnish the soup with sour cream and serve.

Chorizo and Vegetable Soup

MAKES 2 QUARTS | PREPARATION TIME: 45 MINUTES

*C*horizo, a sausage popular in both Mexican and Spanish cuisines, is made from either fresh or smoked pork, seasoned with garlic and powdered chiles. Even a small amount will deliver bold and exciting flavor to a simple delicious vegetable soup.

5 ounces chorizo, diced

1 tablespoon olive oil

1 cup onion, chopped

$1/4$ cup celery, chopped

$1/2$ tablespoon cumin seeds

2 teaspoons garlic, minced

5 cups chicken broth

4 cups canned plum tomatoes

1 cup potatoes, peeled, diced

1 cup red peppers, diced

3 tablespoons tomato paste

1 bay leaf

2 tablespoons parsley, chopped

$1/2$ teaspoon oregano, chopped

1 tablespoon salt, or to taste

$2^3/4$ cups corn kernels, fresh or frozen

$1/2$ teaspoon freshly ground black pepper, or to taste

$1/2$ tablespoon cilantro, chopped

Sauté the chorizo in a large soup pot until browned, about 10 minutes. Transfer to absorbent towels.

Heat the oil in the same pot. Add the onion, celery, cumin seeds, and garlic. Sauté over medium heat until the onions are translucent, about 5–7 minutes.

Add the chorizo, broth, tomatoes, potatoes, peppers, tomato paste, bay leaf, half the parsley, the oregano, and the salt. Simmer until the potatoes are tender, about 15 minutes.

Discard the bay leaf. Stir in the corn and black pepper. Simmer until thoroughly heated, another 5-6 minutes.

Garnish each serving with the cilantro and remaining parsley.

Minestrone

MAKES 2 QUARTS | PREPARATION TIME: 45 MINUTES

*T*his soup bursts with the flavors of fresh vegetables, which can be varied depending on what is seasonally available. Follow this formula for a delicious soup, or create a variation of your own.

2 tablespoons olive oil

1 ounce pancetta, chopped (about 5–6 thin slices) (optional)

1¹/₂ cups green cabbage, chopped

1 cup onions, chopped

1 cup carrots, sliced

1 cup celery, chopped

2 garlic cloves, minced

2 quarts chicken broth

1 cup potatoes, peeled, diced

1 ounce Parmesan cheese rind (about one 3-inch piece) (optional)

³/₄ cup vermicelli or angel hair pasta, broken into 2-inch pieces

¹/₂ cup canned plum tomatoes, drained, chopped

¹/₂ cup cooked or canned chickpeas, drained and rinsed

¹/₂ cup cooked or canned kidney beans, drained and rinsed

1 tablespoon salt, or to taste

¹/₂ tablespoon freshly ground black pepper, or to taste

Freshly grated Parmesan cheese (optional), as needed

Heat the oil in a soup pot over medium heat. Add the pancetta and cook until the fat melts, about 3 to 5 minutes. Do not allow the pancetta to brown.

Add the cabbage, onions, carrots, celery, and garlic. Cook until the onions are translucent, about 6 to 8 minutes.

Add the broth, potatoes, and Parmesan cheese rind, if using. Bring the mixture to a simmer and cook until the vegetables are tender, about 30 minutes. Be sure to not overcook the vegetables.

When the vegetables in the soup are just tender, add the vermicelli, tomatoes, chickpeas, and kidney beans. Remove and discard the Parmesan rind.

Season the soup to taste with the salt and pepper. Garnish the soup with sprinkled cheese if desired.

NOTE: The soup can be made vegan by omitting the pancetta and the Parmesan cheese.

Hlelem
(Tunisian Vegetable and Bean Soup)

MAKES 2 QUARTS | PREPARATION TIME: 35 MINUTES

*P*acked with beans and greens, this slightly spicy vegetable soup is both tasty and good for you. Harissa is a Tunisian hot sauce or paste usually made with hot chiles, garlic, cumin, coriander, caraway and olive oil. It's available in cans, jars, or tubes from Middle Eastern markets and specialty stores.

2 tablespoons olive oil

4 teaspoons garlic, minced

$^1/_4$ cup celery stalk, large outer veins trimmed, diced

$^1/_4$ cup onion, minced

1 quart chicken broth

6 tablespoons tomato paste

$^2/_3$ cup canned lima beans, drained, juices reserved

$^2/_3$ cup canned chickpeas, drained, juices reserved

7 cups Swiss chard leaves, stems removed and cut into 1-inch pieces, leaves shredded, lightly packed

$^1/_2$ cup angel hair pasta, dry, broken into bite-sized pieces

$^1/_2$ tablespoon red curry paste (or harissa)

Salt, to taste

Freshly ground black pepper, to taste

$^1/_4$ cup parsley, chopped

Heat the olive oil in a soup pot over medium heat. Add the garlic, celery, and onion. Cook, stirring occasionally, until the onion is translucent, about 5–7 minutes.

Combine ½ cup of the reserved chickpea liquid with ½ cup of the reserved lima bean liquid. Add the broth, reserved bean liquid, and the tomato paste. Mix together until well blended and bring to a simmer for 10 minutes.

Approximately 10 minutes before serving, add the cooked beans and chickpeas, the Swiss chard, and the pasta. Simmer until the pasta and chard stems are tender, about 10 minutes.

Add the red curry paste and stir until blended. Season to taste with the salt and pepper. Garnish with the chopped parsley.

Mussel Soup

MAKES 2 QUARTS | PREPARATION TIME: 40 MINUTES

*T*he hairy, inedible filaments that protrude from a mussel are known as a "beard." To debeard a mussel, pinch the filaments between thumb and forefinger and pull firmly. Debearding a mussel kills it, so wait until just before cooking to perform this step. You can substitute a variety of seafood for the mussels if you like. Any white fish, such as flounder, halibut, or monkfish, works well, as does shelled and deveined shrimp.

$^1/_2$ cup white wine

1 medium onion, minced

1 bay leaf

2 fresh thyme sprigs (optional)

1–2 cups water, as needed

3 pounds mussels, debearded and scrubbed well under cold running water

2 tablespoons olive oil

1 leek, white and light green parts, finely diced

1 celery stalk, finely diced

2 garlic cloves, minced

2 cups plum tomatoes, drained, seeded, and chopped, juices reserved

1 teaspoon dried basil

Salt, to taste

Freshly ground black pepper, to taste

$^1/_2$ teaspoon lemon zest, grated

$^1/_4$ cup basil or parsley, chopped

In a pot large enough to accommodate the mussels, combine the wine, ¼ cup of the onion, bay leaf, thyme sprig (if using), and enough of the water to raise the liquid level to about 1 inch. Bring to a boil. Add the mussels, cover, and steam until the mussels open, about 5 minutes. Use a slotted spoon to transfer the mussels to a bowl and allow them to cool slightly. Remove the mussels from their shells and set aside. Discard the shells. Strain the cooking liquid, including the liquid released by shucked mussels, through a coffee filter and set aside.

Heat the olive oil in a soup pot over medium heat. Add the remaining onion, leek, celery, and garlic. Cover the pot, reduce the heat to medium-low, and cook until the vegetables are translucent, about 5–7 minutes.

Combine the mussel cooking liquid with the reserved tomato juice. Add enough water to bring the amount of liquid to 4 cups. Add this mixture along with the tomatoes and the dried basil to the soup pot. Bring to a simmer and cook, partially covered, for 10–12 minutes.

Add the mussels and cover the pot. Simmer until the mussels are heated through, about 2 minutes.

Season to taste with the salt, pepper, and lemon zest. Garnish with the basil or parsley.

VARIATIONS: Add $^1/_2$ teaspoon of saffron along with the tomatoes. Substitute $^1/_4$ cup Pernod and $^1/_4$ cup dry vermouth for the white wine.

Add a sachet containing $^1/_2$ teaspoon each of anise seeds and fennel seeds and 1 clove of peeled garlic, at the same time that the tomatoes are added.

Thai Hot and Sour Soup

*T*hai Hot and Sour Soup creates a complex interplay of spicy hot chile and sour citrus flavors on the palate. All of the ingredients are crucial to the overall flavor, so try not to leave anything out. You can find the ingredients at Asian groceries and some specialty markets. Once you have all your ingredients assembled, the soup is a snap to put together.

2 ounces thin rice noodles (vermicelli)

2 quarts chicken broth

1 stalk lemon grass, cut into 2-inch pieces and smashed

2 tablespoons Thai fish sauce (nam pla)

1 tablespoon chili oil

2 teaspoons lime zest

2 tablespoons canned jalapeños, minced

3 tablespoons lemon juice

1½ tablespoons lime juice

½ pound shrimp (30–35 count), peeled and butterflied

8 ounces straw mushrooms, canned, drained

¼ cup cilantro, chopped

Bring a medium-sized pot of water to a boil. Add the rice noodles and boil until tender, about 3–4 minutes. Drain, rinse under cold water, and drain again. Set aside.

Combine the chicken broth with the lemon grass, fish sauce, chili oil, lime zest, jalapeños, lemon juice, and lime juice in a wok or soup pot. Bring to a simmer and cook for 7 minutes.

Strain or use a slotted spoon to remove the lemon grass. Add the shrimp and cook 3 minutes.

Distribute the rice noodles, shrimp, mushrooms, and cilantro evenly between 8 heated soup bowls. Pour the broth into the bowls and serve.

Tortilla Soup

MAKES 2 QUARTS | PREPARATION TIME: 45 MINUTES

*T*his soup, fragrant with cilantro, chili powder and cumin, is both flavored and thickened with corn tortillas. Toasting the tortillas before grinding them helps develop their fullest flavor. Garnished with avocado, cheese, chicken, and toasted tortilla strips, this soup can be the center of a light meal, rounded out with a green salad.

8 corn tortillas, 6-inch diameter

4 teaspoons vegetable oil

1½ cups onion, pureed

2 garlic cloves, large, minced

1½ cups tomato puree

2 tablespoons cilantro leaves

1 tablespoon mild chili powder

2 teaspoons ground cumin

3 quarts chicken broth

2 bay leaves

½ cup cheddar cheese, grated

1 cup chicken breast, cooked, shredded

1 cup avocado, diced

Cut the tortillas into matchsticks. Toast the strips by sautéing them in a dry skillet over medium heat, tossing frequently, for about 7–8 minutes. Reserve about ½ cup of the strips for a garnish. Crush the remainder in a food processor.

Heat the oil in a soup pot over medium heat. Add the onion and garlic and cook, stirring frequently, until they have a sweet aroma, about 5–7 minutes.

Add the tomato puree and continue to cook for another 3 minutes. Add the cilantro, chili powder, and cumin, and cook for another 2 minutes.

Add the broth, crushed tortillas, and bay leaves. Stir well. Bring the soup to a simmer and cook for about 25 minutes. Strain the soup through a sieve.

Serve the soup in heated bowls, garnished with the shredded chicken, cheddar cheese, reserved tortilla strips, and diced avocado.

CHAPTER FOUR

Salads

*F*RESH CONCOCTIONS OF SEASONED HERBS AND LETTUCES HAVE BEEN ENJOYED WORLDWIDE SINCE THE BEGINNING OF RECORD-ED CULINARY HISTORY. THE ANCIENT GREEKS AND ROMANS ENJOYED SEASONED HERBS AND LETTUCES, KNOWN AS HERBA SALATA OR SALT-ed herbs. Today, the versatility of salads, coupled with their contrasting colors, fla-vors, textures, and temperatures provides a pleasant and refreshing accompaniment to the main attraction of the meal; or when enhanced, a salad can serve as a quick-to-prepare and satisfying main course.

Selection

Salad greens include lettuces of all types, as well as other leafy vegetables such as Belgian endive and watercress. The selection of greens and their complementary dressings lend themselves to many forms and appearances. In its most basic form, a green salad is one or two lettuces, tossed with a dressing, and garnished with veg-etables, croutons, or cheeses. More complex or composed salads are usually served as main-course meals or appetizers, rather than an accompaniment.

Today you can feature a wider variety and better quality of greens than ever before in your salad bowl.

Salad greens can be grouped according to their flavors and/or textures:

- MILD GREENS—*Bibb, Boston, green or red leaf, iceberg, mâche, oak, romaine, and various baby varieties of cooking greens*
- SPICY GREENS—*amaranth, arugula, mizuna, tat-soi, and watercress*
- BITTER GREENS AND CHICORIES—*Belgian endive (or witloof), curly endive (known as chicory or frisée), and radicchio*
- HERBS AND FLOWERS—*basil, chives, chervil, mint, parsley, chrysanthemums, nasturtiums, and pansies*

Lettuce blends are readily available in virtually every market. You can select from precut lettuces such as romaine, iceberg, or baby spinach; or try more exotic blends, sometimes referred to by their French name of mesclun. These precut and cleaned greens can be purchased in your local market. A great boon to the time-challenged cook, precut and packaged salad greens need only a quick rinse and a few turns in your salad spinner. If you have a bit more time, you can prepare your own blend from individual greens, using the list above as a flavor guide and your own sense of color to guide you. Using more than one color, flavor, or texture is a great way to make your own custom blend.

Once the greens are selected and prepared, you can add to the artistry of your salad through garnishing. Depending upon what's in season (or in your refrigerator), choose from such items as slices or wedges of tomatoes, cucumbers, carrots, radishes, mushrooms, olives, and peppers. For a more substantial salad, add eggs, cheese, raw or blanched vegetables, potatoes, and cooked meats. These additions give your salads yet another level of interest, in terms of flavor, texture, and nourishment.

Preparation

Nothing is worse than a gritty salad or one that forces your friends and family to use a knife to cut the lettuce. All greens, including prepackaged salad mixes and "triple-washed" bagged spinach, must be washed and dried prior to serving and should be kept properly chilled until ready to eat.

Salad greens are highly perishable and require proper handling. More tender greens, such as Boston lettuce or mâche, last only a day or two; romaine and iceberg are heartier and last much longer. If you purchase your fresh produce at a weekly farmer's market, be sure to enjoy tender greens right away and save the longer-lasting ones for later in the week.

The salad spinner is a relatively inexpensive, key piece of timesaving equipment for salad washing. Through centrifugal force, the salad spinner cleans the greens while spinning away water. This ensures the greens will have better flavor and the dressing will cling to them more evenly.

Wash the greens thoroughly in plenty of cool water to remove all traces of dirt and sand:

- *Separate the greens into leaves, and trim coarse rims or stem ends or ribs.*
- *Fill a large bowl or a clean sink with cold water, then add the lettuce. Swish it gently through the water and lift it away.*
- *Check the bottom of the bowl or sink; if you feel any grit or sand, drain the water and repeat until all traces of grit are gone.*

Dry the greens completely:

- *Greens that are properly dried have more flavor and, when stored, last longer*
- *Fill the basket of a salad spinner and spin until the leaves are dry.*

Store cleaned and dried greens in the refrigerator until ready to dress and serve:

- *Store greens in plastic containers or zipper-lock bags with a piece of paper towel to absorb any excess moisture, or directly in your salad spinner.*
- *Use the greens within a day or two.*

Cut or tear the lettuce into bite-size pieces:

- *Use clean fingers to tear lettuce into pieces or use a knife to cut greens into pieces or to shred them.*
- *Sharpen the blade so you don't bruise or crush the letttuce.*
- *A high-carbon stainless-steel blade won't discolor the leaves.*

Garnish and dress your salad:

- *Dress salads just before you serve them.*
- *Use a lifting and tossing motion to toss the salad until each piece of lettuce is coated completely.*
- *Use just enough dressing for the greens; don't drown the salad.*
- *Use clean hands, tongs, or a salad spoon and fork to toss.*

STEP-BY-STEP | Vinaigrettes

Quick meals can be easily enhanced with the addition of freshly made, flavorful vinaigrettes. Consider making a large batch to have on hand for dressing a salad, marinating grilled or broiled foods, serving as a sauce, or simply brushing on sandwiches. On the other hand, there's nothing keeping you from making just enough to dress one salad. Try mixing the vinaigrette directly in the salad bowl, leaving one less thing to wash.

➡ DETERMINE THE BALANCE OF ACID AND OIL

A good vinaigrette balances the sharpness of the vinegar or juice by combining it with oil. One of the simplest of all recipes, a basic vinaigrette is a combination that you can express as a ratio: three parts oil to one part acid.

This works well as a starting point, but you may find with experience that you prefer a combination that changes the ratio slightly. If your oil is so strongly flavored that is could overpower the vinegar, you may replace some of the intensely flavored oil with a more subtly flavored one. Very sharp or strong vinegars can be adjusted for by either adding a bit of water to dilute them, or a bit of sugar to soften their acidity.

➡ ADD ANY ADDITIONAL INGREDIENTS

When preparing a vinaigrette, add the salt, pepper, herbs, mustard, or other ingredients to the vinegar before adding the oil, so they will be blended evenly throughout the sauce. Fresh herbs give vinaigrettes a wonderful flavor and color. However, if they are added too far in advance, the vinegar can start to discolor their fresh green color and flatten their lively flavors. When preparing a large batch of vinaigrette that you want to last through several meals, you may prefer to add the fresh herbs to the dressing just before you serve it.

➡ GRADUALLY ADD THE OIL

Slowly pour or ladle a few droplets of oil at a time into the bowl, whisking constantly. Once the vinaigrette starts to thicken, you can add the oil more quickly. If the vinaigrette sits for a short time, it will start to separate. Whisk it vigorously before you dress your salad or serve it as a dip.

Use a handheld or countertop blender to make a vinaigrette quickly. Vinaigrettes made with a blender will be thicker, and can hold their emulsion longer than those that are simply whipped together.

➡ CHECK THE SEASONING

To be certain your dressing is balanced, put a few leaves of lettuce in a small bowl and add a teaspoon of the vinaigrette. Toss the greens until they are lightly coated and then taste them. If you taste a vinaigrette full strength, it may seem too strong or biting; once on your greens, however, the flavor may be perfect. Adjust the seasoning or the ratio of oil to vinegar, if necessary, whisk well, and serve.

French Lentil Salad

*L*entils, available in many varieties, are quick-cooking legumes. Substitute red or yellow lentils for the brown French lentils to create a more vibrantly colored salad.

2 cups French lentils

4 cups water

$^3/_4$ cup carrots, small dice

$^1/_2$ cup celery, small dice

1 cup red onion, small dice

$^1/_4$ pound white mushrooms, thinly sliced

2 teaspoons mustard

2 teaspoons salt, or to taste

$^1/_4$ cup cider vinegar

$^1/_2$ cup olive oil

Simmer the lentils in the water until they are tender, about 25 minutes. Rinse the lentils in cold water until they are slightly chilled and drain well.

Combine the lentils, carrots, celery, onion, and mushrooms.

Combine the mustard, salt, and vinegar. Stream in the olive oil while whisking to fully combine.

Toss the dressing with the lentil mixture.

Panzanella
(Bread Salad with Fresh Tomatoes)

MAKES 8 SERVINGS | PREPARATION TIME: 15 MINUTES

Panzanella is an Italian bread and tomato salad made with garlic, basil, parsley, olive oil, and vinegar. While this recipe calls for toasting the bread, other variations include soaking the bread in water before tossing it with the remaining ingredients.

1 baguette, 24-inch, preferably 2 days old

1/2 cup plus 3 tablespoons extra-virgin olive oil

1 tablespoon butter

1/4 cup garlic, chopped

2 pounds tomatoes

1/2 cup balsamic vinegar

2 teaspoons salt, or to taste

1 teaspoon freshly ground black pepper, or to taste

1 bunch basil

1/2 cup parsley, roughly chopped

Cut the baguette into 1-inch by 1-inch cubes. Toast in a 350°F oven for 1–2 minutes or until crisp and dry, stirring occasionally if necessary.

Place the butter and 2 tablespoons of the olive oil into a 10-inch sauté pan over medium low heat. Allow the butter to melt and then add the garlic. Sauté the garlic for 2–3 minutes until it is translucent, but not brown. Toss the cooked garlic, butter, and oil with the diced bread.

Slice the tomatoes and place in a large bowl. Add the vinegar, remaining olive oil, salt, and pepper.

Layer one-quarter of the basil leaves on top of each other and roll into a tight bunch. Thinly slice the bunch of leaves crosswise to create long strips of basil approximately 1/8-inch thick.

Just before serving, toss the bread, basil, and parsley with the tomatoes. Adjust the seasoning with additional salt and pepper if necessary.

Soba Noodle Salad

Soba noodles, of Japanese origin, are made from buckwheat and wheat flours, giving them a dark brownish color and nutty flavor. They are widely available in Asian markets, and come in both dried and fresh forms.

$1/2$ pound soba noodles

2 tablespoons rice vinegar

$1/4$ cup tamari soy sauce

2 teaspoons light miso

6 tablespoons sesame oil

$2^1/2$ tablespoons sesame seeds, plus additional for garnish

$1/2$ teaspoons red pepper flakes

3 carrots, cut into thin strips

1 bunch scallions, thinly sliced on the bias

2 cups snow peas, cut in $1/8$-inch strips on bias

$1/2$ teaspoon salt, or to taste

1 teaspoon freshly ground black pepper, or to taste

Cook the noodles in boiling salted water until al dente. Rinse with cold water, drain, and allow to dry slightly.

To prepare the dressing, stir together the rice vinegar, soy sauce, and miso. Whisk in the sesame oil, sesame seeds, and red pepper flakes.

Toss the carrots, scallions, and snowpeas in the dressing, then toss in the noodles, and adjust the seasoning with salt and pepper. The salad is ready to serve now, or it may be held, covered, under refrigeration. Garnish with additional sesame seeds before serving, if desired.

Cucumber, Tomato, and Feta Salad

MAKES 6 SERVINGS | PREPARATION TIME: 30 MINUTES

*T*his salad is simple to prepare and perfect for a summer lunch, when tomatoes and cucumbers are just waiting to be enjoyed.

3¹/₂ cups cucumbers, sliced and quartered

1¹/₂ cups tomatoes, diced

¹/₄ pound feta cheese

1 cup red onion, thinly sliced

¹/₄ cup red wine vinegar

1 tablespoon oregano, coarsely chopped

1 teaspoon salt, or to taste

1 teaspoon freshly ground black pepper, or to taste

¹/₂ cup extra-virgin olive oil

Combine the cucumbers, tomatoes, cheese, and onion.

Combine the vinegar, oregano, salt, and pepper. Stream in the olive oil while whisking constantly.

Toss the dressing with the salad ingredients and serve.

Mediterranean Salad

MAKES 8 SERVINGS | PREPARATION TIME: 40 MINUTES

*S*imple and delicious, this salad is a delicate combination of sweet vegetables and the sharp Mediterranean flavors of cured olives and Asiago cheese.

3 tablespoons anchovy fillets, minced

1¹/₂ cups Balsamic Vinaigrette (page 128)

1 pound mixed greens, washed and dried

2 cups artichoke hearts, jarred, quartered

2 cups peas, thawed

2 medium carrots, thinly sliced

¹/₂ cup picholine olives, pitted

¹/₂ cup Niçoise olives, pitted

1 cup Asiago cheese, grated

¹/₂ cup parsley, minced

Stir the anchovies into the vinaigrette.

Toss the greens with the vinaigrette. Place a bed of 2 cups mixed greens in the center of each plate. Top with ¼ cup each of the artichoke hearts and peas, about 2 tablespoons

carrots, and about 1 tablespoon each of the picholine and Niçoise olives.

Garnish with 2 tablespoons of the cheese and a sprinkling of parsley.

Spinach Salad
with Tangerines and Mango

MAKES 8 SERVINGS | PREPARATION TIME: 30 MINUTES

Spinach may be purchased pre-washed, making it convenient to use in salads. Also nutritious, spinach is packed with iron, and vitamins A and C.

1¼ pounds spinach, young tender leaves, stems removed

¾ cup Tangerine-Pineapple Vinaigrette (page 127)

1 red onion, sliced into paper-thin rings

5 tangerines, segments only

1 pound mango, small dice

Clean and thoroughly dry the spinach.

Just before serving, whisk the vinaigrette vigorously and adjust the seasoning, if necessary. For each portion, toss 2 cups of spinach with 1½ tablespoons of vinaigrette. Arrange on chilled plates, top with onion rings, tangerine segments, and diced mango. Serve immediately.

Orange and Fennel Salad

MAKES 8 SERVINGS | PREPARATION TIME: 20 MINUTES

Fennel is a mildly anise-flavored plant, delicious both raw and cooked. The sweetness of the oranges, contrasted with the savory flavors of the olives and salt and pepper, makes this simple salad a sure success.

1 fennel bulb

6 oranges

¼ cup extra-virgin olive oil

¾ teaspoon sea salt, or to taste

½ teaspoon freshly ground black pepper, or to taste

½ cup Niçoise olives, pitted

Trim the fennel bulb and wash well. Slice it thinly across the width of the bulb.

Peel the oranges and break them into segments, removing seeds if possible.

Place the fennel, oranges, and olive oil in a bowl and toss to combine.

Season with salt and pepper, if necessary. Divide the salad among 8 plates and garnish with pitted olives.

Mixed Bean and Grain Salad

MAKES 8 SERVINGS | PREPARATION TIME: 40 MINUTES

Mixed Bean and Grain Salad is shown here with Jerk Pork Kebabs (page 153).

*T*his healthy salad is chock full of grains and legumes that not only offer a delicious complement to a variety of entrees, but make nutrition-conscious food both fun and exciting.

$^1/_2$ pound bulgur	2 tablespoons red wine vinegar	$^1/_4$ cup olive oil
$^1/_2$ pound green lentils	$^3/_4$ teaspoon salt, or to taste	$^1/_2$ cup parsley, minced
$^1/_2$ pound chickpeas, canned	$^1/_4$ teaspoon freshly ground black pepper, or to taste	4 sundried tomatoes, minced
3 ounces Israeli couscous		8 parsley leaves, for garnish

Bring about 3 cups of water to a boil. Measure the bulgur in a large bowl, pour the boiling water over it, and let it stand until softened, about 15 minutes. Drain well.

In a medium pot, cover the lentils with water and bring to simmer. Cook the lentils for 20 minutes, or until tender. Drain and reserve.

While the bulgur is soaking, bring 3 cups of water to a boil, add ¼ teaspoon of the salt and the Israeli couscous. Cook the couscous until it is tender, about 10–12 minutes. Drain the couscsous and rinse with cold water until cool.

Rinse and drain the chickpeas.

Mix the vinegar, remaining salt, and the pepper together in a salad bowl, then whisk in the oil and add the parsley. Add the bulgur, couscous, lentils, chickpeas, and sundried tomatoes. Toss until the salad is evenly dressed.

The salad can be served now or chilled in the refrigerator for 15–20 minutes before serving.

Use a 4-ounce ramekin or other small bowl to mold the salad, making an elegant presentation. Garnish with parsley leaves.

Roasted Beet Salad

MAKES 8 SERVINGS | PREPARATION TIME: 40 MINUTES

*T*ake advantage of the amazing variety of beets available in season. Use red, golden, candy-stripe, or a combination of beets for this colorful salad. For a special presentation, alternate the sliced beets with orange slices.

8 beets, green tops trimmed	2 tablespoons lemon juice	5 oranges, skin removed and split into
5 tablespoons olive oil	1 teaspoon salt, or to taste	segments (approximately 40 segments)
2 tablespoons red wine vinegar	pinch cayenne pepper	1 cup goat cheese, crumbled

Preheat oven to 375°F.

Place the beets in a baking dish, add about ¼-inch of water, and cover tightly with foil. Roast the beets until tender, about 20 minutes. Allow to cool slightly, and slip off their skins. Cut the beets into quarters.

Blend together the olive oil, vinegar, lemon juice, salt, and cayenne pepper. Toss the beets in the dressing while they are still warm.

Divide the beets into eight portions and serve each portion with 5 orange segments and 2 tablespoons of crumbled goat cheese.

TO PREPARE THE ORANGES: Cut away both ends of the orange. Using a sharp paring knife, follow the curve of the orange and cut away the skin, pith, and membrane, leaving the flesh completely exposed. Working to release each segment and keep it intact, slice the connective membrane on either side of each orange segment.

Fruit Salad
with Orange-Blossom Syrup

MAKES 8 SERVINGS | PREPARATION TIME: 30 MINUTES

*O*range-blossom water, generally available from health food stores and wholesalers, adds a fragrant touch to the delicious syrup. Orange-blossom water is distilled using bitter orange flowers and is commonly used in beverages, confections, and baked goods.

5 fluid ounces orange-blossom water	2 cups pineapple, diced	$^2/_3$ cup kiwi, diced
2 tablespoons sugar	1$^1/_4$ cups red grapes	$^1/_4$ cup mint, chiffonade
1 orange	1$^1/_2$ cups strawberries, quartered	
1$^1/_4$ cup cantaloupe, diced	1 cup blueberries	

To make the syrup, combine the orange-blossom water and the sugar in a small saucepan. Heat, stirring occasionally, until the sugar completely dissolves. Set aside until needed.

Zest the orange using the smallest holes on a grater. Reserve the orange for another use.

Combine all of the fruits except the kiwi in a large bowl.

Serve immediately or refrigerate until needed.

For individual servings, place 1 cup of the fruit salad in a glass or serving dish. Top with 1 tablespoon of the syrup. Spoon 1 tablespoon of the diced kiwi on top of the fruit. Garnish the fruit with the orange zest and mint chiffonade. Alternately, the fruit salad can be garnished and served in a large bowl.

Warm Salad of Hearty Greens and Blood Oranges
with Tangerine-Pineapple Vinaigrette

MAKES 8 SERVINGS | PREPARATION TIME: 20 MINUTES

A bright and delicate salad to enjoy at the peak of citrus season, when the rich colors and sweetness of blood oranges and tangerines are at their peak. Easy to prepare, this unique salad is an excellent first course.

4 cups frisée, washed and dried

2$^1/_2$ cups radicchio, washed and dried

3 cups arugula, washed and dried

3 cups baby spinach, washed and dried

$^3/_4$ cup Tangerine-Pineapple Vinaigrette, warm (page 127)

1$^1/_4$ pounds blood oranges, sectioned

1 cup slivered almonds, toasted

Tear or cut greens into bite-sized pieces. Combine all of the greens and refrigerate until needed.

Toss the mixed greens with the warm vinaigrette and divide between 8 plates. Garnish the salad with 5–6 blood orange sections and 2 tablespoons of the almonds.

FOCUS ON | Composed Salads

Carefully arranging items on a plate, rather than tossing them together, forms a composed salad. A "main item," such as grilled chicken or shrimp, a portion of cheese or grilled vegetables, and so forth, is often set on a bed of greens. The formulation of a composed salad is rather loose, but the following principles should be kept in mind:

- **CONSIDER THE ELEMENTS:** Contrasting flavors are intriguing . . . conflicting are not.

- **REPETITION OF COLOR OR FLAVOR** can contribute to the dish . . . too much of a good thing is just too much.

- **ALL OF THE COMPONENTS** should be capable of standing alone; however, the composition should be that each part is enhanced in combination with the others.

- **THE SALAD SHOULD BE ARRANGED** in a way that the textures and colors of the food are most attractive to the eye.

Waldorf Salad

MAKES 8 SERVINGS | PREPARATION TIME: 35 MINUTES

This classic salad is credited to Oscar Tschirky, maître d' of the Waldorf Astoria Hotel in New York City. Since the early 1890's there have been a few modifications, but the salad has maintained the same great taste and texture as the original.

2 Red Delicious apples
2 Golden Delicious apples
2 Granny Smith apples
1 cup mayonnaise

1 cup sour cream
$^1/_2$ teaspoon salt, or to taste
$^1/_4$ teaspoon freshly ground black pepper, or to taste

2 teaspoons lemon juice
1 cup celery hearts, medium dice
$^1/_2$ cup walnuts, toasted, roughly chopped

Core and dice the apples.

Mix together the mayonnaise, sour cream, and lemon juice and season to taste with salt and pepper. Fold in the apples, celery, and walnuts.

The salad is ready to serve now or it may be held, covered, under refrigeration for up to 8 hours. This salad should be made the same day it is to be served.

Mixed Green Salad
with Pears, Walnuts, and Blue Cheese

MAKES 8 SERVINGS | PREPARATION TIME: 20 MINUTES

Though easy to prepare, this is an elegant starter for every day or when entertaining guests. Port Wine Vinaigrette provides the perfect finishing touch for this marriage of sweet and piquant flavors.

$1^1/_2$ pounds red leaf lettuce or baby romaine, washed and dried

$^1/_2$ cup Port Wine Vinaigrette (page 128)
6 ripe Seckel pears, quartered and cored

1 cup walnuts, toasted
1 cup blue cheese, crumbled

Toss the lettuce with the vinaigrette. Divide the lettuce between 8 plates. Top with 3 pear quarters and about 2 tablespoons each of the walnuts and blue cheese.

NOTE: Other pears may be used, depending upon seasonal availability.

Frisée with Walnuts, Apples, Grapes, and Blue Cheese

MAKES 8 SERVINGS | PREPARATION TIME: 35 MINUTES

*F*risée, a light green variety of endive with very curly leaves, is the base for a delicious combination of early autumn produce, crunchy walnuts, and pungent blue cheese.

APPLE CIDER VINAIGRETTE

$^3/_4$ cup apple cider

$^1/_4$ cup cider vinegar

$^1/_4$ Granny Smith apple, diced

$^1/_2$ cup peanut oil

1 tablespoon tarragon leaves, chopped

$^1/_2$ teaspoon salt, or to taste

pinch ground white pepper

COMPOSED SALAD

1$^1/_2$ pounds frisée lettuce

2 Granny Smith apples, or other tart apple

1 cup red grapes, cut in half lengthwise

$^1/_2$ cup walnuts, toasted, coarsely chopped

1 cup blue cheese, crumbled

Prepare the vinaigrette by whisking together the ingredients by hand or by mixing with a hand blender.

Clean and thoroughly dry the frisée. Slice the apples ⅛-inch thick. If necessary, hold the apple slices in water that has a splash of lemon juice in it. This will prevent the apple slices from browning.

Just before serving, whisk the vinaigrette vigorously and re-season with salt and pepper, if necessary. Toss the frisée with the vinaigrette. Arrange the frisee on chilled plates, top with apple slices, about 2 tablespoons of grapes, 1 tablespoon of walnuts, and 2 tablespoons of blue cheese. Serve immediately.

NOTE: Mesclun lettuce mix may be mixed with the frisée.

Baked Goat Cheese
with Mesclun, Pears, and Toasted Almonds

MAKES 8 SERVINGS | PREPARATION TIME: 35 MINUTES

*T*he rich and creamy texture of the cheese contrasts nicely with its crispy, baked crust. The almonds add a deep, rich flavor to the dish. The backdrop of the mesclun mix pulls all the elements together.

1¼ pounds goat cheese, well chilled

1 cup dry breadcrumbs

1½ pounds mesclun lettuce mix

¾ cup extra-virgin olive oil

¼ cup lemon juice

Salt, to taste

Freshly ground black pepper, to taste

2 pears, cored, sliced into thin wedges

1 cup almonds, sliced, toasted

Preheat the oven to 400°F. Slice the goat cheese into ½-inch thick discs. Gently coat the goat cheese with the breadcrumbs and place on a baking sheet. Bake the goat cheese in a 400°F oven until lightly browned, about 10 minutes. Allow the cheese to cool slightly while assembling the salads.

Toss the mesclun mix with the olive oil, lemon juice, salt, and pepper. Divide the lettuce into 8 portions and mound each portion on a plate. Top each portion with 3–4 pear slices, about 2 tablespoons of almonds, and 2 goat cheese rounds.

Lemon-Infused Greek Salad
with Grape Leaves

MAKES 8 SERVINGS | PREPARATION TIME: 45 MINUTES

*S*imple Mediterranean flavors come together in this easy-to-make salad. The time needed is mostly for vegetable preparation, which will make an elegant presentation a cinch.

1^1/$_2$ pounds romaine hearts

1 cup Greek olives, pitted and sliced
    in half lengthwise

^{1}/$_2$ cup Lemon-Parsley Vinaigrette (page 126)

4 pita bread, toasted, cut into 16 wedges

1 European cucumber, peeled,
    sliced ^{1}/$_8$-inch thick

1 pound cherry tomatoes, halved

1 yellow pepper, thinly sliced

1 red onion, peeled, sliced ^{1}/$_8$-inch thick

^{3}/$_4$ pound feta cheese, crumbled

16 stuffed grape leaves, purchased

Remove about a third of the stem from the romaine lettuce. Wash and spin-dry. Slice the romaine or tear it into bite size pieces. Place the cleaned romaine into a large serving bowl.

Add the sliced olives, cucumbers, cherry tomatoes, peppers, and red onions; toss with the vinaigrette. Top with the feta cheese and garnish with pita wedges and the stuffed grape leaves.

Romaine and Grapefruit Salad
with Walnuts and Stilton

MAKES 8 SERVINGS | PREPARATION TIME: 30 MINUTES

An excellent starter that combines the bittersweet taste of grapefruit, with the sharp taste of Stilton blue cheese, and crunchy walnuts. This is a great first course to a hearty braised dish, best enjoyed in winter when great citrus is available.

$^1/_4$ cup ruby port wine

2 tablespoons red wine vinegar

2 tablespoons grapefruit juice

4 teaspoons olive oil

1$^1/_2$ pounds romaine, cut into bite-sized pieces

2 white or pink grapefruit

$^1/_4$ teaspoon salt, or to taste

$^1/_4$ teaspoon freshly ground black pepper, or to taste

1 cup Stilton cheese

$^1/_2$ cup walnuts, chopped

Peel the grapefruit and break into sections.

Whisk together the port, red wine vinegar, grapefruit juice and olive oil. Add the salt and pepper.

Toss the romaine with the dressing and divide between 8 plates. Add the grapefruit sections, cheese, and walnuts to each plate.

Spring Herb Salad

*T*ruffle-infused oils are now widely available at markets and specialty food stores that offer a broad selection of flavored oils. Since working with real truffles can be costly, these infused oils are an excellent substitute, with only a small amount needed to impart the flavor of truffle to a dish.

3/4 cup olive oil	Salt, to taste	1 cup parsley, chopped
2 tablespoons truffle oil	Freshly ground black pepper, to taste	1 cup dill, chopped
1/4 cup white wine vinegar	8 cups mesclun mix	1/2 cup chives, sliced 1/2-inch long
1/2 teaspoon sugar	1 cup radicchio, chiffonade	

Prepare the vinaigrette by combining the olive oil, truffle oil, white wine vinegar, and sugar. Season with salt and pepper and reserve.

Clean and thoroughly dry the mesclun mix. Combine the mesclun, radicchio, parsley, and dill and toss thoroughly.

Just before serving, whisk the vinaigrette vigorously and season with additional salt and pepper, if necessary. Toss the salad with the vinaigrette, and arrange on plates. Serve immediately.

Lobster and Roasted Red Pepper Salad

MAKES 8 SERVINGS | PREPARATION TIME: 45 MINUTES

Rich tasting and gorgeous looking, this is an elegant salad that can be assembled in minutes. Serve it as a first course, or accompanied with crusty bread for a light dinner. You can cook the lobster up to 2 days ahead of serving, removing the meat and chilling thoroughly, but wait until serving time to assemble the salad. You can also look for cooked lobster meat at the market.

4 lobsters, 1½ pounds each
8 cups mixed salad greens
4 red bell peppers

1 jalapeño
1 tablespoon lemon juice
1 tablespoon thyme leaves

2 tablespoons extra-virgin olive oil
1 cup corn kernels, fresh or frozen
1 pint cherry tomatoes

Put about 1 inch of water and a steamer insert in a large pot with a lid, cover, and bring to a boil over high heat. Add the lobsters, replace the cover, and steam until the shells are bright red/pink and the flesh is opaque and cooked through, about 10–12 minutes. Remove the lobsters and let them cool until they can be handled.

While the lobsters steam and cool, rinse and spin dry the greens. Keep them in the refrigerator while preparing the rest of the salad.

After the greens are cleaned, roast the peppers over an open flame or in the oven until evenly charred. Place the peppers in a bowl and cover with plastic wrap to steam for about 5 minutes. Peel and de-seed the peppers and cut them into very fine matchsticks.

Slice the jalapeño into thin rings. Be sure to wear gloves to prevent irritation.

Use kitchen shears or a heavy duty knife to cut through the lobster shell. Pull the meat out of the tail and cut it into medallions. Remove the claws from their shells and leave them whole.

Whisk together the lemon juice, thyme, and oil in a large non-reactive bowl. Add the greens and gently toss to coat. Remove the greens and briefly let the dressing drain back into the bowl, then put the dressed greens onto plates or a platter. Add the peppers, corn, and jalapeño to the dressing left in bowl and toss to coat them thoroughly. Arrange the vegetables and the tomatoes on top of greens. Lean one of the claws against the salad and fan half of a lobster tail next to the claw.

Grilled Steak Salad
with Horseradish Dressing

MAKES 6 SERVINGS | PREPARATION TIME: 30 MINUTES

*T*he minimal time required to prepare this flank steak allows time for the assembly of a salad packed with hearty flavors that is both easy to prepare and beautiful to present.

1½ pounds flank steak

1 teaspoon salt, or to taste

½ teaspoon freshly ground black pepper, or to taste

¼ cup sour cream

½ cup mayonnaise

1–2 tablespoons prepared horseradish

1 tablespoon lemon juice

⅔ cup blue cheese, crumbled

6 cups romaine lettuce, washed and drained, cut into bite size pieces

1 teaspoon lemon zest

⅔ pint cherry tomatoes, sliced lengthwise

½ cup red onion, thinly sliced

Season the beef generously with salt and black pepper. Grill the steak to desired doneness, about 3–4 minutes per side for medium rare.

Meanwhile, in a small bowl, mix together the sour cream, mayonnaise, horseradish, lemon juice, and ½ teaspoon pepper using a hand held wire whisk. Season the dressing with salt and pepper, if necessary, and reserve.

In a large bowl, toss together the lettuce, lemon zest, tomatoes, half the cheese, and the dressing. Divide the mixture among 6 individual plates.

Cut the steak across the grain into thin slanting slices.

Place the sliced steak around the salad and top with the onion slices and remaining cheese.

Niçoise-Style Grilled Tuna

MAKES 8 SERVINGS | PREPARATION TIME: 45 MINUTES

*O*riginating in Nice, France, this salad gained its name and popularity from its specific combination of ingredients and the inclusion of an olive known also as "Niçoise", a variety native to the Mediterranean region.

2 pounds tuna fillet, trimmed
   of silverskin

16 baby red potatoes, halved

6 tablespoons olive oil

2 tablespoons salt, or to taste

1 tablespoon freshly ground black pepper,
   or to taste

1 pound mixed salad greens

1 pound haricots verts, cooked

½ cup Port Wine Vinaigrette (page 128)

1 quart cherry tomatoes

32 Niçoise olives

4 hard-boiled eggs, cut into eighths

1 cup Tomatillo Salsa (page 16)

Preheat the oven to 350°F.

Cut the tuna into eight 4-ounce portions and refrigerate until needed.

Coat the potatoes in the olive oil and about half of the salt and pepper. Roast the potatoes in a 350°F oven for 30–35 minutes, or until tender.

When the potatoes are about halfway cooked, toss 2 cups of the greens and ½ cup haricots verts with 3 tablespoons of the vinaigrette. Mound the greens and beans on a plate. Arrange ½ cup cherry tomatoes, 4 olives and 4 pieces of egg on the greens. Assemble the remaining salads while the potatoes are cooking.

Season the tuna with the remaining salt and pepper. When the potatoes are finished cooking, grill the tuna to the desired doneness, about 2–3 minutes on each side for medium rare. Slice the tuna into ¼-inch thick slices and fan the tuna on top of the greens. Spoon 2 tablespoons of the tomatillo salsa across the tuna. Place 4 of the potato halves around the tuna on each plate.

Grilled Tuna
with Spring Herb Salad and Marinated Tomatoes

MAKES 8 SERVINGS | PREPARATION TIME: 40 MINUTES

*Y*ellowfin tuna, also known as ahi, has a pale-pink flesh and a more intense flavor than albacore. Accompanied by this delicate mix of greens, spring herbs, and ripe cherry tomatoes, the tuna is the highlight of this delicious lunch or light dinner.

1 quart cherry tomatoes

3 tablespoons extra-virgin olive oil

1 tablespoon plus 1/4 teaspoon salt, or to taste

1 teaspoon freshly ground black pepper, or to taste

2 pounds yellowfin tuna fillet, trimmed, whole

6 tablespoons chives, cut into 1/8-inch lengths

3/4 cup parsley leaves

1 1/2 pounds mesclun greens

2 tablespoons lemon juice

Pre-heat the grill on the highest setting until it is very hot.

Slice the tomatoes lengthwise and place in a stainless steel bowl. Add 1 tablespoon of olive oil and 1/4 teaspoon of salt and toss together to coat. Refrigerate until ready to serve.

Dry the whole tuna fillet well using paper towels. Season the tuna generously with 1 tablespoon salt and 1 teaspoon freshly cracked black pepper. Drizzle 2 tablespoons of olive oil across one side and turn to coat all sides.

Place the tuna on the grill and cook with the grill cover closed for 2 minutes to mark the first side. Rotate the tuna 90° on the same side to create the cross-hatch marking. Grill the tuna for an additional minute.

Turn the tuna over and grill on the second side for 2 minutes. Rotate the tuna on this side to mark with a second cross-hatch, and finish grilling, an additional minute.

Remove the tuna from the heat and cool slightly to allow for easier slicing. While the tuna is cooling, combine the herbs and mesclun and toss thoroughly.

Drizzle 2 tablespoons of good-quality extra-virgin olive oil across the salad. Add the lemon juice and season with salt. Toss the mixture to coat evenly.

Cut the tuna into 24 slices. Arrange about 2 cups of seasoned salad mixture and 1/2 cup of marinated tomatoes on a plate and top with three slices of grilled tuna.

Spinach Salad
with Marinated Shiitakes and Red Onions

MAKES 8 SERVINGS | PREPARATION TIME: 25 MINUTES

*S*autéed shiitake mushrooms add an earthy flavor and heartiness to this salad, making it perfect for an autumn lunch.

2 tablespoons peanut oil

3 cups shiitake mushrooms, sliced

2 teaspoons reduced-sodium soy sauce

1 tablespoon cider vinegar

1/8 teaspoon salt, or to taste

1/8 teaspoon freshly ground black pepper, or to taste

Dash Tabasco sauce

2 teaspoons olive oil

1/2 cup red onion, diced

6 cups fresh spinach, trimmed, washed, and torn

2 cups radicchio, chiffonade

1/4 cup Balsamic Vinaigrette (page 128)

Heat the peanut oil in a sauté pan.

Add the mushrooms and sauté for 2 minutes. Add the soy sauce and cook until dry. Remove from the heat and add the vinegar, salt, pepper, and Tabasco sauce. Cool completely.

Sweat the onion in the olive oil until translucent, about 5–7 minutes. Allow to cool.

Toss the mushrooms, onions, spinach, and radicchio together with the vinaigrette. Adjust the seasoning with salt and pepper to taste. Serve immediately.

Grilled Chicken Caesar Salad

MAKES 8 SERVINGS | PREPARATION TIME: 30 MINUTES

According to culinary lore, this salad as created by Caesar Cardini in 1924 at his restaurant in Tiajuana, Mexico. Today, Caesar salads may be served as a plated first course or main course garnished with sliced grilled chicken.

3 pounds chicken breast halves, boneless and skinless

1 cup Parmesan cheese, grated, plus additional for garnish, if desired

1/2 teaspoon freshly ground black pepper, or to taste

1/2 teaspoon salt, or to taste

2 tablespoons dried basil

1/2 cup olive oil

1/4 cup lemon juice

1 teaspoon anchovy paste

1 teaspoon Dijon mustard

2 garlic cloves, finely minced

1 1/4 pounds romaine lettuce, washed, drained, and cut into bite size pieces

4 cups Homemade Croutons (recipe follows)

Lemon slices for garnish (optional)

Spray the grill or broiler rack with nonstick spray and preheat.

In a shallow bowl, combine the chicken, half of the Parmesan cheese, pepper, salt, and basil. Turn the chicken breasts in the cheese mixture, making sure to coat completely.

Grill or broil the chicken 5 inches from the heat, turning occasionally until cooked through, about 10–12 minutes. Watch the chicken carefully because the cheese burns easily. Allow the chicken to cool slightly.

Meanwhile, in a large bowl, whisk the oil, lemon juice, anchovy paste, mustard, and garlic to blend. Add the lettuce, remaining cheese and croutons; and toss to coat. Divide the salad among 8 individual plates.

Cut each chicken breast diagonally into 5 strips; carefully arrange one sliced breast atop each salad. Garnish with additional Parmesan cheese and lemon slices, if desired.

Homemade Croutons

MAKES 8 SERVINGS | PREPARATION TIME: 15 MINUTES

Homemade croutons enliven any salad or soup with a satisfying crunch. You can substitute other dried herbs for the rosemary, or omit the herbs altogether for plain croutons.

4 cups bread, cut into 1/2-inch cubes

Olive oil, as needed

Salt, to taste

Freshly ground black pepper, to taste

Dried rosemary, to taste

Preheat the oven to 350°F.

Toss the bread with enough olive oil to coat, add salt, pepper, and dried rosemary to taste. Spread the croutons in an even layer on a baking sheet. Bake until golden brown, stirring occasionally so the croutons bake evenly. Allow to cool. Croutons will keep well in an airtight container for several days.

Traditional Cobb Salad

MAKES 8 SERVINGS | PREPARATION TIME: 35 MINUTES

*C*obb Salad was created at the Brown Derby Restaurant in Hollywood, California. Various interpretations may call for either chicken or turkey. The garnish suggestions here are typical, but some versions have included watercress, celery, Cheddar cheese, hard-boiled eggs, black olives, or alfalfa sprouts.

2 pounds chicken breasts, boneless and skinless

2 teaspoons salt, or to taste

1 teaspoon freshly ground black pepper, or to taste

1 tablespoon vegetable oil

16 bacon slices

1 pound romaine lettuce, washed, dried, and torn into pieces

$^1/_2$ cup Cobb Salad Vinaigrette (page 126)

$1^1/_2$ cups tomatoes, diced

2 cups blue cheese, crumbled

2 avocados, halved, cut into $^1/_4$-inch-thick slices

$^1/_2$ cup scallions, sliced on bias

8 eggs, hard-boiled, quartered

Preheat the oven to 400°F.

Season the chicken breasts with salt and pepper. Heat the vegetable oil in a large sauté pan over medium-high heat and sauté the chicken breasts until golden brown, about 2–3 minutes on each side. Place the pan in a 400°F oven and finish cooking the chicken to an internal temperature of 165°F. Cool and cut into ¼-inch-thick slices on the bias.

Sauté the bacon until crisp. Drain on absorbent paper and crumble into small pieces.

Toss the romaine with the vinaigrette and divide between 8 plates. Top with 5–6 chicken slices, 3 tablespoons diced tomato, ¼ cup blue cheese, ¼ avocado, 1 tablespoon scallions, 4 hard-boiled egg quarters, and 2 tablespoons crumbled bacon.

Grilled Chicken and Pecan Salad

MAKES 8 SERVINGS | PREPARATION TIME: 45 MINUTES

*N*utty, sweet, bitter, and tart elements combine well in this meal-size salad. Substitute walnuts or almonds for the pecans, but be sure to use walnut oil in the dressing—it contributes a great deal of flavor.

2 pounds chicken breasts, boneless, skinless

2¼ teaspoons salt, or to taste

2¼ teaspoons freshly ground black pepper, or to taste

1 cup apple cider

2 tablespoons cider vinegar

1 teaspoon Worcestershire sauce

1 teaspoon hot pepper sauce

1 teaspoon thyme, chopped

2 tablespoons walnut oil

4 cups arugula, torn, rinsed, and dried

3 cups mixed salad greens, rinsed, and dried

2 Belgian endive heads, thinly sliced

2 Granny Smith apples, cored and thinly sliced

½ cup pecans, toasted

Spray the grill or broiler rack with nonstick spray and pre-heat. Season each chicken breast with ¼ teaspoon salt and ¼ teaspoon pepper. Grill or broil the chicken 5 inches from the heat, turning occasionally, until cooked to an internal temperature of 165°F, about 10–12 minutes. Allow the chicken to cool before thinly slicing it on the diagonal.

Bring the cider to a boil in a small saucepan and simmer until it reduces by two-thirds, about 5 minutes. Transfer the cider to a bowl; add the vinegar, Worcestershire sauce, hot pepper sauce, thyme, and the remaining salt and pepper. Gradually whisk in the oil.

Combine the arugula, mixed greens, and endive in a large bowl; add the apples and half of the dressing, and gently toss to coat. Arrange the salad on plates and top with the chicken and pecans. Drizzle the chicken with the remaining dressing and serve at once.

NOTE: If desired, add 2 tablespoons of blue cheese to each salad for an added layer of complexity.

Lemon-Parsley Vinaigrette

MAKES 2 CUPS | PREPARATION TIME: 15 MINUTES

*S*imilar to many store-bought varieties, this homemade version is quick and easy to make and well worth the extra effort.

$^3/_4$ cup lemon juice

2 tablespoons balsamic vinegar

$^3/_4$ cup canola oil

$5^1/_2$ tablespoons olive oil

$1^1/_2$ tablespoons parsley, chopped

1 teaspoon salt, or to taste

$^1/_2$ teaspoon freshly ground black pepper, or to taste

Combine all of the ingredients in a large bowl and use a whisk or hand blender to mix the ingredients until thoroughly incorporated.

Cobb Salad Vinaigrette

MAKES 2 CUPS | PREPARATION TIME: 10 MINUTES

*T*his vinaigrette, while perfect for the Cobb Salad, is also versatile enough for most green salads.

$^1/_4$ cup water

6 tablespoons red wine vinegar

$^1/_2$ teaspoon sugar

$2^1/_2$ teaspoons lemon juice

$1^1/_4$ teaspoons salt, or to taste

$^1/_2$ teaspoon freshly ground black pepper, or to taste

$^1/_2$ teaspoon coarse grain mustard

2 garlic cloves, minced

$1^1/_4$ cups extra-virgin olive oil

Blend together all of the ingredients except for the olive oil. Allow the flavors to marry for 5 minutes.

Add the olive oil and whisk thoroughly. It may be necessary to blend the dressing together again before serving.

Tangerine-Pineapple Vinaigrette

MAKES 2 CUPS | PREPARATION TIME: 15 MINUTES

*I*n this vinaigrette, the fruitiness of the tangerine and pineapple juice is contrasted by the sharpness of the Dijon mustard.

1/2 cup plus 2 tablespoons tangerine juice

5 tablespoons pineapple juice

1 tablespoon lemon juice

1 teaspoon balsamic vinegar

1 teaspoon Dijon mustard

1/2 teaspoon garlic, minced

1/2 cup plus 2 tablespoons vegetable oil

5 tablespoons olive oil

1 teaspoon salt, or to taste

1/2 teaspoon freshly ground black pepper,
   or to taste

Combine the juices, vinegar, mustard, and garlic.

Whisk in the oils gradually.

Adjust the seasoning with salt and pepper.

Whisk together the port, vinegar, salt, and pepper.

Lime-Cilantro Vinaigrette

MAKES 2 CUPS | PREPARATION TIME: 10 MINUTES

*T*he flavors of lime and cilantro give this vinaigrette a Southwestern flair, perfect on a green salad or with Black Bean Salad (page 282).

1/2 cup lime juice

1/2 teaspoon honey

1/4 cup cilantro, chopped

1 teaspoon salt, or to taste

1/2 teaspoon freshly ground black pepper,
   or to taste

3/4 cup peanut oil

3/4 cup vegetable oil

Combine all of the ingredients except the oils. Allow the flavors to blend for 5–6 minutes.

Gradually whisk in the oils.

Port Wine Vinaigrette

MAKES 2 CUPS | PREPARATION TIME: 5 MINUTES

*P*ort, a sweet fortified wine from Portugal, adds a luscious sweetness to this vinaigrette.

$\frac{1}{2}$ cup tawny port

$\frac{1}{2}$ cup red wine vinegar

1 cup vegetable oil

$\frac{1}{4}$ teaspoon salt, or to taste

Freshly ground black pepper, or to taste

Whisk together the port and the vinegar. Gradually whisk in the oil. Season with the salt and pepper if necessary.

Refrigerate until needed. Whisk to recombine before using.

Balsamic Vinaigrette

MAKES 2 CUPS | PREPARATION TIME: 5 MINUTES

*T*his vinaigrette features the distinctive sweet taste of balsamic vinegar. Balsamic vinegar is a speciality of the town of Modena in Italy, where it is aged in wooden barrels for several years, resulting in its characteristic dark caramel color and rich flavor.

$\frac{1}{4}$ cup red wine vinegar

$\frac{1}{4}$ cup balsamic vinegar

1 teaspoon salt

$\frac{1}{4}$ teaspoon freshly ground black pepper

$1\frac{1}{2}$ cups extra-virgin olive oil

Whisk together the red wine vinegar, the balsamic vinegar, and the salt and pepper.

Gradually whisk in the oil. Adjust seasoning as desired. Refrigerate until needed. Whisk to recombine before using.

CHAPTER FIVE

Meat

Certain cuts of meat, such as tenderloin of beef, sug-
gest time and effort in the kitchen. However, with just
a few pieces of basic information, you'll be able to select
several cuts of meat that will work interchangeably in
your recipes, resulting in delicious dishes that are both quick and easy. The table on
pages 130–131 provides information on the best cuts of meat for quick cooking. Use
this valuable guide when cooking meat.

When shopping for meat, it is important to be aware that cuts of meat that are
difficult to find are often times in the butcher's case, but hiding behind an unfa-
miliar name. A boneless top loin steak might be labeled strip steak, Kansas City
steak, New York strip steak, hotel cut strip steak, ambassador steak, or club sirloin
steak, depending upon the region of the country or the store where you are shopping. The best recourse is to find a reliable market or butcher and ask questions.

Trimming Meat

Trimming meat before cooking results in a finished dish with better texture. Remember to always use a clean cutting board and knife when cutting meat, and then
wash all equipment and your working surface thoroughly before preparing any
other ingredients. Purchase meat from a reputable market, avoid storing it for more
than one day, and cook it to the proper temperature (see table, page 133). Since heat-

ing meat to specific temperatures will kill bacteria, be sure to check for doneness with a thermometer.

If you buy larger cuts of meat, you may find gristle and excess fat that need to be removed. Although a small amount of fat adds flavor and helps keep meat tender, too much will make meat look and taste unpleasant. Gristle, a general term for cartilage and tough tissue, will ruin the mouth-feel of even the most tender cut of meat. Feel the meat for hard spots and cut

them away carefully. Some cuts, such as rack of lamb, have an even layer of fat enclosing the major muscles. These can often be removed by gripping a corner of the fat layer and peeling it back firmly. For thicker fat coverings, use a sharp knife and cut slowly with small movements to be sure that only fat is removed and not the meat itself. Pull away the fat as you cut it, holding it to reveal the line of separation between the fat and the meat. You may also choose to leave a thin layer of fat over a

AT A GLANCE | Best Quick Cooking Methods for Meat

	CUT	QUICK COOKING METHODS
BEEF	Ribeye Steak (bone-in or boneless)	Grilling, broiling, sautéing
	Porterhouse ot T-bone Steak	Grilling, broiling, sautéing
	Tenderloin Steak (filet mignon)	Grilling, broiling, sautéing
	Striploin/Shell/Top Loin Steak (bone-in or boneless)	Grilling, broiling, sautéing
	Tri-tip Steak	Grilling, broiling, sautéing, stir-frying
	Top Sirloin Steak (bone-in or boneless)	Grilling, broiling, sautéing, stir-frying
	Flank Steak	Grilling, broiling, sautéing, stir-frying
	Skirt Steak	Grilling, broiling, sautéing
	Hangar Steak	Grilling, broiling, sautéing
	Flat Iron/Top Blade Steak	Grilling, broiling, sautéing, stir-frying
	Shoulder London Broil	Grilling, broiling
	Top Round London Broil	Grilling, broiling

roast, to allow for self-basting as it cooks. In this case, use a sharp knife to shave all but a ¼-inch-thick layer of fat. Smaller cuts may also have excess fat that require trimming to ensure a neat appearance, even cooking and a more healthful diet.

Removing the Silverskin

Be sure to remove the silverskin completely before cooking a piece of meat. This tough membrane, named for its silvery translucent appearance, tends to shrink when exposed to heat, causing uneven heating as well as an unpleasant texture and appearance. It is most likely to appear on the tenderloin of beef, pork, veal, and lamb; top round of beef and veal; and venison loin. Work the tip of a boning knife under the silverskin membrane. Grip the end of the silverskin, holding it taut at a low angle over the meat, and glide the knife blade just underneath the membrane. Angle the blade upward

	CUT	QUICK COOKING METHODS
VEAL	Loin chops	Grilling, broiling, sautéing
	Cutlets	Grilling, broiling, sautéing, pan frying
	Rib/Rack Chops	Grilling, broiling, sautéing
	Tenderloin	Grilling, sautéing
PORK	Loin Roast (boneless)	Roasting
	Loin Chops, center-cut or end (bone-in or boneless)	Grilling, broiling, sautéing, roasting
	Rib/Rack Chops	Grilling, broiling, sautéing, roasting
	Tenderloin	Grilling, roasting
	Cutlets	Sautéing, pan frying, stir-frying
	Blade Steak	Grilling, broiling
LAMB	Rack	Roasting
	Rib/Rack Chops (single or double)	Grilling, broiling, sautéing, roasting
	Shoulder Chops	Grilling, broiling, sautéing
	Loin chops (bone-in or boneless)	Grilling, broiling, sautéing
	Leg, butterflied (boneless)	Grilling
	Top Round	Broiling, roasting

slightly to cut away only the silverskin. If the silverskin is wide or if it wraps around the contours of a rounded piece of meat, you may need to remove the membrane in several narrow strips.

Testing Meat for Doneness

Combine temperature and touch to test meat while it cooks. Generally, cuts of meats that are more tender, like a beef tenderloin, require less cooking time; while tougher meats, like a beef shank, require longer cooking time.

Temperature is the most accurate method for judging the doneness of meat. You can use either an instant-read thermometer or a meat thermometer with a probe that stays in the meat while it cooks. It is important to remember that meat retains heat and continues to cook after it is taken off the grill or out of the oven. This "carry-over cooking" can account for an increase of up to 10°F, so it is essential to take

meat out of the oven before it reaches its desired doneness. For example, if you like your beef tenderloin medium rare (145°F), take it out of the oven at 135°F, so that it will carry over to a perfect medium rare, rosy pink and juicy. See the table on the following page for helpful tips.

Touching meat to judge its firmness offers a helpful guideline to gauge the progression of cooking. With the tip of one finger, press the meat in the center to judge its resistance. The less done a piece of meat is, the softer and more yielding it will feel. Practice recognizing the feel of meat cooked to various stages of doneness by using your own hand as a guide. Hold one hand open, palm up, with your fingers relaxed and slightly curled. Touch the flesh at the base of your thumb. It will feel soft and yielding; this is how rare meat will feel. As you gradually spread your fingers open and flat, the flesh will become increasingly firm and unyielding, just as meat will feel as it cooks to well done.

| Doneness Temperatures and Tests

DESIRED DONENESS:	REMOVE FROM COOKING MEDIUM AT:	CARRY-OVER TO:	MEAT SHOULD LOOK:
Beef, Veal, and Lamb			
Rare	125°F	135°F	Red and shiny interior.
Medium rare	135°F	145°F	Rosy pink interior, juicy.
Medium	150°F	160°F	Pink only at center, pale pink juices.
Well done	160°F	170°F	Evenly brown throughout, no traces of red or pink, moist but no juices
Pork			
Medium	150°F	160°F	Opaque throughout, slight give, juices with faint blush
Well done	160°F	170°F	Slight give, juices clear

STEP-BY-STEP | Sautéing

The term "sautéing"—cooking food quickly in a pan, in a small amount of oil over direct heat—is often used interchangebly with the term "frying," though sautéing is generally thought of as a quicker cooking method in less oil, making it an ideal technique for use in the quick kitchen. Observing a few simple steps will ensure successful sautéing.

➥ GET THE INGREDIENTS READY

Once you put the pan on the heat, you'll be moving rapidly so it's important to have everything ready to go in the pan. If something needs to be minced or chopped, pounded or dredged, do that first. Add seasonings, marinades, or rubs a minimum of 15 minutes before you start to sauté.

➥ GET THE PAN HOT FIRST

Foods cook quickly and end up with better flavor and color if the pan is hot. Allow a few minutes over medium heat for most pans on most stoves. As soon as the oil goes into the pan, it comes to cooking temperature very quickly.

➥ ADD THE INGREDIENTS TO THE PAN

When you put the food in the pan, put the best looking side down first so that it browns evenly. This is the side that should be face-up on the plate when you serve it. Turn the food over when it is cooked halfway. You can sometimes see a slight change in color around the edges as the first side cooks. Turn the sautéed food over to finish cooking. Have a pan or plate ready to hold sautéed foods while you complete the dish. It's a good idea to allow a little leeway so that the heat the food holds finishes it to perfection while you complete a quick sauce in the pan.

➥ DEGLAZE THE SAUTÉ PAN WITH LIQUID TO MAKE A PAN SAUCE

A pan sauce lets you capture every last bit of flavor using a technique called deglazing. Add a little liquid—flavorful liquids make more flavorful sauces, so opt for broth, wine, or beer. Stir and scrape the pan to release the browned drippings (*fond*), then swirl in a bit of butter, oil, cream, or a puree (such as pesto or tomato sauce) for a light sauce that clings beautifully. You can add any number of additional ingredients, cut into fine slivers or minced, to garnish or flavor the sauce, including fresh herbs, pureed garlic, roasted peppers, sun-dried tomatoes, toasted nuts, chiles, mushrooms, or ham.

See the step-by-step photographs accompanying the recipe for Veal Saltimbocca with Fettuccine (page 149).

Stir-Fry Citrus Beef

MAKES 8 SERVINGS | PREPARATION TIME: 30 MINUTES

*S*tir-frying is a quick cooking method that produces delicious results and eye-appealing presentations. If you're not in the mood for beef, substitute 2 pounds of boneless, skinless chicken breasts, cut into ¼-inch-thick slices.

2 pounds oranges

6 tablespoons dry sherry

6 tablespoons soy sauce

1 tablespoon vegetable oil

2 pounds sirloin, trimmed of fat and cut across the grain into $^1/_4$-inch-thick slices

$^1/_4$ cup ginger, minced

$^1/_2$ teaspoon red pepper flakes

3 cups bean sprouts

3 cups snow peas, ends and strings removed

8 cups steamed rice

2 teaspoons sesame oil (optional)

4–6 tablespoons cilantro leaves

Zest half of the oranges and juice them all. Measure the juice and add enough water to equal 2 cups. In a small bowl, stir together zest, juice, sherry and soy sauce. Reserve.

Heat a wok or nonstick pan over high heat. When pan is hot, add the oil, then add the beef, ginger, and pepper flakes. Cook, stirring occasionally until beef is browned, about 3–4 minutes. With a slotted spoon, transfer beef to a bowl. Pour off any excess oil

Pour orange juice mixture into wok and bring to a simmer. Add bean sprouts and pea pods; cook, stirring, until pea pods turn a brighter green (about 1 minute).

Return the beef and any juices to the pan and cook long enough to reheat the beef. Serve over steamed rice. If desired, finish with sesame oil. Garnish with cilantro.

Reuben Sandwich

The Reuben Sandwich is shown here with Coleslaw (page 276).

This classic combination of corned beef, Swiss cheese, and sauerkraut is reportedly named for the New York delicatessen owner who created it. Paired with a cup of hearty soup or a crisp, refreshing salad, it makes a satisfying meal.

4 tablespoons butter, softened

16 slices rye bread

16 slices Swiss cheese

1¼ pounds corned beef brisket, thinly sliced

1 pound sauerkraut

½ cup Russian Dressing (recipe follows)

Butter one side of 8 slices of the bread, and place the slices buttered-side down on a lined baking sheet. Top each with a slice of Swiss cheese, then divide half of the corned beef among them.

Divide the sauerkraut among the sandwiches, and top each with 1 tablespoon of Russian dressing. Add another layer of corned beef and a second slice of Swiss cheese to each sandwich. Finish with the remaining bread slices, buttered on one side, buttered-side facing out.

Preheat a sandwich griddle or frying pan to medium heat. Cook the sandwiches on one side until the bread is golden brown. Use a spatula to carefully flip the sandwiches over and finish cooking on the second side. Cut the sandwiches in half before serving.

Russian Dressing

⅔ cup mayonnaise

3 tablespoons ketchup

1 tablespoon prepared horseradish

1 teaspoon Worcestershire sauce

Salt, to taste

Freshly ground black pepper, to taste

Combine all of the ingredients thoroughly and hold under refrigeration until needed.

Grilled Flank Steak

MAKES 6 SERVINGS | PREPARATION TIME: 30 MINUTES

Grilled Flank Steak is shown here with Corn, Pepper, and Jicama Salad (page 313) and Oven-Roasted Potatoes (page 304).

*F*lank steak on the grill is ever so versatile. Sliced flank steak may be wrapped up in flour tortillas, or served as a garnish for a delicious composed salad.

2¼ pounds flank steak, trimmed,
   excess fat removed

MARINADE

4 tablespoons extra-virgin olive oil

4 teaspoons freshly ground black pepper,
   or to taste

4 teaspoons salt, or to taste

2 cloves garlic, bruised

2 teaspoons paprika (optional)

Mix together all of the ingredients for the marinade. Place the flank steak into a zipper-lock bag, and pour the marinade in. Seal the bag and toss the meat with the marinade until it is completely coated. Hold under refrigeration for 20 minutes, or longer if desired.

Heat a grill to high. Grill to desired doneness (2–3 minutes on each side for medium rare). If a grill is not available, the steak can also be broiled in the oven.

Allow the grilled steak to rest for 3–5 minutes before slicing. Holding the knife at a 45-degree angle, carve the steak across the grain into thin slices.

Satay of Beef
with Peanut Sauce

MAKES 8 SERVINGS | PREPARATION TIME: 45 MINUTES

*W*hile the beef pairs nicely with the peanut sauce, lamb or chicken are excellent substitutions.

Bamboo skewers, 8-inch, as needed

3 pounds top round of beef or beef flank
    steak, cut 1 x 5 inches and thinly sliced

MARINADE

4 teaspoons ginger, finely chopped

8 garlic cloves, minced

1 teaspoon crushed red pepper flakes

2 1/2 tablespoons curry powder

2 tablespoons honey

1/2 cup fish sauce

1/2 cup soy sauce

PEANUT SAUCE

1 1/2 teaspoons peanut oil

1 1/2 teaspoons garlic, minced

1/4 teaspoon crushed red pepper flakes

1/4 cup coconut milk

2 tablespoons lemon juice

1/2 cup smooth peanut butter

1 tablespoon soy sauce

1/4 cup water

Soak the skewers in water while you prepare the marinade. Combine the beef with the marinade ingredients in a zipper-lock bag and seal. Gently toss the beef with the marinade in the bag until coated evenly. Allow the meat to marinate for 30 minutes. (You may marinate the meat overnight, if desired.)

While the beef is marinating, combine the ingredients for the Peanut Sauce in a small saucepan and bring to a slow boil.

Simmer 4–5 minutes, adjusting consistency with more water or peanut butter as needed, and adjusting seasoning as needed.

Thread a piece of the marinated beef on each skewer. Grill or broil the skewered meat, cooking about 3–4 minutes per side. Serve with the warm Peanut Sauce.

Tenderloin of Beef
with Blue Cheese and Herb Crust

MAKES 6 SERVINGS | PREPARATION TIME: 30 MINUTES

Tenderloin of Beef with Blue Cheese and Herb Crust is shown here with Potato Gratin (page 304)
and Pan-Steamed Lemon Asparagus (page 280).

Simple and elegant, this dish is a sure winner. Whether serving an intimate dinner for two or a number of guests, the delicious flavors of Madiera and blue cheese are a perfect choice with the beef tenderloin.

3 tablespoons butter, softened	2¼ pounds beef tenderloin	¼ cup chives, chopped
3 tablespoons all-purpose flour	¼ cup breadcrumbs	¼ teaspoon black peppercorns, crushed
3 cups beef broth	6 tablespoons blue cheese	1 tablespoon olive oil
6 tablespoons Madeira wine	¼ cup parsley, chopped	

Combine the butter and flour together.

Bring the beef broth and Madeira to a boil. Whisk in the butter and flour mixture until completely dissolved. Simmer for about 15–20 minutes, until the liquid is thickened and reduced by half. While the sauce is simmering, preheat the oven to 350°F. Spray the rack of a roasting pan with nonstick spray and place in the pan.

Slice the tenderloin into 6 portions that are approximately 3 inches in diameter and 1½ inches thick. Tie butcher's twine around the beef medallions so they maintain their shape while cooking, if desired.

Combine the breadcrumbs, blue cheese, parsley, chives, and pepper to form a paste.

Heat the olive oil in a nonstick skillet over high heat. Sear the medallions until just browned, 2–3 minutes on each side. Arrange the medallions in a roasting pan. Coat the top side of each medallion with 3 tablespoons of the blue cheese and herb crust.

Roast until the crust is golden brown and the meat is cooked as desired, about 6 to 8 minutes for medium-rare, depending on the size of the medallions. If butcher's twine was used, be sure to remove it. Serve the medallions on a pool of the warm Madeira sauce.

Beef Tenderloin
with Southwestern-Style Sauce

MAKES 8 SERVINGS | PREPARATION TIME: 30 MINUTES

Beef Tenderloin with Southwestern-Style Sauce is shown here with
Jalapeño Jack Polenta (page 311) and Tarragon Green Beans (page 274).

*T*his versatile Southwestern-Style Sauce, with its zesty blend of black peppercorns and Creole mustard, is a perfect match for beef tenderloin, or other meats, like Sautéed Pork Medallions (page 156).

3 pounds beef tenderloin, trimmed

Salt, to taste

Freshly ground black pepper, to taste

2 tablespoons olive oil

SOUTHWESTERN-STYLE SAUCE

2 garlic cloves, minced

3 tablespoons shallots, minced

1½ tablespoons tomato paste

3 tablespoons Creole mustard

1½ teaspoons black peppercorns, crushed

2 cups chicken broth

3 tablespoons maple syrup

¼ cup cider vinegar

2¾ teaspoons salt, or to taste

1 teaspoon freshly ground black pepper, or to taste

2½ teaspoons cilantro, chopped

1½ tablespoons jalapeño, finely diced, for garnish

Trim the beef and cut into eight ½-inch thick medallions, about 6 ounces each.

Season the medallions with salt and pepper and brush with olive oil. Cover and refrigerate until needed.

Heat ½ tablespoon of the oil in a sauté pan over medium-high heat. Sauté the garlic and shallots until aromatic, 1–2 minutes. Add the tomato paste and cook until slightly browned, about 2 minutes. Add the mustard, black peppercorns, chicken broth, maple syrup, vinegar, salt, and pepper.

Simmer until mixture reduces to a sauce consistency, about 10 minutes.

Heat the oil in a skillet on medium-high heat. Sauté the medallions to the desired doneness, 1½ minutes for the first side and approximately 1 minute for the second side for medium.

Finish the sauce with the cilantro and serve over the tenderloin. Garnish with the jalapeño.

Veal Scallopine
with Lemon and Capers

MAKES 8 SERVINGS | PREPARATION TIME: 30 MINUTES

Veal Scallopine with Lemon and Capers is shown here with Bulgar and Lentil Pilaf with Caramelized Onions (page 302)

and Pan-Steamed Zucchini with Yellow Squash Noodles (page 281).

*V*eal top round is the ideal cut for this veal dish. Its delicate texture, combined with lemon and capers, enhance the velvety finish of this longtime favorite.

3 pounds boneless veal cutlets

1 teaspoon salt, or to taste

$\frac{1}{2}$ teaspoon freshly ground black pepper, or to taste

$\frac{2}{3}$ cup flour, or as needed

2 tablespoons olive oil, plus more as needed

1 tablespoons butter, plus more as needed

LEMON-CAPER SAUCE

4 tablespoons water

6 tablespoons capers, rinsed, drained

6 tablespoons lemon juice

2 tablespoons lemon zest

2 tablespoons butter

Salt and pepper, to taste

Pound cutlets to an even thickness of about ¼ inch between two pieces of plastic wrap. Season the pounded veal generously with salt and pepper. Dredge the cutlets in flour and shake off excess.

Place a large sauté pan over high heat. Add 2 tablespoons of olive oil and 1 tablespoon of butter to the pan.

Sauté the veal in batches, adding more butter and oil as needed. Place the veal in the pan and sauté 1–2 minutes, until lightly golden. Flip the veal over, and continue to cook it for an additional minute. Remove and hold warm. Keep the oil/butter in the pan, add the remaining oil and an additional

tablespoon of butter. Add the second batch of veal, and sauté in same manner as first batch. Remove and hold warm.

Deglaze pan with about 4 tablespoons of water, and add the capers. Gently scrape browned bits from the bottom of the pan. Add the lemon juice, and stir in the remaining 2 tablespoons of butter to emulsify the sauce. Add the lemon zest, and heat for 1 minute, while swirling the sauce in the pan. Adjust the seasoning with salt and pepper. Serve the veal immediately with the lemon-caper sauce.

Pan-Fried Veal Cutlets

MAKES 8 SERVINGS | PREPARATION TIME: 35 MINUTES

*T*hese simple breaded cutlets are delicious, and very straightforward to prepare. Be sure to serve them immediately after cooking, as they will become soggy as they sit.

3 pounds boneless veal cutlets

1 tablespoon salt, or to taste

1½ teaspoons freshly ground black pepper, or to taste

½ cup all-purpose flour

1 cup breadcrumbs

2 eggs, beaten

2 cups oil (vegetable or olive), or more as needed

8 lemon wedges

Pound cutlets to an even thickness of about ¼ inch between two pieces of plastic wrap.

Place the flour on one plate and breadcrumbs on another. Put the eggs into a bowl. Blot cutlets dry and season generously with salt and pepper. Press each cutlet into the flour and shake off excess. Dip each into the beaten eggs and drain off excess. Press each into the breadcrumbs and hold on a separate plate.

Pour ⅛ inch of oil into a large sauté pan. Heat over moderate heat until oil is very hot (about 350°F). A few breadcrumbs will sizzle when dropped into the oil, but they should not turn black or sink to the bottom of the pan.

Add the breaded cutlets to the hot oil in batches, being sure not to crowd them in the pan. Pan fry on the first side for 2–3 minutes or until golden brown and the cutlets release easily from the pan. Turn the cutlets once and finish cooking on the second side, 2–3 minutes. Remove the cutlets from the pan, and drain briefly on absorbent paper towels. If the oil in the pan begins to darken while cooking, carefully pour it off, wipe out the pan with paper toweling, add fresh oil, and bring back to 350°F before cooking the remaining cutlets.

Serve the veal cutlets hot, garnished with lemon wedges.

Veal Saltimbocca
with Fettuccine

MAKES 8 SERVINGS | PREPARATION TIME: 45 MINUTES

*I*ndulge yourself in the velvety, rich flavors of veal, butter, white wine, and prosciutto. Pounding the cutlets thin enhances the delicate texture of this dish. If desired, substitute pork cutlets for the veal.

2 pounds fettuccine noodles

2 tablespoons olive oil

3 pounds boneless veal cutlets

4 teaspoons sage, finely chopped

1 teaspoon salt, or to taste

1 teaspoon freshly ground black pepper, or to taste

16 prosciutto slices, paper-thin

2 cups all-purpose flour

1/2 cup olive oil

1 cup dry white wine

1 1/2 cups butter, chilled and cubed

1/2 teaspoon salt, or to taste

1/4 cup parsley, coarsely chopped

1 lemon, cut into eighths

Bring a large pot of salted water to a boil. Cook the pasta in the boiling water for 8–10 minutes, or until tender to the bite. Toss with 2 tablespoons olive oil and keep warm.

Pound cutlets to an even thickness of about ¼ inch between two pieces of plastic wrap. Season the veal with sage, salt, and pepper. Place 1 slice of prosciutto atop each cutlet.

Dredge veal in flour; shake off excess. Heat 2 tablespoons olive oil in heavy, large skillet over medium-high heat. Add 4 pieces of veal and cook until golden, 3–4 minutes per side. Transfer veal to a platter and keep warm.

Pour off fat from skillet and discard. Add fresh oil as needed until all of the veal is cooked. *(continued on next page)*

ABOVE, LEFT TO RIGHT: Season the item to be sautéed and dredge with flour. Preheat the pan and add the cooking fat. Add the food, presentation side down; sauté until golden on the first side before flipping the item to finish cooking; remove the cooked item from the pan.

Pour off excess fat, add the wine to the skillet, and bring to a boil, scraping up any browned bits. Boil until liquid is reduced to ¼ cup, about 3–4 minutes. Reduce heat to low. Whisk in the chilled butter, 2 tablespoons at a time.

Season sauce with salt, pepper and chopped parsley.

Serve the completed veal immediately accompanied by the fettuccine. Pour ¼ cup sauce over the top of each portion and garnish with a lemon wedge.

ABOVE, LEFT TO RIGHT: Make a sauce from the pan drippings: deglaze the pan with the white wine to remove the fond from the bottom; finish, season, and garnish the sauce; serve over the sautéed item. Opposite, the completed Veal Saltimbocca served with fettuccine.

Cider-Braised Pork Medallions

MAKES 8 SERVINGS | PREPARATION TIME: 40 MINUTES

"Medallions" refers to small, round pieces of meat usually cut from the tenderloin. Serve the braised pork medallions with the Warm Vegetable Slaw (page 276) for the complementary flavors and colors.

3 pounds pork tenderloin

$^1/_2$ cup all-purpose flour

1 teaspoon salt, or to taste

$^3/_4$ teaspoon freshly ground black pepper, or to taste

$^1/_4$ cup vegetable oil

1 cup apple cider

2 tablespoons cider vinegar

2 teaspoons lemon zest

Cut the tenderloin into 24 equal medallions, about 2 inches across and ½-inch thick.

Combine the flour with the salt and ½ teaspoon of the pepper in a zipper-lock plastic bag. Add the medallions to the bag a few at a time, seal, and turn to coat the medallions well with flour. Remove the medallions from the bag and shake off any excess flour.

Heat 2 tablespoons of oil in a large nonstick skillet on high heat, then add half of the medallions. Sauté until lightly browned, 1–2 minutes on each side. Remove the medallions to a warm platter. Add the remaining 2 tablespoons of oil to the pan and sauté the remainder of the medallions.

Reduce the heat to medium and add the cider to the pan. Return the medallions to the pan and simmer, covered, until they are cooked through, about 15 minutes. Transfer the medallions to a warm platter.

Add the vinegar and lemon zest to the pan and bring to a boil. Cook, stirring occasionally, until slightly thickened, about 5 minutes. Season with the remaining ¼ teaspoon of pepper.

To serve, place three medallions on each plate and spoon about 2 teaspoons of the sauce over them.

Jerk Pork Kebabs

MAKES 8 SERVINGS | PREPARATION TIME: 45 MINUTES

See photograph on page 96.

*J*erk seasoning originated in Jamaica, but it is used on grilled meats throughout the Caribbean. Jerk seasoning varies from cook to cook, but it usually includes hot chiles, onion, and allspice, which is known as "pimento" in Jamaica.

JERK SEASONING

5 scallions, chopped

1/2 cup cilantro, leaves and stems, chopped

1-inch piece of ginger, peeled, chopped

3 garlic cloves, chopped

1 1/2 teaspoons ground allspice

2 teaspoons dried thyme

2 teaspoons Creole mustard

1/2 teaspoon cinnamon

1 jalapeño, seeded, chopped

1 teaspoon salt, or to taste

Freshly ground black pepper, to taste

2 tablespoons Worcestershire sauce

2 tablespoons lime juice

3 tablespoons canola oil

3 pounds boneless pork loin, cut into 12 equal pieces

2 red peppers, cut into 1-inch pieces

2 yellow peppers, cut into 1-inch pieces

2 red onions, cut into 1-inch pieces

To make the jerk seasoning, combine the scallions, cilantro, ginger, garlic, allspice, thyme, mustard, cinnamon, salt, and pepper in a food processor. Pulse the machine on and off until the mixture is coarsely chopped. Drizzle in the lime juice, then the oil, with the machine running, until a paste forms.

Transfer this mixture to a zipper-lock bag, with the pork. Press out the air, seal, turn, and gently squeeze the bag several times until the pork is evenly coated. Let the pork marinate at room temperature for at least 10 minutes before preheating the grill.

Thread the pork, peppers, and onion on skewers and grill over medium-high heat, turning as necessary, until the pork is fully cooked and the vegetables are hot and tender, about 15 minutes total. Serve at once.

Roasted Pork Tenderloin
with Honey-Mustard Sauce

MAKES 8 SERVINGS | PREPARATION TIME: 45 MINUTES

Roasted Pork Tenderloin with Honey-Mustard Sauce is shown here with Sautéed Apples (page 290),
Sweet Potato Cakes (page 307), and Haricots Verts with Walnuts (page 287).

*D*elicate and lean, pork tenderloin is an excellent cut that can be roasted whole or sliced into medallions. This recipe will allow you to prepare the rest of the meal while the tenderloin is roasting in the oven.

3 pounds pork tenderloin, whole	2 tablespoons shallots, minced	1^1/$_2$ teaspoons thyme, chopped
1^1/$_2$ teaspoons salt	1 tablespoon tomato paste	^{1}/$_2$ teaspoon salt
^{3}/$_4$ teaspoon freshly ground black pepper	2 tablespoons whole-grain mustard	1 teaspoon black peppercorns, crushed
2 tablespoons vegetable oil	2 tablespoons honey	1^1/$_3$ cups vegetable or chicken broth
2 garlic cloves, minced	2^1/$_2$ tablespoons red wine vinegar	

Preheat the oven to 425°F. Place a rack in a roasting pan, spray with nonstick spray, and place in oven. Remove any excess fat or silverskin from the tenderloin. Season the tenderloin with salt and pepper.

Heat the vegetable oil in a large sauté pan over medium-high heat. Sear the tenderloin until it is golden brown on all sides, approximately 5 minutes.

Remove the tenderloin and place it on the rack in the roasting pan. Roast to the desired doneness. (Pork is safely cooked when it reaches an internal temperature of 160°F.) This will take approximately 15–20 minutes. While the tenderloin is roasting, return the sauté pan to medium heat. Add the gar-lic and shallots; cook until fragrant, about 1 minute. Add the tomato paste and cook until slightly browned. Add the mustard, honey, vinegar, thyme, salt, pepper, and chicken broth. Bring to a boil, then simmer until the mixture reduces to a sauce consistency, about 10 minutes. Keep warm.

Remove the tenderloins from the oven and let stand 5–10 minutes before slicing. Carefully skim and discard the fat from the pan juices. Pour the degreased pan juices into the sauce. Bring the sauce to a boil, reduce the heat, and simmer until it is slightly reduced.

Slice the roast and serve with the warm honey-mustard sauce.

Sautéed Pork Medallions
with Southwestern-Style Sauce

MAKES 6 SERVINGS | PREPARATION TIME: 35 MINUTES

*T*his sauce, also served with Beef Tenderloin (page 144), is excellent with pork medallions as well. The addition of zucchini and yellow squash makes a well-rounded meal.

2¼ pounds pork loin, trimmed

1 recipe Southwestern-Style Sauce
(page 144)

2½ tablespoons vegetable oil

1½ teaspoons salt

¾ teaspoon pepper

2 garlic cloves, minced

2 red peppers, cut into thin strips

1 zucchini, cut into thin strips

1 yellow squash, cut into thin strips

1½ tablespoons jalapeño, finely diced

Slice the pork loin into 12 pieces.

Prepare the Southwestern-Style Sauce as directed. While the sauce is reducing, heat a sauté pan with 1 tablespoon of oil over medium-high heat.

Season the pork with salt and pepper. In two batches, sauté the pork medallions until golden brown and cooked throughout, about 3–4 minutes each side. Remove the pork from the pan and hold it in a warm place.

Add the garlic to the pan and sauté for one minute. Add the red pepper, zucchini, and yellow squash and sauté for roughly 3–4 minutes. Deglaze the skillet with 3 tablespoons of the reduced sauce.

Season the vegetables with salt and pepper as needed.

Finish the sauce with cilantro as directed in the recipe. Serve the pork on a bed of the sautéed vegetables with the sauce spooned on top. Garnish with jalapeño.

Sautéed Pork Medallions
with Apple Chutney

MAKES 8 SERVINGS | PREPARATION TIME: 35 MINUTES

*C*hutney is a general term that refers to a cooked mixture of fruit, vinegar, sugar, and spices. This recipe combines the delicious seasonal fruits of autumn with walnuts and spices. The result is a bold, slightly spicy condiment that is the perfect accompaniment to the tender pork medallions.

¼ cup light brown sugar, lightly packed	1½ teaspoons ginger, grated	2½ cups Granny Smith apple, peeled, cored, medium dice
¼ onion onion, diced	1 teaspoon jalapeño, minced	1 tablespoon salt, or to taste
¼ cup golden raisins	½ teaspoon lemon zest, grated	½ teaspoon freshly ground black pepper, or to taste
1½ tablespoons walnuts, toasted and chopped	½ clove garlic, minced	3 pounds pork loin, boneless
1 tablespoon cider vinegar	⅛ teaspoon ground mace	¼ cup vegetable oil
1½ teaspoons lemon juice	⅛ teaspoon ground clove	

Combine brown sugar, onion, raisins, walnuts, vinegar, lemon juice, ginger, jalapeño, lemon zest, garlic, mace, and clove in a saucepot, cover, and simmer over low heat for 10 minutes. Add the apples and simmer until the apples are very tender and the juices are reduced and slightly thickened, 10–15 minutes. Season with salt and pepper. Hold warm until needed.

While the apples are cooking, slice the pork loin into 12 pieces. Season the pork with salt and pepper.

Heat one tablespoon of oil in a skillet over medium-high heat. In two batches, sauté the pork medallions until golden brown and cooked throughout, about 3–4 minutes each side.

To serve, place three medallions on each plate and spoon about 3 tablespoons of the apple chutney over them.

Fennel and Chorizo Strudels

MAKES 8 SERVINGS | PREPARATION TIME: 40 MINUTES

*T*hese strudels are very hearty and rustic, full of delicious and robust flavors. Phyllo dough is very easy to use, but all the ingredients should be ready before assembling the strudels in order to prevent drying of the delicate sheets.

3/4 cup butter, melted

2 shallots, minced

4 ounces chorizo, sliced thin, skin on

1²/₃ cups fennel bulb, diced

1¹/₂ tablespoons tarragon leaves, minced

¹/₂ tablespoon chives, minced

1 egg

1 cup breadcrumbs

1 teaspoon salt, or to taste

¹/₄ teaspoon freshly ground black pepper, or to taste

8 sheets phyllo dough, thawed

Preheat the oven to 400°F

Heat about 2 tablespoons of the butter in a sauté pan over medium heat. Add the shallots and sauté them until they are translucent.

Add the chorizo, lower the heat, and allow some of the fat to render. Add the fennel and gently cook until tender. It may be necessary to reduce the heat slightly so that the mixture does not burn.

Allow the mixture to cool to room temperature. Add the tarragon leaves, chives, egg and enough breadcrumbs (about ½ cup) to lightly bind the mixture. Adjust the seasoning with salt and pepper.

To assemble each strudel, lay a sheet of phyllo dough on your work surface with the longer edge of the dough parallel to the edge of the work surface. As you work, keep the unused sheets of phyllo covered with plastic wrap to keep them from drying out.

Brush the dough with melted butter and sprinkle with about 1 to 1½ teaspoons of breadcrumbs. Top with another sheet of phyllo dough and repeat this process until a stack of 4 buttered phyllo sheets is formed.

Mound half of the chorizo-fennel mixture along the bottom of the phyllo, leaving a 2-inch border at the edges. Beginning with the bottom edge, carefully roll up the dough and filling, and seal. Repeat with the remaining dough and filling to make a second strudel. Transfer the strudels seam-side down to a parchment paper-lined baking sheet. Brush with the remaining melted butter, and score the dough on a bias to indicate 4 portions.

Bake in a 400°F oven until golden brown, about 10–15 minutes. Slice and serve immediately.

Roasted Pork Loin
with Apricot-Armagnac Compote

MAKES 8 SERVINGS | PREPARATION TIME: 45 MINUTES

Armagnac is a renowned brandy from Gascony, France. Aged in dark oak, the spirit is silky smooth and hearty.

3 pounds pork loin

1½ teaspoons freshly ground black pepper, or to taste

2 teaspoons salt , or to taste

1 tablespoons vegetable oil

1 cup onion, diced

¼ cup Armagnac

1 cup dried apricot, diced

1 teaspoon sage leaves, dried, crumbled

Preheat the oven to 350°F. Spray the rack of a roasting pan with nonstick spray and place in pan. Season the pork loins with the salt and 1 teaspoon of the pepper. Heat 2 teaspoons of the oil in a large sauté pan until almost smoking. Add the pork loins and sauté until the meat is golden brown on all sides, about 6–8 minutes. Remove the loins and place them in the roasting pan. Roast the loins until they are cooked through, about 30–35 minutes, or until an internal temperature of 165°F for well done, and 155°F for slightly pink.

Heat the remaining 1 teaspoon oil in a nonstick skillet and add the onion. Sauté, stirring frequently, until the onion is lightly browned, 6–7 minutes.

Deglaze the pan with the Armagnac. Bring the liquid to a simmer and add the apricot, sage and remaining pepper. Allow the mixture to simmer until most of the liquid has evaporated, about 5- 7 minutes.

After removing the roasted pork loin from the oven, allow it to stand 10 minutes before carving. Carve the loin into slices and serve with the warm apricot compote.

Thai-Spiced Loin Chops
with Hot-Sweet Mustard

MAKES 8 SERVINGS | PREPARATION TIME: 10 MINUTES

This delicious recipe, inspired by the bold flavors of Thai cuisine, is about as simple as it gets. Serve these tangy chops with an aromatic Herbed Basmati Rice (page 327) for a quick and healthy meal.

3 pounds boneless center-cut
    pork loin chops, $1/2$-inch thick,
    trimmed of fat

1 teaspoon salt, or to taste

1 teaspoon freshly ground black pepper,
    or to taste

2 tablespoons Thai red curry paste

Cilantro sprigs, as needed

$1/2$ cup hot-sweet mustard,
    prepared

Lightly oil the grill and preheat to high heat. Season the pork chops with salt and pepper. Spread ¼ teaspoon of the curry paste on each side of each chop.

Place the pork chops on the hot grill. Cook, turning once, until pork is done, about 3–3½ minutes per side.

Garnish the pork chops with cilantro sprigs. Serve with the hot-sweet mustard.

Eggplant and Prosciutto Panini

MAKES 8 SANDWICHES | PREPARATION TIME: 30 MINUTES

"Panini" is the Italian word for rolls or sandwiches. Today "panini" usually refers to rustic sandwiches that are grilled.

1 cup ricotta cheese

1 teaspoon freshly ground black pepper, or to taste

2 tablespoons basil, chopped

22 ounces eggplant caponata, jarred

8 sandwich rolls (hoagie, ciabatta, sourdough), sliced in half lengthwise

¼ pound prosciutto, thinly sliced

In a bowl, combine the ricotta cheese, pepper, and basil. Mix well and refrigerate until ready to use.

Preheat a grill or sandwich press to high.

Spread the eggplant caponata evenly on one half of each roll. Spread the ricotta mixture evenly on the other half. Top the ricotta side with the prosciutto slices, and invert the eggplant side on top.

Grill each sandwich for 3–4 minutes. Slice each sandwich into 4 pieces, and serve.

Broiled Lamb Chops
with White Bean and Rosemary Ragout

MAKES 8 SERVINGS | PREPARATION TIME: 40 MINUTES

Broiled Lamb Chops with White Bean and Rosemary Ragout are shown here
with Summer Squash Sauté (page 280).

A simple ragout of cannellini beans and fresh, pungent rosemary provides an ideal accompaniment to the full flavor of roasted lamb. This elegant, easy-to-prepare dish is great for entertaining.

6 tablespoons reduced-sodium soy sauce

2 tablespoons Dijon mustard

2 tablespoons Worcestershire sauce

2 tablespoons vegetable oil

1 teaspoon freshly ground black pepper, or to taste

2 tablespoons rosemary, chopped

4 teaspoons thyme, chopped

4 teaspoons sage, chopped

16 double lamb chops (rib or loin), frenched

1³/₄ cup cannellini beans, drained, juices reserved

1 tablespoon demi-glace concentrate

1 teaspoon lemon zest

Salt, to taste

Freshly ground black pepper, to taste

Combine the soy sauce, mustard, Worcestershire sauce, vegetable oil, 1 teaspoon pepper, 1 tablespoon rosemary, and the thyme and sage in a zipper-lock bag; add the lamb. Squeeze out the air and seal the bag; turn to coat the lamb with the marinade ingredients. Refrigerate for 30 minutes.

While the lamb is marinating, prepare the white bean ragout. Combine the cannellini beans, ½ cup of their reserved juices, 1 tablespoon rosemary, the demi-glace concentrate, and the lemon zest in a saucepan.

Bring the mixture to a simmer, stirring constantly. Reduce the heat to medium low and continue to simmer the ragout for 10 minutes, stirring occasionally. If the ragout becomes too thick, add 2 to 3 tablespoons of the reserved juices from the beans to restore consistency. Keep warm.

Spray the broiler rack with nonstick cooking spray; preheat the broiler.

Remove the lamb chops from the marinade. Discard the marinade and brush off any excess herbs that may have stuck to the lamb. Be sure to wipe any excess marinade off the bones or else they will burn under the broiler. Season the chops with salt and pepper.

Broil the lamb chops 5 inches from the heat until done to taste, 2–3 minutes on each side for medium.

Spoon about ¼ cup of the white bean ragout onto a warm plate and nestle 2 of the lamb chops in the sauce.

CHAPTER SIX

Poultry

THE FAMOUS SEVENTEENTH-CENTURY FRENCH GASTRONOME
Jean Anthelme Brillat-Savarin wrote: "Poultry is for
the cook what canvas is to the painter." Sold fresh and
frozen, available throughout the year, bred to be leaner,
more tender, and less expensive than ever, poultry continues to rise in popularity.
Statistics indicate that the average American ate 96.7 pounds of poultry in 1999,
and that amount has been steadily increasing, with projections of 113.3 pounds per
person by the year 2009.

While roasting a whole turkey requires substantial cooking time, poultry is
available in various sizes and forms, making it swift and effortless to prepare. This
chapter features a wide range of poultry, from duck breast to chicken thighs to
ground turkey.

White and Dark Meat

Dark meat, such as chicken thighs or duck breast, stays moist longer than white
meat and generally requires longer cooking time. White meat, by contrast, requires
shorter cooking times and a more careful eye, as it may become tough and dry if
overcooked. One of the great challenges when cooking whole poultry is to get leg
(dark) meat fully cooked without overcooking breast (white) meat. By cooking a
cut-up chicken or a combination of leg and breast portions you can eliminate this

problem. Start the leg portions first, then add the breast portions to the pan or grill several minutes later. Then, the dark and white portions are done at the same time, perfectly cooked and moist.

Safety

When working with any type of poultry, keep all tools and work surfaces clean to avoid cross-contamination of other foods with bacteria commonly found in poultry. Wash cutting boards and knives thoroughly with hot, soapy water before and after you use them to cut poultry. Rinse poultry with cold water and pat dry with absorbent paper towels before cooking. Store uncooked birds in leak-proof containers in the refrigerator. Never place raw poultry directly above cooked meat or fresh vegetables. This will prevent raw juices from dripping onto these other ingredients.

AT A GLANCE | Best Quick Cooking Methods for Poultry

BIRD	QUICK COOKING METHODS
Cornish Game Hen	Grilling, broiling, roasting
Chicken Pieces:	
White meat	
Bone-in breast, with skin	Grilling, broiling, pan frying, roasting
Boneless, skinless breast	Grilling, sautéing, deep-frying
Dark meat	
Bone-in leg, thigh, wing	Suitable for all cooking techniques
Duckling:	
Boneless breast	Grilling, sautéing, pan searing

AT A GLANCE | Doneness Temperatures and Tests

DESIRED DONENESS:	REMOVE FROM COOKING MEDIUM AT:	CARRY-OVER TO:	MEAT SHOULD LOOK:
Whole birds	170°F	180°F	Legs move easily in sockets and when pierced in the thigh, juices run clear. Juices in an unstuffed bird's cavity no longer have a red or pink hue.
Breasts	160°F	170°F	Meat becomes opaque and firm throughout.
Legs, thighs, and wings	170°F	180°F	Meat releases easily from the bone.
Stuffing	155°F	165°F	For stuffing cooked separately or inside a whole bird.
Ground poultry	155°F	165°F	Even opaque color throughout, no hint of pink.

Butterflying Boneless Cuts

By carefully cutting a boneless chicken breast nearly in half and then opening it like a book (or a butterfly), you create a cut that is thin enough for cooking rapidly with high heat or for rolling around a filling. Place the breast flat on a work surface. Put your guiding hand flat on the breast; this will keep breast stable and also help you keep the blade parallel to work surface. With a sharp knife, make long but shallow cuts into the curved side of the breast. Keep your knife's blade parallel to the work surface and cut almost through to the other side, stopping ½ to 1 inch short. This intact portion creates the "hinge" that allows you to open the breast into a flat, thin piece. If desired or directed in a recipe, after butterflying the breast, place it between 2 sheets of plastic or parchment paper and pound it lightly with a mallet or meat pounder to an even thickness.

Testing for Doneness

A reliable way to determine doneness in poultry is to use a thermometer. Use the table above as a reference. Remember, as with any meat, poultry will continue to cook after it is removed from its cooking medium.

Chicken Breast
with Artichokes and Mustard Sauce

MAKES 8 SERVINGS | PREPARATION TIME: 40 MINUTES

*T*his recipe brings together the flavors of two mustards: Dijon and whole-grain. Dijon mustards—ranging from mild to hot—are made from brown or black mustard seeds and usually include white wine. Whole-grain mustards come in many styles, from hot to sweet and mild.

3 tablespoons olive oil

1 tablespoon butter

1½ cups white onion

3 pounds chicken breast, boneless, skinless, ¾-inch dice

2 tablespoons whole-grain mustard

1 tablespoon Dijon mustard

1½ cups white wine, or as needed

8 artichoke hearts, canned or frozen, quartered

1 tablespoon tarragon, chopped

Salt, to taste

Freshly ground black pepper, to taste

Heat a Dutch oven. Swirl in the oil and butter, then add the onions. Sauté until translucent, about 5 minutes. Add the chicken and cook until opaque, about 5 minutes, stirring occasionally.

Stir in the whole-grain mustard, Dijon mustard, and white wine. Cover and simmer for about 20–25 minutes, adding additional wine if needed. Uncover, and simmer the mixture until it reduces to a sauce consistency, about 10 minutes.

Add the artichoke hearts and tarragon 5 minutes before completion; cook until heated through.

Season with salt and pepper.

STEP-BY-STEP | Grilling

Grilling is a great way to make dinner in minutes. It requires minimal preparation and the cleanup is effortless as there are no pots and pans to scrub.

➡ SEASON OR MARINATE THE MAIN ITEM

Choose tender, portion-size cuts for grilling like poultry breasts, portion-size steaks, chops or cutlets, or cubes threaded on skewers. Remove excess fat that might cause the grill to flare up. Grilling is a quick cooking method that relies upon intense dry heat. Adding seasonings and marinades in advance gives poultry, meats, and fish a chance to develop a good, full flavor. Add salt a few minutes before you are ready to grill, but to give marinades and rubs a chance to penetrate, add them before you preheat the grill so they will have at least 15 or 20 minutes. (If you wish to marinate foods longer, put them in the refrigerator.)

➡ PREHEATING THE GRILL

Grills must be well cleaned and maintained. Scour the grill well with a stiff brush between uses to remove any charred particles. Preheat a gas grill, or use a chimney starter to start coals and let smolder until covered with white ash. You can set up a hotter and cooler area in the grill: For charcoal grills, arrange the coals to one side of the center of the grill; for gas grills, keep the heat lower or leave it off on one side. If you are using skewers, oil metal ones to prevent sticking, or soak wooden ones to keep them from burning.

➡ PUTTING THE FOOD ON THE GRILL

Place the best-looking side of the food face down on the grill. When the food comes into contact with the heated rods, distinct marks are charred onto its surface. Let foods cook undisturbed on the first side until it is time to turn; when the food releases easily from the grill and can be lifted without tearing or sticking, it is usually ready to turn over. This develops better flavor and allows the food to release naturally from the grill. Grill baskets make it easier to manage large batches, for instance, sliced vegetables for the grill. They are also very helpful when you want to grill a more delicate food, like fish.

Chefs will often give foods a quarter turn on the grill to mark them with a crosshatch prior to flipping them over. This also provides an opportunity to move the food to a cooler area of the grill, so that it won't scorch or char. Lift the food up after the first side is already marked and stiffened and move it to a new area on the grill. As you set it down, rotate the food 90 degrees.

➡ ADDING A GRILLING SAUCE OR GLAZE

Because many grilling sauces and glazes contain sugar (which burns easily), cook the food partially before applying them so that they will brown lightly but not burn. Brush a single coat on each side, or build up an appealing, crusty coating by turning the food more frequently and applying a thin layer each time you turn the food over.

➡ FINISHING

Larger pieces of meat may require transfer to a cooler part of the grill to cook through more slowly and evenly. Remove meat, poultry, and fish when slightly underdone, as even thin pieces retain enough heat to continue cooking even after you take them from the grill.

See the step-by-step photographs accompanying the recipe for Lemon-Ginger Grilled Chicken (page 180).

Grilled Chicken Sandwich
with Pancetta, Arugula, and Aïoli

MAKES 8 SANDWICHES | PREPARATION TIME: 25 MINUTES

*E*asy components can give you outstanding results. Cook the chicken, pancetta and bread all at the grill. Mix the aïoli and assemble. This flavorful grilled sandwich has an elegant twist with garlicky mayonnaise and the light peppery flavor of arugula.

AÏOLI

1 cup mayonnaise

1 garlic clove, minced

3 pounds chicken breasts, boneless, skinless

3 teaspoons salt, or to taste

2 teaspoons freshly ground black pepper, or to taste

5 tablespoons olive oil

16 slices sourdough bread

16 slices pancetta, sliced 1/8-inch thick

1 bunch arugula, trimmed, washed, and dried

Combine the mayonnaise and garlic to make the aïoli. Reserve.

Pound the chicken breasts to an even thickness. Season generously with salt and pepper, and brush with 3 tablespoons of the olive oil.

Preheat the grill on the highest setting.

Lightly brush the slices of bread with the remaining olive oil. Grill over moderate heat until golden and crispy on the outside, but soft on the inside. Reserve.

Grill the chicken breasts until cooked through, about 5–6 minutes on each side. While the chicken is cooking, grill the pancetta until crispy.

Spread 1 tablespoon of the aïoli on each side of the grilled bread. Place a few leaves of arugula, 2 slices of crispy pancetta, and the chicken breast on one side of the bread. Top with the other half of bread and slice diagonally.

Moroccan Lemon Chicken
with Mango Chutney

MAKES 8 SERVINGS | PREPARATION TIME: 45 MINUTES

Moroccan Lemon Chicken is shown here with Herbed Basmati Rice (page 327).

*F*resh lemon, chickpeas and a dash of spice create the Moroccan flavors in this one-skillet meal. The chicken, combined with its seasonings, actually improves with time, so don't worry about preparing it a day in advance if necessary.

1 lemon	2 teaspoons curry powder	2 bunches asparagus, white and green
8 chicken breast halves, boneless	2 tablespoons olive oil	1½ cups chickpeas, drained and rinsed
1 tablespoon salt, or to taste	2 cups onion, thinly sliced	Mango Chutney (recipe follows)
Freshly ground black pepper, to taste	1¼ cups chicken broth or water	¼ cup parsley, chopped

Bring a large pot of salted water to a boil. Cut the lemon in half. Juice one half and thinly slice the remaining half in rounds. Reserve.

Season the chicken with salt, pepper, and a little curry powder Heat the oil in a large nonstick skillet over medium-high heat. Add the chicken and cook until golden, about 2 minutes per side. Transfer the chicken to a platter.

Pour off excess fat from the pan and return to the heat. Add the onion, the remaining curry powder, and ½ cup of broth or water to the skillet. Bring to a boil, scraping up browned bits from the bottom. Cover and cook over medium heat, stirring occasionally, until onions are almost tender, about 5 minutes.

Return the chicken to the pan, along with ¾ cup broth or water, the reserved lemon slices, and ½ teaspoon salt. Bring to a boil. Reduce the heat, cover, and simmer 15–20 minutes, turning the chicken and stirring occasionally during cooking.

Meanwhile, trim 1–2 inches off the asparagus, and cook in boiling salted water until just tender. Drain the asparagus and reserve.

Stir the chickpeas and ⅓ cup of the mango chutney in with the chicken. Simmer for 5 minutes or until the chickpeas are heated through. Stir in the reserved lemon juice to taste.

Serve the chicken with the chickpeas, garnished with chopped parsley and the asparagus, with additional mango chutney on the side.

NOTE: The chicken breast cut shown on the opposite page is known to chefs as a *suprême*. The skin is left on and the first joint of the wing is left attached. Use a sharp knife to scrape away the meat from the wing bone.

Spicy Mango Chutney

MAKES 1¾ CUPS | PREPARATION TIME: 20 MINUTES

2 cups mango, chopped (about 2 medium)

⅔ cup dark brown sugar

2 tablespoons cider vinegar

½ cup raisins

1 tablespoon jalapeño, minced

1 tablespoon garlic, minced

1 tablespoon ginger, minced

¼ teaspoon salt, or to taste

⅛ teaspoon freshly ground black pepper, or to taste

Combine the mangos and brown sugar in a 2½ quart sauce-pan. Add the vinegar, raisins, jalapeño, garlic, ginger, salt, and pepper, bring to a boil and simmer 15 minutes.

Transfer to clean storage container. Cover and refrigerate for up to 2 weeks.

Grilled Chicken Burritos

MAKES 6 SERVINGS | PREPARATION TIME: 45 MINUTES

*F*or an easy summer meal, roll flour tortillas into burritos with this cilantro-lime marinated chicken. Serve with Tomatillo Salsa (page 16) or Tomato Salsa (page 24) for a zesty finish.

¼ cup olive oil

1½ teaspoons lime juice

2 teaspoons cilantro, chopped

2 garlic cloves, chopped

¼ shallot, chopped

2 teaspoons salt, or to taste

½ teaspoon black peppercorns, crushed

2¼ pounds chicken breasts, boneless, skinless

6 flour tortillas (12-inch diameter)

1 cup Guacamole (page 18)

1 cup Tomato Salsa (page 24)

Combine the olive oil, lime juice, cilantro, garlic, shallot, salt, and peppercorns in a zipper-lock plastic bag; add the chicken. Squeeze out the air and seal the bag; turn to coat the chicken. Refrigerate, turning the bag once, for at least 30 minutes.

Preheat the grill to the highest setting. Shake any excess marinade from the chicken. Grill, until cooked through, about 7 minutes on the first side, and 5 minutes on the second side.

Heat a large skillet or nonstick sauté pan and heat the tortillas for 15 seconds on each side until warm. Alternatively, tortillas can be grilled lightly, about 15 seconds per side.

Thinly slice the chicken breasts on a bias. Spread each warmed tortilla with about 2 tablespoons of the guacamole and fill with one sliced chicken breast. Roll the tortillas and serve each with 2 tablespoons of the salsa.

Jerk Chicken

Scotch bonnets, along with the closely related (and equally potent) Jamaican hots and habaneros, are small, fiery-hot chiles that are irregularly shaped and range in color from yellow to orange to red. Use gloves when handling Scotch bonnets to prevent irritation, and be sure not to inadvertently rub your eyes or face.

2 teaspoons allspice, ground

1 teaspoon cinnamon, ground

1/2 teaspoon nutmeg, ground

1 onion, large, cut into eighths
   (about 1/2 pound)

4 scallions, cut into fourths

1 Scotch bonnet chile, seeded

1/2 teaspoon dark rum

1 teaspoon salt, or to taste

1 teaspoon freshly ground black pepper,
   or to taste

8 chicken breasts, boneless, skinless

Preheat the oven to 375°F.

Combine the allspice, cinnamon, nutmeg, onion, scallions, chile, rum, salt, and pepper in a food processor. Process until the mixture forms a thick salsa-like mixture.

Rub the mixture on each chicken breast and place the chicken in a zipper-lock plastic bag. Squeeze out the air and seal the bag. Refrigerate for 10 minutes.

Spray the rack of a roasting pan with nonstick spray and place in the pan.

Arrange the chicken on the rack, and bake for 12 minutes. Flip the chicken and cook another 15 minutes until cooked through. Serve warm.

Whole Wheat Quesadillas
with Chicken, Jalapeño Jack, and Mango Salsa

MAKES 8 SERVINGS | PREPARATION TIME: 45 MINUTES

Whole Wheat Quesadillas with Chicken, Jalapeño Jack, and Mango Salsa are shown here with
Black Bean Salad with Lime-Cilantro Vinaigrette (page 282).

*N*owadays, tortillas and wraps come in dozens of variations. Look for whole wheat flour tortillas in the refrigerated section of your supermarket. Serve these healthy quesadillas with Black Bean Salad seasoned with Lime-Cilantro Vinaigrette for a tasty meal.

2 tablespoons vegetable oil

3 pounds chicken breasts, boneless, skinless

2 teaspoons salt, or to taste

1 teaspoon freshly ground black pepper, or to taste

4 mangoes, diced

1 papaya, diced

1 chipotle pepper, canned, minced

¹/₄ cup orange juice

¹/₄ cup lime juice

4 cups Jalapeño Jack cheese, grated

6 cups scallions, thinly sliced

1 cup peanuts, toasted, roughly chopped

16 whole wheat flour tortillas

3 tablespoons peanut oil

Preheat the oven to 400°F.

Heat the vegetable oil over high heat in a large sauté pan. Season the chicken with the salt and pepper. Cook the chicken breasts until golden brown on all sides, about 8–10 minutes. Place the chicken in the oven until cooked through, about 10–12 minutes total.

Allow the chicken to cool for 5 minutes. Shred the chicken into bite-sized pieces.

While the chicken is cooking, combine the mango, papaya, chipotle pepper, orange juice, and lime juice. Reserve under refrigeration until needed.

To assemble the quesadillas, place ¾ cup chicken, ½ cup Jalapeño Jack cheese, ¾ cup scallions, and 2 tablespoons peanuts on a tortilla. Top with another tortilla. Repeat with the remaining ingredients to make 8 quesadillas.

Heat about 1 teaspoon peanut oil in a large sauté pan. Place 1 quesadilla in the pan and lightly brown on both sides, making certain that the cheese is melted in the middle before removing from the heat. Repeat with remaining quesadillas, adding more peanut oil when necessary.

Cut each quesadilla into fourths and serve with the mango salsa.

Lemon-Ginger Grilled Chicken

MAKES 8 SERVINGS | PREPARATION TIME: 20 MINUTES

Lemon-Ginger Grilled Chicken is shown here with Boiled Potatoes with Saffron and Parsley (page 310).

*I*nspired by the Lemon Chicken which is a Chinese-restaurant favorite, this heavenly, slightly tart dish can be made on the grill or under the broiler, and is delicious served hot or cold.

4 tablespoons lemon zest

²/₃ cup lemon juice

4 teaspoons ginger, peeled and minced

4 teaspoons light brown sugar, firmly packed

1 tablespoon peanut oil

1 tablespoon salt, or to taste

4 Szechuan chili peppers, dried, seeds removed

3 pounds chicken thighs, boneless, skinless

Combine the lemon zest, lemon juice, ginger, brown sugar, salt, and chiles in a zipper-lock plastic bag. Add the chicken, squeeze out the air, and seal the bag; turn to coat the chicken. Refrigerate, turning the bag occasionally, at least 15 minutes.

Spray the grill or broiler rack with nonstick spray. Preheat the grill or broiler on high. If broiling, position the rack about 5 inches from the heat source. Grill or broil the chicken until cooked through, about 6 minutes per side.

FROM LEFT: Place the item, presentation side down, on a preheated grill; turn the food over and continue cooking to desired doneness.

Herb-Breaded Chicken
with Creamy Mustard Sauce

MAKES 8 SERVINGS | PREPARATION TIME: 40 MINUTES

*T*his chicken is dipped in buttermilk, dredged in an herbed breading, and baked. The result is a crispy, low-fat alternative to fried chicken. The creamy, sweet-and-sour sauce makes a fine contrast of flavor and texture.

2 cups chicken broth

1¼ cup all-purpose flour

2 tablespoons butter

½ cup evaporated milk

¼ cup Dijon mustard

1 tablespoon honey

¼ teaspoon freshly ground black pepper, or to taste

¼ cup parsley, chopped

¼ cup tarragon, chopped

¼ cup basil, chiffonade

¼ cup chives, chopped

⅔ cup cornmeal

⅔ cup cornflake crumbs

1 cup buttermilk

4 eggs

4 teaspoons salt, or to taste

2 teaspoons freshly ground black pepper, or to taste

8 chicken breasts, boneless, skinless

3 tablespoons vegetable oil

Preheat the oven to 400°F.

Bring the chicken broth to a simmer.

Combine ¼ cup of the flour with the butter, and mix to form a paste. Whisk the paste into the simmering chicken broth. Allow the mixture to simmer until thickened, about 10 minutes.

Add the evaporated milk, mustard, honey, and pepper. Simmer for an additional 5–10 minutes, or until the flavors have combined, skimming as necessary. Season to taste with salt and pepper and keep warm.

While the sauce is simmering, combine the parsley, tarragon, basil, and chives in a small bowl. Combine the cornmeal and corn flake crumbs on a sheet of wax paper; add one-half of the herb mixture.

Whisk the eggs into the buttermilk. Combine the remaining herbs with the buttermilk and transfer to a shallow dish.

Season the chicken breasts liberally with salt and pepper. Dredge each chicken breast in the remaining flour. Dip each chicken breast in the buttermilk mixture. Coat the chicken on both sides with the cornmeal mixture, shaking off excess.

Heat 1½ tablespoons of the oil in a large sauté pan over medium-high heat. Sauté the chicken in 2 batches, cooking until golden brown, about 4–5 minutes per side. Place the cooked chicken on a baking sheet while sautéing the rest in the remaining oil. Place all of the chicken in the oven for 10–12 minutes, or until cooked through. Serve with the reserved creamy mustard sauce.

Chicken Curry with Almonds

MAKES 8 SERVINGS | PREPARATION TIME: 30 MINUTES

*C*urry powders are mixtures of various combinations of ground spices, originally of Indian origin; curry refers to the sauce-based dishes they are used to prepare. Depending on the origin and composition of the curry powder, curries can range from sweet and mild to sweet and moderately hot or pungent and very hot.

1 cup almonds, sliced

1 cup water, hot

1 tablespoon vegetable oil

6 black peppercorns

5 green cardamom pods

1 cinnamon stick

1/4 cup onion, minced

1 teaspoon garlic, minced

1 teaspoon ginger, minced

1 tablespoon curry powder

3 pounds chicken thighs, boneless, skinless, cut into 1-inch pieces

1 1/4 pounds Yukon potatoes, cut into small cubes

1/2 cup chicken broth

3/4 cup milk or cream

1 teaspoon salt, or to taste

1/4 cup cilantro, chopped

1/4 cup almonds, toasted, for garnish

Soak the almonds in the hot water for 15–20 minutes.

While the almonds are soaking, heat the oil in a large pan, add the peppercorns, cardamom pods, and cinnamon stick. Fry until the cardamom pods turn pale brown, about 3 minutes. Remove the peppercorns, cardamom pods, and cinnamon stick from the oil.

Add onion and sauté until golden, about 2 minutes.

Add garlic, ginger, and curry powder, and continue to cook for another minute. Remove from heat.

Drain the almonds, reserving the liquid. Blend the almonds in a food processor and gradually add the reserved liquid. The final result should be a smooth puree with a consistency similar to cream.

Return the pan with the onion mixture to medium heat. Stir in the almond puree, thoroughly incorporating it into the onion mixture, and stirring continually, cook until fragrant, about 1 minute.

Add the chicken and simmer for about 5 minutes.

Add the potatoes, chicken broth, milk, and salt, and cook, covered, over medium-high heat for about 15 minutes, or until the chicken is cooked and the sauce is thick and creamy.

Remove from the heat, place on a large platter and top with chopped cilantro and toasted almonds.

Pesto-Stuffed Chicken Breasts
with Tomato Relish

MAKES 6 SERVINGS | PREPARATION TIME: 45 MINUTES

Pesto-Stuffed Chicken Breast with Tomato Relish is shown here
with Wild Rice Pilaf (page 320) and Grilled Vegetables (page 284).

*P*esto is a paste usually made from garlic, oil, pine nuts, basil, and Parmesan cheese. Rich in flavor, it adds an exciting twist to simple boneless, skinless chicken breasts. Complement these flavors with a touch of tomato relish and you have a winner.

TOMATO RELISH

4 plum tomatoes, seeded and chopped

1 tablespoon extra-virgin olive oil

2 teaspoons balsamic vinegar

$1/4$ teaspoon salt, or to taste

$1/8$ teaspoon freshly ground black pepper, or to taste

PESTO

3 garlic cloves, peeled

2 cups basil, packed

1 lemon, zested and juiced

5 tablespoon pine nuts, toasted

$2/3$ cup Parmesan cheese, grated

$1/4$ cup extra-virgin olive oil

$2^1/4$ pounds chicken breast, boneless, skinless

Butcher's twine or wooden toothpicks

1 teaspoon salt, or to taste

$1/2$ teaspoon freshly ground black pepper, or to taste

2 tablespoons vegetable oil

Combine the tomatoes, 1 tablespoon olive oil, vinegar, ¼ teaspoon salt, and ⅛ teaspoon pepper in a small bowl; refrigerate, covered, until chilled.

Preheat the oven to 400°F. Spray a baking sheet with nonstick spray.

Combine the garlic, basil, lemon juice and zest, pine nuts, Parmesan, ¼ teaspoon salt, and a pinch of pepper in a food processor; pulse until finely chopped. Add the remaining ¼ cup olive oil in a thin stream until fully incorporated and a thick paste forms.

Place the chicken breasts, skinned side down, between 2 sheets of wax paper and pound to ¼-inch thickness using a meat mallet. Remove and discard the top sheet of wax paper. Spread each chicken breast with about 2 tablespoons of the pesto mixture. Starting with the narrower end, roll each breast around the filling; discard the wax paper.

Tie each breast with butcher's twine or secure with toothpicks to prevent it from unrolling. Season the chicken with salt and pepper.

Heat the vegetable oil in a large sauté pan over medium-high heat. Sauté the chicken until golden brown on all sides, about 8–10 minutes total. Place the chicken in the oven and roast until cooked through, about 10–15 minutes.

Remove the chicken from the oven and let stand 5 minutes. Remove and discard the string or toothpicks, and slice each chicken breast on the bias into four pieces. Arrange the slices on individual plates, and garnish with some of the tomato relish.

Walnut Chicken

MAKES 8 SERVINGS | PREPARATION TIME: 30 MINUTES

Walnut Chicken is shown here with Sweet and Sour Green Beans (page 286).

*H*ere, chicken is cooked along with a pilaf of bulgur and walnuts. Bulgur wheat—wheat kernels that have been steamed, dried, and crushed—is available in most supermarkets, and comes in coarse, medium, and fine grinds.

2 teaspoons vegetable oil

3 pounds chicken breasts, boneless, skinless, cut into chunks

1 teaspoon salt, or to taste

1 teaspoon freshly ground black pepper, or to taste

2 onions, chopped

4 carrots, chopped

1 teaspoon cumin seeds

1 teaspoon caraway seeds

2 cups chicken broth

2 tablespoons walnuts, chopped

$^1/_2$ cup golden raisins

$1^1/_2$ cups bulgur wheat

$^1/_2$ teaspoon cinnamon, ground

Heat 1 teaspoon of oil on medium-high heat in a large non-stick skillet. Season the chicken chunks with ½ teaspoon of salt and ½ teaspoon of pepper. Sauté the chicken for approximately 5 minutes, until it is browned. Transfer to a plate and reserve.

Add 1 teaspoon of oil to the skillet. Add the onions, carrots, cumin seeds, and caraway seeds. Sauté for approximately 3–5 minutes, or until the onions are translucent and the carrots are tender.

Add the chicken broth, scraping any residual brown bits from bottom of the skillet. Add the walnuts, raisins, and bulgur wheat. Bring to boil then lower to simmer and adjust the heat to medium low. Add the cinnamon, ½ teaspoon of salt, and ½ teaspoon of pepper. Cover and cook for 10 minutes. Add the reserved chicken chunks and cook for 5 minutes more.

Adjust the seasoning with salt and pepper, if necessary, and serve at once.

Spicy Szechuan Chicken Stir-Fry

MAKES 8 SERVINGS | PREPARATION TIME: 35 MINUTES

*T*he subtly complex Szechuan spice of this dish is ideally partnered by Asian-style noodles or brown rice. Longer marinating of the chicken will intensify the overall flavor.

1 teaspoon Szechuan seasoning

2 teaspoons sugar

1 teaspoon salt, or to taste

3 pounds chicken breasts, boneless, skinless, cut into thin strips

$^1\!/_4$ cup peanut oil

8 scallions, thinly sliced

1$^1\!/_2$-inch piece ginger, peeled and minced

3 cups mushrooms. thinly sliced

3 cups bok choy, thinly sliced

1 cup water chestnuts, sliced

2 tablespoons reduced-sodium soy sauce

Combine the Szechuan seasoning, sugar, and salt in a zipper-lock plastic bag; add the chicken. Squeeze out the air and seal the bag; turn to coat the chicken. Refrigerate, turning the bag occasionally, 15 minutes or longer. While the chicken is marinating, prepare the vegetables.

Heat a nonstick wok or skillet over high heat until a drop of water skitters. Pour in 1 tablespoon of the oil and swirl to coat the pan, then add the chicken. Stir-fry until the chicken is cooked through, 1–3 minutes. Remove the chicken from the pan and keep warm.

Return the wok or skillet to the heat. Pour in the remaining oil and swirl to coat the pan, then add the scallions and ginger. Stir-fry until the scallions are softened, about 2 minutes. Add the mushrooms and stir-fry until the liquid that the mushrooms release has evaporated, 3–4 minutes. Add the bok choy and stir-fry until wilted, 3–4 minutes. Add the chicken, water chestnuts, and soy sauce. Stir the mixture gently until heated through, 3–4 minutes. Serve at once.

Smoked Turkey and
Roasted Red Pepper Sandwich

MAKES 8 SERVINGS | PREPARATION TIME: 40 MINUTES

*T*his is a delicious sandwich that is quick to prepare. If you're short on time, substitute jarred roasted red peppers which have been drained well.

2 red bell peppers

2 tablespoons balsamic vinegar

2 tablespoons water

2 sprigs rosemary, chopped

2 focaccia loaves

½ cup mayonnaise or Aïoli (page 172)

2 pounds smoked turkey, thinly sliced

16 basil leaves

Preheat the broiler. Broil the bell peppers 5 inches from the heat, turning frequently with tongs until the skin is shriveled and darkened, about 10 minutes. Place the peppers in a bowl, cover with plastic wrap, and let steam 5 minutes. When cool enough to handle, peel, seed, and then slice the peppers into thin strips (about ¼ inch thick).

Combine the vinegar, water, and rosemary in a zipper-lock bag; add the pepper strips. Squeeze out the air and seal the bag; turn to coat the peppers. Refrigerate, turning the bag occasionally, for 20 minutes, or the peppers may be marinated overnight.

Cut the focaccia into 3½-inch square × 1-inch high pieces. Slice the pieces in half along the center.

Drain the pepper strips, reserving the marinade. Add 3 tablespoons of the marinade to the mayonnaise.

To assemble the sandwiches, spread 1 tablespoon mayonnaise on one side of one half of the bread. Layer 4 ounces of turkey, 4–5 of the red bell pepper strips, and 2 basil leaves. Top with the other half of the focaccia and serve.

Turkey Burger

MAKES 8 SERVINGS | PREPARATION TIME: 30 MINUTES

A lean and healthy base for a wide variety of toppings, this recipe is full of flavor. Top it our way or as you desire.

2 pounds ground turkey

1 garlic clove, minced

1/2 teaspoon salt, or to taste

1/4 teaspoon freshly ground black pepper, or to taste

2 tablespoons parsley, chives, or basil, chopped

2 teaspoons vegetable oil

8 provolone or Monterey Jack cheese, sliced

8 sandwich rolls, split and toasted

BURGER GARNISH ITEMS (OPTIONAL)

1 avocado, sliced just before serving

1 tomato, sliced

1 red onion, sliced

8 romaine lettuce leaves

Preheat the grill. Gently blend the ground turkey with the garlic, salt, pepper, and herbs. Shape into 8 patties and chill in the refrigerator until the grill is very hot.

Brush the grill rods with the oil. Grill the turkey burgers on the first side until browned, about 5 minutes. Carefully flip the burgers over, and grill on the second side until browned and cooked through, another 5 minutes. Top with the cheese during the final 2–3 minutes of grilling.

Serve the burgers on the toasted buns, topped with sliced avocado, tomato, onion, and lettuce.

Duck, Shrimp, and Andouille Gumbo

MAKES 2 QUARTS | PREPARATION TIME: 45 MINUTES

*G*umbo is a stew-like dish that was created in Louisiana and is now recognized and enjoyed in many varieties. Originally, it combined meat and shellfish, okra, tomatoes, bay leaf, and hot pepper. Make and eat it the same day, or enjoy it a day later, as the taste improves after the flavors have had time to marry.

2 tablespoons butter

$^1/_4$ cup all-purpose flour

2 tablespoons vegetable oil

$1^1/_2$ onions, diced

3 celery stalks, diced

1 green bell pepper, diced

4 garlic cloves, minced

2 tablespoons tomato paste

$^1/_4$ cup white wine

1 quart chicken broth

1 cup tomato puree

1 ham hock

$^3/_4$ cup okra, trimmed, cut into $^1/_4$-inch slices

$^1/_2$ pound andouille sausage, sliced into $^1/_4$-inch pieces

2 duck breasts (preferably smoked), skinless

2 teaspoons salt, or to taste

1 teaspoon freshly ground black pepper, or to taste

$^1/_2$ pound shrimp, peeled and deveined

3 plum tomatoes, seeded, diced

$^1/_2$ teaspoon hot sauce

In a small saucepan, combine the butter and flour to form a roux, and cook over medium heat until dark brown, stirring frequently, about 8–10 minutes.

While the roux is cooking, sauté the onions, celery, and bell pepper in the vegetable oil over medium to medium-high heat until golden brown, about 12–15 minutes.

Add the garlic and cook for 2 more minutes, or until the aroma of the garlic is noticeable. Add the tomato paste and cook to a rich red-brown color, stirring constantly, about 3–4 minutes. Deglaze the pan with the white wine and allow the wine to reduce by half.

Bring the chicken broth to a simmer. Whisk the roux into the hot broth, making sure there are no lumps, then add the vegetable mixture. Add the tomato puree, ham hock, and the okra and simmer for 15–20 minutes.

While the gumbo is simmering, cook the andouille in a sauté pan over medium-high heat until browned and cooked through, about 4–5 minutes. Remove the andouille from the pan and reserve the fat. Season the duck breasts with ½ teaspoon salt and ¼ teaspoon pepper, and sauté in the andouille fat over medium-high heat until cooked thoroughly. Once cool enough to handle, cut into medium dice.

Season the shrimp with ½ teaspoon salt and ¼ teaspoon pepper. Dry sear the shrimp in a separate pan over high heat until cooked through, about 2–3 minutes. Add the shrimp, andouille, and duck to the gumbo along with the tomatoes. Continue to simmer until all the ingredients are heated through. Season with the remaining salt and pepper, and hot sauce, to taste.

Sautéed Duck Breast
with Pinot Noir Sauce

MAKES 6 SERVINGS | PREPARATION TIME: 45 MINUTES

Sautéed Duck Breast with Pinot Noir Sauce is shown here with Potato Puree (page 305)
and Broccoli Rabe with Toasted Pine Nuts (page 278).

*D*uck has a thick layer of fat under its skin that helps keep this aquatic bird warm. Most recipes for duck involve a step designed to render away much of this fat, leaving the skin deliciously crisp.

1 bottle Pinot Noir wine (750 ml)

6 cups chicken broth

2 tablespoons vegetable oil

1 onion, diced

4 celery stalks, diced

2 carrots, diced

3 tablespoons tomato paste

1 crushed garlic clove, 4 parsley stems, 6 black peppercorns, $1/4$ teaspoon dried thyme, 1 bay leaf, tied in a cheesecloth to make a pouch

$1/2$ teaspoon olive oil

$2^3/4$ teaspoons salt, or to taste

2 teaspoons freshly ground black pepper, or to taste

$2^1/4$ pounds duck breast, boneless, skin on, trimmed of excess fat

3 tablespoons butter

Preheat the oven to 400°F.

Bring the wine and the broth to a boil separately and reduce for 10 minutes.

While the liquids are reducing, heat the vegetable oil in a large sauté pan over medium-high heat. Add the onions and cook for 5 minutes, or until slightly translucent. Add the celery and the carrot and sauté until lightly caramelized, about 10 minutes.

Add the tomato paste to the caramelized vegetables and cook to a deep red-brown, stirring constantly, about 5 minutes.

Deglaze the pan with the reduced wine and simmer until reduced by half. Add the reduced broth and the cheesecloth

pouch and simmer until the sauce lightly coats the back of a spoon, about 15–20 minutes.

While the sauce is simmering, heat the olive oil over medium heat in a large sauté pan. Season the duck with half of the salt and pepper. Sauté the duck breasts, skin side down, until the fat has rendered and the skin is dark golden brown, about 8–10 minutes. Turn the duck breasts skin side up and roast in the oven until cooked through, about 5–6 minutes. Hold the duck in a warm place if the sauce is not ready.

Season the sauce with the remaining salt and pepper, and swirl in the butter just before serving.

Turkey Club Sandwich

MAKES 8 SERVINGS | PREPARATION TIME: 20 MINUTES

Turkey Club Sandwich is shown with Steak Fries (page 308).

Never forget a quick-but-classic favorite that is delicious by itself, or served with a cup of warm soup on a cool day.

24 slices sandwich bread

1 cup mayonnaise

16 leaves green leaf lettuce, washed, dried, and sized to bread

1 pound roast turkey breast, thinly sliced

1 pound smoked ham, thinly sliced

4 plum tomatoes, thinly sliced

16 strips bacon, cooked and drained, cut in half

For each sandwich, toast 3 pieces of bread. Using 2 tablespoons of mayonnaise per sandwich, spread the mayonnaise on the top of each slice. Top one piece of toast with a lettuce leaf and 2 ounces each of both turkey and ham. Cover with a second piece of toast.

Top with 1 lettuce leaf, 3 tomato slices, and 4 half strips of bacon. Top with the remaining piece of toast, mayonnaise side down. Cut each sandwich on the diagonal into 2 triangles and serve.

CHAPTER SEVEN

Seafood

*V*ERSATILE, FLAVORFUL, HEALTHY, AND FAST-COOKING, SEA-FOOD MAKES A PERFECT CENTERPIECE FOR QUICK MEALS. GREAT SEAFOOD DISHES HIGHLIGHT THE FISH'S ABSOLUTE FRESH-NESS AND NATURAL TENDERNESS. GENERALLY, FISH AND SHELLFISH don't require excess preparation or a long cooking time, making it easy to get a sea-food meal on the table in minutes.

Shopping for Seafood

To enjoy great fish consistently, you need a great fish market, whether it is a shop specializing in fish, or a section of a larger store. All great fish markets have certain characteristics. First off, a fish market should smell of the seashore, without any unpleasant or "fishy" odors. Also, when shopping for fish check to make sure that the fish looks fresh, with moist flesh and skin, that all the fish and shellfish are iced or cooled, and the entire display is clean and orderly. The staff should handle the fish safely by keeping all work surfaces and scales clean and sanitized.

Select from familiar varieties of fish, but don't be afraid to try new varieties with confidence. See the tables on the following pages for tips on cooking different types of fish. Don't be afraid to ask questions at the fish counter. If you're uncomfortable portioning fish yourself, ask the person behind the counter to do so for you.

Make your stop at the fish shop, counter, or freezer case the last one you make before heading home, to keep your purchase as cold as possible. Once home, keep fresh fish in the coldest part of your refrigerator and remember to put a plate or dish underneath any packages that might drip or leak.

Many fish are now frozen right on the fishing ships using blast freezers. The fish freezes very quickly without the large ice crystals that form when you try the same thing in your home freezer. When you examine the packaging, check that it is intact and that there aren't a lot of ice crystals in the package (that's a sign the fish may have thawed at some point during its trip from the ship to your store).

As long as the fish or seafood is properly thawed, there is relatively little difference between the flavor, moisture, and texture of a frozen fish and a fresh one. Keep frozen fish or seafood in the freezer until you are ready to thaw it. Most fish thaws evenly and safely overnight in the refrigerator.

Market Forms of Fish and Shellfish

Whole or pan-dressed fish are usually big enough for a single portion. They are typically gutted and scaled. The head, tail, and fins are sometimes removed.

Steaks are cut from large fish such as tuna, salmon, or halibut. They normally contain some of the backbone; the skin may be removed or not. Although scales are generally removed before the fish is cut into steaks, it's a good idea to check your steaks for any stray scales before cooking.

Fillets are boneless cuts. Salmon or halibut fillets are often cut into individual portions, but you may prefer to buy the intact fillet to cut yourself; since there aren't any bones, it is very simple if you have a good sharp knife. Fish with relatively tough skin such as catfish or perch are skinned before they are sold as fillets. For some fish, however, you might prefer to leave the skin on for a crisp, flavorful contrast to the flesh, especially if you are grilling or pan searing the fish.

AT A GLANCE | Best Quick Cooking Methods for Shellfish

ITEM	QUICK COOKING METHODS
Clams	Steaming, grilling, deep-frying
Oysters	Broiling, stewing, pan frying
Lobster	Boiling, steaming, roasting, broiling, grilling
Mussels	Steaming, roasting, stewing
Scallops	Sautéing, baking, roasting, broiling, grilling
Shrimp	Suitable for all techniques

| Best Quick Cooking Methods for Fish

ITEM	CHARACTERISTICS	QUICK COOKING METHODS
Bass	Moderately fatty, fairly firm, smooth	Excellent steamed or en papillote, also grilled, but suitable for all techniques
Bluefish	Oily, flaky, soft, strong taste	Roasting, broiling, grilling
Catfish	Moderately fatty, firm, sweet	Excellent pan-fried, but suitable for all techniques
Cod	Lean, firm, mild taste	Poaching, braising, stewing, steaming
Flounder	Lean, flaky, mild taste	Shallow-poaching, steaming, deep-frying
Grouper	Lean, firm, mild taste	Sautéing, pan frying, steaming, shallow-poaching
Halibut	Lean, fine texture, flaky, mild taste	Pan frying, braising,, poaching
Perch	Lean, delicate, sweet flavor	Steaming, poaching, deep-frying
Pompano	Moderately fatty, firm, full flavor	Broiling and en papillote
Salmon	Moderately fatty, firm, rich flavor	Excellent poached, baked, and grilled, but suitable for all techniques
Shad	Lean, flaky, sweet	Sautéing, pan frying
Snapper	Lean, firm	Excellent en papillote or baked, but suitable for all techniques
Sole	Lean, flaky, delicate flavor	Shallow poaching, pan frying, braising
Swordfish	Lean, very firm	Grilling, broiling, roasting
Trout	Moderately oily, flaky	Pan frying, roasting, poaching
Tuna	Moderately oily, firm	Roasting, broiling, grilling

Oysters, clams, and mussels are sold live by the dozen or by weight. Lobsters and crab are sold live by the pound, as well as frozen in the shell or as cooked meat, pasteurized and tinned or frozen. Shrimp is sold according to a system known as "count" that identifies the size by counting the number of shrimp in a pound; it is generally frozen before sale. Many larger markets also offer live lobster or crab which they will cook to order.

A form of steaming, cooking en papillote is suited to naturally tender foods like fish and shellfish or chicken. Parchment paper is the classic wrapper for a dish en papillote, but aluminum foil creates a similar effect.

➡ PREPARE THE INGREDIENTS

Trim or cut the food to the appropriate size or shape. Foods prepared en papillote are typically thin and portion-size. Vegetables and aromatics can be sliced very thin, cut into matchsticks, or minced so that they cook properly in the relatively short cooking time and develop a great flavor. Season the ingredients before putting them into the packet.

➡ PREPARE THE PARCHMENT PACKET

Cut the parchment or foil into a heart shape large enough to allow all the ingredients to fit without crowding on one of the halves. Be sure to leave at least 2 inches of margin all the way around the edge. Lightly oil or butter the paper on both sides to prevent it from burning.

➡ SEAL THE INGREDIENTS IN THE PACKET

Place the food on one half of the cut-out heart. Fold the other half over the food and align the edges. Fold and crimp the edges together securely to seal the packet and prevent steam from escaping. Make small, tight folds all along the edge of the paper and when you come to the bottom of the heart, give it a twist.

➡ COOK IN A MODERATE OVEN

Preheat a large baking sheet or ovenproof platter in the oven. Arrange the packets on the baking sheet and cook them at a moderate temperature (350–375°F). Recipes for seafood prepared en papillote rely upon properly cut and prepared ingredients so that they finish cooking at the same time that the parchment puffs up high and turns brown.

➡ OPEN THE PACKETS TABLESIDE

Serve them as soon as possible to be sure the packets are dramatically puffy when they come to the table. Cut the packages open with scissors or a sharp paring knife in front of everyone so they can enjoy the clouds of aromatic steam released from each packet.

See the step-by-step photographs accompanying the recipe for Bass and Scallops en Papillote (page 223).

Flounder Sauté
à la Meunière

MAKES 8 SERVINGS | PREPARATION TIME: 25 MINUTES

À *la meunière*—in the style of the miller's wife—means to dredge in flour, sauté in butter, and serve with brown butter sauce and parsley. Browning the butter gives it a rich, nutty flavor that pairs well with mild flounder. Serve with lightly garnished boiled potatoes and steamed vegetables.

3 pounds flounder fillet

2 tablespoons extra-virgin olive oil

7 tablespoons butter

1 teaspoon salt, or to taste

1/2 teaspoon freshly ground black pepper, or to taste

1/2 cup all-purpose flour

Juice of 1 lemon

1/4 cup parsley, chopped

Cut the flounder into eight 6-ounce portions.

Season the flour with salt and pepper.

Heat the oil and 3 tablespoons butter in a large sauté pan.

Season the fish with some of the salt and pepper, and dredge in the flour.

Sauté the fish for 1–2 minutes on each side, until lightly browned and crisp. Transfer the fish to a heated platter or plates and keep warm. Be very careful not to overcook fish.

Pour out any excess oil from pan, if necessary.

Add the remaining butter to the sauté pan and place over medium-high heat until the butter turns brown and has a nutty aroma, 2 minutes. Add the lemon juice and parsley and swirl the pan to blend the sauce. It should be almost foamy.

Spoon or pour the sauce over the flounder and serve at once.

FOCUS ON | ## Cutting Up a Whole Fillet into Individual Servings

Diagonal cuts of fish are a simple way to create elegant individual servings. Tranches are wide, angled slices cut from larger fillets of salmon, halibut, or tuna. Though this cut is normally associated with sautéed or pan-fried dishes, a tranche is also ideal for grilling or broiling. To prepare tranches, hold a very sharp knife at an angle while cutting, to expose more surface area and to give the fish a larger appearance. Cut across the fillet at approximately a 45-degree angle. The greater the angle of the knife, the more surface area will be exposed.

Sea Bass
with Gingered Broth

MAKES 8 SERVINGS | PREPARATION TIME: 30 MINUTES

*T*his lightly spicy broth is an innovative way to showcase delicate sea bass. Gently poaching the fish in this delicious broth results in an easy presentation, fully garnished and ready to serve after just a few minutes in the oven.

GINGERED BROTH

2 cups water

1 cup dry white wine

2 tablespoons cider vinegar

1 two-inch piece ginger, peeled, cut into matchsticks

2 teaspoons salt, or to taste

1/2 teaspoon freshly ground black pepper, or to taste

3 pounds sea bass fillet

1/2 head of bok choy

4 ounces shiitake or white mushrooms

1 red pepper

1 carrot

1 stalk celery

1 bunch scallions

Preheat the oven to 325°F.

Prepare the broth by combining the water, wine, vinegar, ginger, and some of the salt and pepper in a saucepan over medium heat. Simmer the mixture until it is flavorful, about 15 minutes. Remove the ginger.

Cut the fish into eight 6-ounce portions and season generously with salt and pepper. Keep cold until needed.

Thinly slice the bok choy, mushrooms, and red pepper. Slice the carrot, celery, and scallion very thin on the bias. Combine the vegetables in a large baking dish. Place the fish on top of the vegetables. Pour the broth over the fish and cover the baking dish with foil. Place the baking dish in the oven and bake until the fish is opaque and the vegetables are very hot, about 12 minutes.

Serve the fish on a bed of the vegetables in a heated pasta or soup bowl. Ladle the broth over the fish.

Spicy Asian Grilled Shrimp

MAKES 8 SERVINGS | PREPARATION TIME: 35 MINUTES

Spicy Asian Grilled Shrimp is shown here with Broccoli with Orange-Sesame Sauce (page 291) and Asian Rice Pilaf (page 318).

*T*he bold flavors that come together in this marinade take very little time to enhance the flavor of these grilled shrimp. This dish is best suited with a relatively plain rice dish that allows for the showcasing of the Asian flavor profile.

3 pounds shrimp, peeled, cleaned, and butterflied (21/25 count)

MARINADE

2 garlic cloves, minced

1$\frac{1}{2}$ tablespoons rice wine vinegar

$\frac{1}{2}$ teaspoon Chinese five spice powder

1 teaspoon ginger juice (grate the ginger and squeeze out the juice)

4 teaspoons Tabasco sauce

4 teaspoons oyster sauce

4 teaspoons sesame oil

Combine the shrimp with the marinade ingredients and refrigerate for 15 minutes.

While shrimp is marinating, preheat the grill on the highest setting.

Shake any excess marinade from the shrimp and place them onto metal skewers, or bamboo skewers that have been pre-soaked in cold water (to avoid burning.)

Grill for 1–2 minutes on each side until the shrimp are opaque and cooked through. Serve at once.

Seared Salmon
with a Moroccan Spice Crust

MAKES 8 SERVINGS | PREPARATION TIME: 25 MINUTES

*T*he impact of this bold spice mixture is a fantastic match for salmon which has its own rich flavor. Easy to prepare, the spices are pressed onto the salmon steaks as a coating before they are seared in a very hot pan. The salmon should be cooked through without overcooking so that the texture is still tender inside and the spicy exterior is browned from the searing.

3 pounds salmon steaks

1¹/₂ teaspoons curry powder

1¹/₂ teaspoons coriander seeds

1¹/₂ teaspoons cumin seeds

1¹/₂ teaspoons caraway seeds

1¹/₂ teaspoons anise seeds

1¹/₂ teaspoons black peppercorns

1 teaspoon salt, or to taste

¹/₂ teaspoon freshly ground black pepper, or to taste

4 tablespoons olive oil

Combine the curry powder, coriander, cumin, caraway, anise, and peppercorns in a small bowl. Coarsely grind the mixture in a spice grinder or mortar and pestle.

Season the steaks generously with salt and pepper.

Rub both sides of each salmon piece with a generous amount of the spice mixture.

Add about 2 tablespoons of olive oil to a preheated pan. The oil should get very hot and shimmer but not smoke.

Add half the salmon and cook, turning once, until the fish is browned on the outside and opaque in the center, about 4 minutes per side. Remove to a warm platter, and repeat with the remaining olive oil and salmon. Serve at once.

Scallop and Mushroom Gratin

MAKES 8 SERVINGS | PREPARATION TIME: 30 MINUTES

*T*his is a very useful cooking method that allows the scallops to be cooked at the last minute to preserve their delicate flavor and moisture. The top of the gratin crisps slightly to provide a contrast in texture to the sabayon underneath, much in the same way that the mushrooms contribute a different texture than the scallops.

2 tablespoons butter

12 ounces mushrooms, sliced

2 tomatoes, seeded and diced

3 pounds sea scallops

$^1/_2$ teaspoon salt, or to taste

$^1/_4$ teaspoon freshly ground black pepper, or to taste

2 egg yolks

1 tablespoon water

2 tablespoons dry white wine

1 tablespoon shallots, minced

$^3/_4$ cup sour cream

2 tablespoons Dijon mustard

Preheat the oven to 450°F.

Heat a sauté pan over medium-high heat. Add the butter. When it stops foaming, add the sliced mushrooms and sauté until they are tender and any juices they release have cooked away, about 5 minutes. Transfer to an ovenproof dish and spread in an even layer. Top with the diced tomatoes.

Pull the tabs from the sea scallops and arrange them on the mushroom mixture. Season with salt and pepper.

Bring a small amount of water (about ½ inch) to a simmer in a large saucepan. Mix together the egg yolks, water, wine, and shallots in a stainless steel mixing bowl. Set the bowl over the simmering water and whisk constantly until a thick foam forms, about 8 minutes. Remove the bowl from the heat, fold in the sour cream and mustard, and spoon over the scallops.

Place the scallops in the oven and bake until the scallops are nearly cooked through, about 6–8 minutes. If the top is not browned, turn on the broiler and broil the scallops just long enough to make the top golden brown, 1–2 minutes. Serve at once.

Sautéed Shrimp
with Penne Pasta and Puttanesca Sauce

*P*uttanesca is an Italian sauce that sometimes includes tomatoes, onions, capers, olives and anchovies and is generally served with pasta. This version adds delicious sautéed shrimp for a quick and easy, yet hearty, pasta dish.

2 tablespoons olive oil

4 garlic cloves, minced

28 ounces diced tomatoes, canned

3 tablespoons Niçoise olives, pitted, chopped

3 tablespoons capers, drained

½ cup parsley, chopped

2 teaspoons red pepper flakes

Salt, to taste

1 pound penne pasta

1 pound shrimp, peeled, deveined (31–40/count)

Parmesan cheese, grated, to taste (optional)

Bring a large pot of salted water to a boil for the pasta. Heat 1 tablespoon of the oil in a large sauté pan over low heat; add 2 teaspoons of garlic and cook, stirring, for 1 minute. Add the tomatoes, olives, capers, ¼ cup of parsley, and the red pepper flakes. Increase the heat to medium and bring the mixture to a simmer. Cook, uncovered, stirring occasionally until thickened, about 10 minutes. Set the sauce aside.

Meanwhile, cook the pasta in the boiling water until tender to the bite, approximately 10–12 minutes. Drain well. .

Heat the remaining oil in a large sauté pan over medium heat. Add the reserved garlic and cook for 1 minute. Add the shrimp and the remaining parsley, sauté for 1–2 minutes and add the tomato sauce. Cook the shrimp for an additional 3–5 minutes, or until opaque in the center.

Add the sauce and shrimp mixture to the drained pasta and top with grated cheese, if desired.

Peanut-Crusted Catfish
with Creole Rémoulade Sauce

MAKES 8 SERVINGS | PREPARATION TIME: 25 MINUTES

*F*arm-raised catfish has a delicate flavor and a moist, light texture. This preparation takes the delicious flavors of Creole cuisine from America's South and brings it together with a variety of fish whose popularity and availability has spread beyond that region. This dish is excellent as a dinner entrée or even a tasty lunch.

CREOLE RÉMOULADE SAUCE

1 1/2 cups mayonnaise

2 tablespoons dill pickle relish

1/2 teaspoon lemon juice

1/4 cup Creole mustard

Hot sauce, to taste

3 pounds catfish fillets (4 large fillets), cut into 8 pieces each

1 tablespoon salt, or to taste

1 teaspoon freshly ground black pepper, or to taste

1/2 teaspoon cayenne pepper, or to taste

1 tablespoon paprika

1 cup all-purpose flour

3 eggs, lightly whipped

1 cup roasted peanuts, finely chopped

2 tablespoons canola oil

2 lemons, cut into wedges

To make the rémoulade, mix the mayonnaise, dill relish, lemon juice, Creole mustard, and hot sauce until smooth. Refrigerate until needed.

Clean the catfish fillet of all bones and fat.

Combine the salt, pepper, thyme, cayenne, and paprika. Use the spice mixture to thoroughly season catfish fillets.

Season the flour and eggs with salt and pepper. Coat the fish in the flour, dip it in the egg mixture, and coat with the chopped peanuts.

Heat the oil in a large sauté pan over medium-high heat. Add the catfish to the pan and cook for 5–6 minutes per side, or until crispy and golden brown.

Place the catfish on a large platter, garnish with lemon wedges, and serve with the Creole rémoulade sauce.

Seared Tuna
with Salsa Verde

Seared Tuna with Salsa Verde is shown here with Black Bean Salad (page 282) and Cornbread (page 316).

MAKES 6 SERVINGS | PREPARATION TIME: 40 MINUTES

*I*n this simple dish, we prefer the fish rare; simply increase the cooking time if you like your fish more well-done. This dish makes an impressive entrée for guests, yet it's deceptively simple to prepare.

2¼ pounds yellowfin tuna fillet

Ground cumin, to taste

Salt, to taste

Freshly ground black pepper, to taste

3 tablespoons olive oil

SALSA VERDE

½ cup tomatillos, finely chopped

½ jalapeño, seeded, finely chopped

½ cup onions, finely chopped

1 garlic clove, finely chopped

½ tablespoon honey

Juice of ½ lime

½ bunch cilantro, rinsed, dried, finely chopped

2 teaspoons parsley, finely chopped

Clean the skin and bloodline from the tuna, if necessary. Slice the tuna into 6 even portions. Season the fish with cumin, salt, and pepper. Refrigerate until needed.

To make the salsa verde, heat 2 tablespoons of the oil in a large sauté pan over medium heat. Cook the tomatillos, jalapeño, and onion until very brown, about 8–10 minutes. Add the garlic and cook briefly.

Season to taste with honey, lime, salt, and pepper. Stir in the cilantro and parsley. Reserve until needed.

Heat the remaining oil in a large sauté pan over very high heat until the oil is almost smoking. Gently lay the tuna steaks in the pan and brown on each side for about 1 minute, for rare tuna. Place the tuna on warm plates and spoon about 1½ tablespoons of the salsa verde on top.

Seared Scallops
with Fiery Fruit Salsa

Seared Scallops with Fiery Fruit Salsa are shown here with Coconut Rice with Ginger (page 324).

MAKES 6 SERVINGS | PREPARATION TIME: 30 MINUTES

*S*earing scallops keeps them plump and tender on the inside, crisp and golden on the outside. When buying scallops, ask to smell them; scallops should have the pleasant briny scent of the ocean. Keep them refrigerated or on ice until cooking time.

TROPICAL FRUIT SALSA

$^2/_3$ cup mango, peeled, diced

$^1/_2$ cup papaya, peeled, diced

$^1/_4$ cup pineapple, canned or fresh, cored, peeled, diced

$^1/_4$ cup red bell pepper, diced

$^1/_3$ cup red onion, diced

1 tablespoon cilantro, chopped

$^1/_2$ tablespoon lime juice

$^1/_2$ tablespoon white wine vinegar

1 teaspoon jalapeño, seeded, minced

$^1/_2$ teaspoon extra-virgin olive oil

$^1/_8$ teaspoon salt, or to taste

Freshly ground black pepper, to taste

2 pounds sea scallops

2 tablespoons vegetable oil

Combine all the ingredients for the salsa in a bowl. Allow the salsa to sit for 15 minutes before serving.

Remove the muscle tabs from the scallops; blot the scallops dry. Heat a sauté pan on medium-high heat. Add the oil to coat bottom of pan. Place the scallops in the pan and sauté on the first side for about 2–3 minutes, or until golden brown. Turn the scallops once and sauté on the second side. Do not overcrowd the scallops in the pan. If necessary, cook the scallops in batches, holding those that are cooked in a warm oven. Serve the scallops with the tropical fruit salsa.

NOTE: The scallops will release from pan when properly browned. Do not try to pry the scallop from the pan as they will tear. The pan should not be too hot because the scallops will get scorched before they're cooked.

VARIATION: This salsa can be turned from savory to sweet by changing just a few ingredients. Serve the sweet style salsa as dessert, or serve it for brunch with muffins, pancakes, French toast, or as a filling for crêpes.

To make a sweet salsa: substitute mint for the cilantro, strawberries for the red pepper, honey for the olive oil, and leave out the vinegar, salt, and pepper.

Salmon en Papillote

MAKES 8 SERVINGS | PREPARATION TIME: 45 MINUTES

*T*his elegant presentation of salmon baked inside parchment unites the delicious combination of parsley, tarragon, white wine and delicate red bliss potatoes for an all-in-one presentation that is sure to impress your dining companions.

3 pounds salmon fillet	2 teaspoons salt, or to taste	4 teaspoons tarragon, chopped
Parchment paper	3 lemons, peeled, thinly sliced	2 pounds red bliss potatoes, thinly sliced
2 teaspoons olive oil	8 celery stalks, cut into thin 2-inch strips	$1/4$ cup dry white wine
1 teaspoon freshly ground black pepper, or to taste	4 shallots, thinly sliced	1 egg, beaten
	$1/4$ cup parsley, chopped	

Cut the salmon into eight 6-ounce portions. Refrigerate until needed.

Preheat the oven to 400°F.

See page 223–24 for the illustrated technique of preparing foods en papillote. Cut or tear eight 16-inch sheets of parchment paper. Fold the sheets in half. Starting at the folded edge, cut each paper into a half-heart shape.

Unfold the 8 paper hearts and brush them with olive oil. Place one portion of salmon on one half of each paper heart. Season the salmon with pepper and salt, top each portion with 3–4 slices of lemon, ¼ cup of celery, 1 tablespoon of shallots, and 1 tablespoon of the herbs. Place ¾ cup of sliced potatoes around the salmon and vegetables.

Sprinkle some white wine onto each piece of salmon and brush the outside edges of the parchment paper with the beaten egg. Fold the paper over the top of the salmon and crimp the paper to seal the edges.

Bake the salmon in a 400°F oven until the paper pouch puffs up and the outside becomes golden brown, approximately 15–20 minutes.

Serve the salmon in the paper and open at tableside, making a slit in the pouche with scissors or a paring knife.

Oyster Po' Boy
with Rémoulade

MAKES 8 SERVINGS | PREPARATION TIME: 45 MINUTES

*T*here are several explanations about its origin, but one popular theory reports that the po' boy sandwich—a true New Orleans specialty—was invented in 1920 by Benny and Clovis Martin at Martin Brother's Grocery, where it was offered to streetcar workers then on strike. In this version, oysters are rolled in fresh breadcrumbs, sautéed, and served in French rolls with a classic rémoulade sauce.

$^1/_2$ cup mayonnaise

2 scallions, minced

$^1/_4$ cup celery, minced

2 tablespoons parsley, minced

2 tablespoons dill pickle relish

2 tablespoons red wine vinegar

4 teaspoons Dijon mustard

4 teaspoons capers, drained, finely chopped

2 teaspoons Worcestershire sauce

4 dashes hot pepper sauce (optional)

$1^1/_2$ cup breadcrumbs

$^3/_4$ cup all-purpose flour

$1^1/_2$ teaspoon freshly ground black pepper, or to taste

$1^1/_2$ teaspoon cayenne pepper

$3^1/_2$ pounds oysters, shucked

4 eggs, beaten

$^1/_2$ cup vegetable oil

8 crusty French rolls, cut in half

$^1/_2$ pound tomatoes, thinly sliced

1 cup romaine, shredded

2 lemons, cut into wedges

To prepare the rémoulade, combine the mayonnaise, scallions, celery, parsley, relish, vinegar, mustard, capers, Worcestershire sauce, and pepper sauce, if using, in a non-reactive bowl.

Combine the breadcrumbs, flour, pepper, and cayenne, toss with your fingertips to combine. Drain the oysters of any liquid and dry thoroughly. Dip the oysters, one at a time, into the beaten egg, then roll each in the crumb mixture. Heat ¼ cup of the oil in a large, nonstick skillet, then add half of the oysters. Fry, turning once, until the oysters are browned and cooked through, about 4–5 minutes. Repeat with the remaining oil and oysters.

Toast the roll halves. Layer the oysters, tomato, and lettuce evenly on 8 halves and top with the remaining halves. Serve with the rémoulade and lemon wedges.

Mussels
in Saffron and White Wine Broth

MAKES 8 SERVINGS | PREPARATION TIME: 25 MINUTES

*T*his recipe is one of the simplest and most delectable recipes in the book. The flavor of the mussels pairs beautifully with the unique flavor that the saffron imparts to the broth. You will find yourself making this recipe again and again.

2 teaspoons butter

3 garlic cloves, chopped

1 cup dry white wine

2 tablespoons half and half

2 1/2 teaspoons saffron threads

1 cup clam juice

4 scallions, thinly sliced

3 tomatoes, seeded, and chopped

3 tablespoons lemon juice

8 pounds mussels, scrubbed and debearded

2 1/2 tablespoons chives, chopped

Melt the butter in a large pot, then add the garlic. Sauté until the garlic is fragrant, about 1 minute. Add the wine, half and half, and saffron; simmer for 5 minutes. Add the clam juice, scallions, tomato, and lemon juice; simmer for 5 minutes.

Add the mussels, cover, and steam until they open, about 5–7 minutes. Shake the pot, holding down the lid with a kitchen towel, to redistribute the mussels. Discard any mussels that do not open. Divide the mussels into eight bowls; distribute the broth equally among the bowls, and top each with fresh chives.

FOCUS ON | Cleaning Mussels

Hold the mussel under cold running water. Use a brush with stiff bristles to thoroughly scrub the mussel and remove grit, sand, and mud from the shell's exterior. Mussels—especially non-farmed ones—often have a dark, shaggy beard extend-ing from each shell. Remove them for a neater appearance in the finished dish. After scrubbing a mussel, pull the beard away from the shell until taut, and then pull the beard down sharply toward the dark hinge. It will snap away easily. Removing its beard will kill the mussel, so perform this step just before cooking.

Grilled Swordfish
with Lentil Ragout

MAKES 8 SERVINGS | PREPARATION TIME: 45 MINUTES

*T*his lentil ragout offers a unique accompaniment to meaty grilled swordfish steaks. Lentils cook quickly because of their small size. Make sure there is enough cooking liquid for the entire cooking time.

LENTIL RAGOUT

1 slice bacon, diced

1 cup onion, diced

1 carrot, diced

1 celery stalk, diced

1 garlic clove, minced

2 tablespoons tomato paste

2 cups chicken broth

1 cup water

$^{1}/_{2}$ cup lentils

$^{1}/_{2}$ teaspoon lemon zest

2 tablespoons white wine

1 tablespoon sherry vinegar

$^{3}/_{4}$ teaspoon salt, or to taste

$^{3}/_{4}$ teaspoon freshly ground black pepper, or to taste

3 pounds swordfish fillet

Render the bacon in a soup pot over low heat. Sweat the onions, carrot, and celery, until the onions are translucent, about 5 minutes. Add the garlic and cook for another minute.

Add the tomato paste and sauté, stirring frequently, until rust colored, 2–3 minutes.

Add the broth, water, lentils, and lemon zest. Simmer until the lentils are tender, about 30 minutes.

Add the wine, vinegar, and ½ teaspoon each salt and pepper.

Cut the swordfish into eight 6-ounce portions.

Preheat the grill to high heat.

Season the swordfish with salt and pepper. Grill the swordfish until thoroughly cooked, about 3–4 minutes on each side.

Serve the swordfish with the warmed lentil ragout.

NOTE: French lentils are the best variety to use in this recipe because they maintain their shape, preventing the sauce from becoming too thick. Other lentils may be used, however. Red lentils cook very rapidly and should be carefully watched to avoid overcooking.

Risotto
with Scallops and Asparagus
MAKES 8 SERVINGS | PREPARATION TIME: 45 MINUTES

Sautéed scallops are paired with a creamy Asiago cheese risotto in this elegant seafood entrée. You may substitute the more delicate bay scallops for sea scallops, if desired, being sure to shorten the cooking time slightly.

4 cups chicken broth

1/4 cup olive oil

1 cup onion, finely chopped

2 cups Arborio rice, uncooked

2 cups white wine

1/4 teaspoon freshly ground black pepper, or to taste

2 tablespoons butter

1/2 cup Asiago cheese, grated

24 asparagus spears, thin, cut diagonally into 1-inch pieces

2 1/2 pounds sea scallops, muscle tabs removed

Salt, to taste

Bring the broth to a boil in a medium saucepan. Reduce the heat and simmer.

Heat 2 tablespoons of the oil in a large saucepan. Add the onion, reduce the heat, and sauté for 1 minute. Add the rice and cook, stirring to coat, about 2 minutes.

Add half of the simmered chicken broth to the rice and cook, stirring constantly, until the rice absorbs all the broth, about 6–8 minutes. Add the remaining broth and simmer, stirring, until the broth is absorbed, 6–8 minutes more. Add the wine and simmer, stirring, until the risotto has a creamy consis-

tency and the rice is tender, about 6–8 minutes more. Stir in the pepper and add the butter and Asiago cheese in the final minutes of cooking.

Steam the asparagus until tender, about 4 minutes.

Meanwhile, pat the scallops dry with paper toweling and season them with salt and pepper. Sauté the scallops in the remaining olive oil over very high heat until they are golden brown, about 2 minutes per side. When the scallops are done, serve them at once on a bed of the risotto with the asparagus.

Grilled Herbed Salmon
with Southwest White Bean Stew

MAKES 8 SERVINGS | PREPARATION TIME: 45 MINUTES

*T*he bold flavor of grilled salmon is complemented by the spicy yet aromatic flavor profile of southwest cuisine. A unique accompaniment for salmon steaks, this white bean stew offers an excellent alternative to the usual side dishes.

3 pounds salmon fillets or steaks

MARINADE

3 tablespoons lime juice

2 tablespoons olive oil

2 tablespoons parsley, chopped

2 tablespoons chives, chopped

1 teaspoon thyme, chopped

1 teaspoon black peppercorns, crushed

SOUTHWEST WHITE BEAN STEW

1 tablespoon corn oil

$^1/_2$ onion, diced

$^1/_4$ cup celery, diced

$^1/_2$ green pepper, diced

1 tablespoon jalapeño, seeded and minced

2 garlic cloves, minced

1 teaspoon ground cumin

1 14-ounce can cannellini beans, rinsed and drained

1 plum tomato, cored and diced

1$^1/_4$ cup chicken broth or water

1 tablespoon red wine vinegar

2 tablespoons cilantro, chopped

$^1/_2$ teaspoon salt, or to taste

$^1/_4$ teaspoon freshly ground black pepper, or to taste

Combine the marinade ingredients in a zipper-lock bag. Add the salmon and seal the bag, turning to coat the salmon evenly with the marinade. Refrigerate for 15 minutes.

Preheat the grill.

Prepare the white bean stew. Heat the oil in a saucepan or skillet with deep sides. Add the onions, celery, pepper, jalapeños, and minced garlic. Sauté over medium-high heat until limp and translucent, about 3 minutes, stirring frequently. Add the cumin and sauté until fragrant, about 30 seconds.

Add the beans, tomato, and enough water or broth to just cover the beans. Stew, stirring frequently, over medium heat, until flavorful, about 20 minutes. Use the back of a wooden spoon to mash some of the beans in order to thicken the stew as it cooks.

Add the vinegar and simmer until the vinegar's raw taste dissipates, about 2 minutes.

Stir in the cilantro just before serving. Season with salt and pepper.

Remove the salmon from the marinade and scrape off any excess. Grill each portion of salmon to the desired doneness, about 2–3 minutes per side.

Serve with the warm bean stew.

Bass and Scallops
en Papillote

MAKES 8 SERVINGS | PREPARATION TIME: 41 MINUTES

The French term *en papillote* refers to baking the ingredients inside of a parchment paper parcel shaped like a half-heart. As the food heats and creates steam, the papillote puffs up. In this recipe the *papillote* is filled with bass and scallops, along with a julienne of vegetables. Cut the parcels open at the table to release the savory aroma from the *papillote* and lend a unique presentation.

1½ pounds sea bass fillet

3 cups vegetable broth

1 cup dry vermouth

2 quarts celeriac, cut into thin strips

3 cups baby red potatoes, thinly sliced

1½ cups carrots, cut into thin strips

2 cups seedless cucumber, peeled, cut into thin strips

GREMOLATA

2 tablespoons garlic, finely minced

2 tablespoons lemon zest, grated

¾ cup parsley, chopped

Parchment paper

¼ cup butter

1½ pounds sea scallops, muscle tabs removed

1 teaspoon black peppercorns, crushed

Salt, to taste

Cut the bass into eight portions. Refrigerate until needed.

Combine the broth and vermouth in a large saucepan and bring it to a simmer. Individually cook the celeriac, potatoes, and carrots in the stock mixture until tender. Drain the vegetables and toss them together with the cucumber.

Combine the gremolata ingredients and reserve until needed.

Cut or tear eight 16-inch sheets of parchment paper. Fold the sheets in half. Starting at the folded edge, cut each paper into a half-heart shape. Unfold the 8 paper hearts and lightly grease both sides of the paper with butter. *(continues next page)*

ABOVE, LEFT TO RIGHT: Season the item to be cooked and prepare the vegetables; cut the parchment paper hearts. Butter the parchment paper hearts and place the food to be cooked in the center of one side of the heart. Fold the parchment paper over the fish.

Place about 1 cup of the vegetables on half of each paper heart. Top the bed of vegetables with one portion of bass, and 3 ounces of the scallops. Top the scallops with 2 teaspoons of the gremolata and sprinkle with the peppercorns and salt.

Fold the top of each heart over the fish and the vegetables. Crimp the edges of the paper to seal tightly. Refrigerate until needed.

For each serving place 1 parchment package on a baking sheet and bake in a 425°F oven for 12–15 minutes. The package should be puffy and the paper brown. For a dramatic presentation, cut the packages open at the table.

ABOVE, LEFT TO RIGHT: Crimp the edges of the parchment paper heart with the food inside. Break open the parchment paper package to reveal the cooked food inside. Opposite, presentation of the completed Bass and Scallops en Papillote.

Grilled Halibut
with Roasted Red and Yellow Pepper Salad

MAKES 8 SERVINGS | PREPARATION TIME: 45 MINUTES

*H*alibut steaks can be purchased in most seafood departments. The lean white flesh is mild in flavor and has an excellent texture for grilling, holding together nicely and ensuring ease in flipping the pieces without breaking them.

2 red bell peppers, or 1 cup of prepared roasted peppers

2 yellow bell peppers, or 1 cup of prepared roasted peppers

¼ cup olive oil

½ onion, thinly sliced

3 tablespoons garlic, thinly sliced

2 tablespoons capers, chopped

1 tablespoon sherry vinegar

½ teaspoon ground cumin

¼ teaspoon red pepper flakes

⅛ teaspoon ground coriander

1 teaspoon salt, or to taste

½ teaspoon freshly ground black pepper, or to taste

3 pounds halibut fillet

Rub the peppers with 2 tablespoons of the olive oil and roast them in a 350°F oven for 25–30 minutes, or until the skins start to fall off. Place the peppers in a bowl and place a piece of plastic wrap over them. Allow them to steam for 5 minutes.

Peel the skin off of the peppers and remove the stems and seeds. Slice the peppers into thin strips. (Alternately, 2 cups of prepared roasted peppers may be substituted.)

Heat the remaining olive oil in a large sauté pan over medium-high heat. Add the onion and cook until lightly caramelized, about 8–10 minutes. Add the garlic and cook until aromatic.

Add the capers, vinegar, cumin, red pepper flakes, and coriander. Season with about ¼ teaspoon salt and a pinch of black pepper. Add the onions to the peppers and keep warm.

Cut the halibut into eight 6-ounce portions. Season the halibut with salt and pepper. Grill the halibut until just cooked through, about 2–3 minutes per side. Serve each portion with ¼ cup of the roasted pepper salad.

Crabmeat and Shrimp Sandwich

Nowadays it's easy to find shrimp and crabmeat of excellent quality that is already cooked and prepared for delicious sandwiches. Check with your local fish market or favorite supermarket for the days these prepared items are freshest.

$1/2$ pound crabmeat, cooked, picked over for shells

$1/2$ pound shrimp, cooked, peeled, diced

$1/2$ cup mayonnaise

$1/4$ cup sour cream

1 tablespoon white wine vinegar

1 garlic clove, minced

2 teaspoons Dijon mustard

2 teaspoons curry powder

$1/4$ teaspoon salt, or to taste

$1/4$ teaspoon freshly ground black pepper, or to taste

8 pitas

1 tomato, thinly sliced

1 red onion, thinly sliced

1 avocado, thinly sliced (optional)

1 container alfalfa sprouts

Place the picked crabmeat and diced shrimp in a mixing bowl.

In a small bowl, stir together the mayonnaise, sour cream, vinegar, garlic, mustard, curry powder, salt, and pepper. Stir the mayonnaise mixture in to the crabmeat and shrimp until combined. Split open the pitas and line each with the tomato, onion, and avocado (if using). Divide the crabmeat mixture evenly between the pitas and tuck some of the alfalfa sprouts into each.

Seared Cod
in a Rich Broth with Fall Vegetables

MAKES 6 SERVINGS | PREPARATION TIME: 45 MINUTES

One of the more common varieties of fish, here cod is seared after being coated with a fine powder of ground, dried shiitake mushrooms. Autumn vegetables and pasta garnish this rich broth for an uncommon twist to a common fish.

1¼ pounds fettuccine pasta

2¼ pounds cod fillet

4 ounces dried shiitake mushrooms

½ teaspoon salt, or to taste

½ teaspoon ground white pepper

2 tablespoons olive oil

5 cups vegetable broth

1 pound haricots verts, cut into 1-inch lengths, blanched

5 ounces carrot, cut into thin strips, blanched

5 ounces yellow turnip, cut into thin strips, blanched

5 ounces white turnip, cut into thin strips, blanched

1 tablespoon ginger, minced

3 ounces enoki mushrooms, cut into 1½-inch lengths

3 tablespoons chives, cut into ½-inch lengths

3 tablespoons scallions, thinly sliced

Preheat the oven to 450°F.

Bring a large pot of salted water to a boil. Cook the pasta for 8–10 minutes, or until tender to the bite. Reserve.

Cut the cod into six portions. Refrigerate until needed.

Grind the dried shiitake mushrooms to a powder in a spice grinder. Blot the cod pieces with paper toweling to remove excess moisture, and season with a small amount of salt and pepper. Dredge each piece in the ground mushrooms. Add the oil to a preheated sauté pan over medium-high heat, and sauté the cod until browned, about 2 minutes per side.

Transfer the cod to a baking dish and bake in the 450°F oven until thoroughly cooked, about 6–7 minutes.

While the cod is baking, bring the broth to a simmer in a saucepan. Add the pasta, haricots verts, carrots, turnips, and ginger. Simmer until heated through, 3–4 minutes.

Transfer the broth, pasta, and vegetables to large soup plates. Arrange the pasta to make a bed for the cod in the center of the plate. Place the cod on the pasta and garnish with the enoki mushrooms and ¾ teaspoon of both chives and scallions.

Classic Boiled Lobster

MAKES 8 SERVINGS | PREPARATION TIME: 40 MINUTES

*A*vailable throughout the year, fresh lobsters should be purchased live and stored for only a few hours prior to cooking. It is imperative that lobster be cooked live or killed just prior to cooking. Here a fragrant lemon-herb dipping sauce complements the creamy white meat of the lobster.

1 cup butter

2 tablespoons lemon juice

4 teaspoons parsley, minced

4 teaspoons tarragon, minced

4 teaspoons watercress, minced

1/2 teaspoon salt, or to taste

1/4 teaspoon freshly ground black pepper, or to taste

8 lobsters, 1 1/2 pounds each

4 lemons, cut into wedges

Melt the butter in a skillet; add the lemon juice, parsley, tarragon, watercress, salt, and pepper. Transfer the dipping sauce to a bowl.

Fill an 8-quart stock pot two-thirds full of salted water and bring to a rolling boil. Add the lobsters, cooking in batches if necessary, and boil until they are bright red, 10–11 minutes. Replenish the salted water as necessary and be sure to bring the water to a boil in between every batch.

Use tongs to place the lobsters on a platter. Serve with the lemon-herb dipping sauce and lemon wedges.

TIPS FOR FABRICATION:

If fabricating the lobsters, wait for the first batch of lobsters to cool until they can be handled. The second batch of lobsters can be cooked while the first is cooling.

Separate the lobster in between the tail and the torso area. Make sure to do this over the sink or a bowl as there is quite a bit of liquid that will release from the lobster.

Separate the claws from the torso, as well as the knuckles from the claws.

Using kitchen shears, cut each edge of the underside of the tail shell and remove. The tail can be served in the shell or can now be removed in one piece.

Cut one side of the claw shell away using kitchen shears. The claw meat can be removed in one piece or served in the shell.

If desired, crack the shells of the knuckles with the heel of a chef's knife or lobster (or nut) cracker and remove the meat.

Broiled Swordfish
with Tomatoes, Anchovies, and Garlic

MAKES 8 SERVINGS | PREPARATION TIME: 30 MINUTES

Swordfish, which is found in the waters off both the Atlantic and Pacific coasts, is wonderful grilled or broiled. The Provençal flavors in this quick recipe make a delightful contrast to the mild flavor and meaty texture of the fish.

3 pounds swordfish fillet

1 tablespoon shallots, chopped

$1\frac{1}{2}$ teaspoons garlic, minced

$\frac{1}{2}$ cup dry white wine

$3\frac{1}{3}$ cups plum tomatoes, seeded, diced

6 anchovies, minced

1 tablespoon olive oil

Salt, to taste

Freshly ground black pepper, to taste

$1\frac{1}{4}$ tablespoon basil, chiffonade

Cut the swordfish into eight portions. Refrigerate until needed.

Sweat the shallots and garlic in the wine until the shallots are translucent, about 2–3 minutes. Remove the pan from the heat and stir in the tomatoes and anchovies. Set the mixture aside.

Brush each portion of swordfish with ¼ teaspoon of the oil. Season the portions with salt and pepper. Place the fish on a rack in a broiling pan, about 2 inches from the heat source.

Broil the fish until golden brown on the edges and slightly firm with a moist surface. Turn the fish after 3–5 minutes and broil the other side until the fish is cooked through, another 3–5 minutes.

While the swordfish is broiling, heat the tomato mixture in a small sauce pan. Remove the mixture from the heat and stir in the basil.

Serve the swordfish with the tomato mixture.

Grilled Swordfish
with Peppered Pasta

MAKES 8 SERVINGS | PREPARATION TIME: 45 MINUTES

*E*ach element of this dish is quick and easy to prepare. Swordfish takes little more than 10 minutes on the grill, and cappellini is one of the fastest cooking pastas because it is delicate and thin. The entire ensemble is terrific for an everyday meal or for preparing during grilling season.

3 pounds swordfish fillet

3 tablespoons olive oil

4 garlic cloves, minced

6 tablespoons shallots, minced

3 tablespoons parsley, minced

3 tablespoons chives, minced

3 tablespoons thyme leaves

1¹/₂ pounds tomatoes, coarsely chopped

¹/₂ cup kalamata olives, pitted, halved

5 ounces balsamic vinegar

1 tablespoon salt, or to taste

1¹/₂ teaspoons freshly ground black pepper, or to taste

2 teaspoons basil, chiffonade

1 pound capellini pasta

Cut the swordfish into eight 6-ounce portions. Refrigerate until needed.

Bring a large pot of salted water to a boil.

Preheat the grill to high heat.

Heat 1½ tablespoons of olive oil in a small sauté pan over medium heat. Sweat half of the garlic and shallots in the oil just until translucent, about 3–4 minutes. Remove from the heat and add the parsley, chives, and thyme.

Heat the remaining oil in a large sauté pan. Add the other half of the garlic and shallots and sweat until translucent. Add the tomatoes and olives. Sauté until heated, about 6–8

minutes. Add the vinegar, about 1 teaspoon salt, ½ teaspoon pepper, and the basil. Toss to fully incorporate. Keep warm.

Cook the pasta in the boiling water until just tender.

Toss the capellini with the tomato mixture and keep warm.

Season the swordfish with the remaining salt and pepper. Grill the swordfish until thoroughly cooked, about 4–5 minutes on each side.

Serve the swordfish on a bed of 1 cup of the cooked pasta mixture, with 1 tablespoon of the herb mixture spooned over the fillet.

CHAPTER EIGHT
Vegetarian

Growing interest in ethnic cuisines based on foods derived from plants, moral issues surrounding animal consumption, and the perception that a vegetarian-based diet is healthier than a diet which includes meat products, have led to the wide acceptance of vegetarian cuisine. Gone are the days of the stereotypical brown rice and tofu vegetarian plate. Plant-based dishes showing the same level of care and attention given to all other menu options are now appearing everywhere. The recipes included in this chapter are not only inventive and delicious, they are also quick and easy to prepare.

Vegetable-based menu items require more than simply replacing the meat in a traditional dish or offering a sampler composed of all the side dishes from the meat-based entrées. When designing vegetable-based dishes, the concept of incorporating a variety of foods becomes crucial for both sound nutrition and aesthetic appeal. Integration is an important concept in preparing plant foods. Main ingredients should be chosen for the color, texture, and flavor elements they bring to a dish, and garnishes should be used to unify the main ingredients.

If the decision is made to classify a dish as vegetarian, then care should be taken to be sure that it truly qualifies as such. While there are numerous kinds of vegetarians, the three types that you need be most concerned with are vegans, lacto-vegetarians, and lacto-ovo-vegetarians. Of all the vegetarians, vegans adhere to the

strictest diet. They do not eat any foods of animal origin, preferring instead to base their diets exclusively on vegetables, fruits, grains, nuts, and legumes. Lacto-vegetarians consume the same foods as vegans, plus dairy products. Lacto-ovo-vegetarians eat plant foods, dairy foods, and eggs.

When classifying a dish as vegetarian, be on the lookout for ingredients of hidden animal origin in a preparation that might otherwise seem to be vegetarian. An obvious example of this is a vegetable soup that might call for chicken broth. More difficult to identify, though, are the ingredients that people often overlook as being animal products. For example, anything with honey in it is off-limits for true vegans. Other ingredients to be aware of include pasta made with eggs, and Worcestershire sauce, which contains anchovies.

Before any food is identified as vegetarian, all of the ingredients used in the preparation should be vigilantly reviewed for these hidden animal sources. One of the biggest challenges in creating this type of cuisine is in compensating for the loss of the savory flavors of meats, poultry, and fish. Care should be taken to avoid the overuse of high-fat dairy products in these instances. Certain plant foods that are also high in fat, like nuts and tofu, should be used only in moderation. Instead, spices and ingredients with complex flavors, such as dried chiles, mushrooms, and roasted garlic or peppers, can be used. In order to make the dish satisfying, complex carbohydrates should make up the bulk of the calories.

Ethnic cuisines that have traditionally relied on plant-based foods are excellent sources for creative inspiration; for examples, look at the Thai-influenced Tofu with Red Curry Paste (page 240) or the Mexican-style Vegetable Fajitas (page 245). In addition to the classical vegetable dishes that these cuisines offer, their characteristic spice and flavor principles can be adapted for use in original creations. You can also look to existing recipes that can be modified to provide additional choices, for instance, a dish could be offered with or without chicken, or tofu could be substituted.

FOCUS ON | Tips for Making Vegetarian Meals in Minutes

Purchase canned beans for your dishes, as they do not require soaking or cooking before being used in a recipe. Be sure to rinse and drain them—they are often laden with salt.

Choose quick-cooking grains and legumes, such as bulgar and lentils.

Cut vegetables in small pieces in order to reduce overall cooking time.

Keep flavorful condiments and spreads on hand. See the recipes for Hummus (page 21) and Guacamole (page 18) for inspiration.

| Stir-Frying

Stir-frying is a method of quickly cooking food which has been cut up into small pieces—the smaller pieces enable the food to cook much faster—in a large pan over very high heat, while constantly stirring the food around the pan.

➡ PREPARE ALL THE INGREDIENTS

A successful stir-fry depends upon a complete preparation. Every ingredient needs to be ready to go into the wok or skillet. You should have it close to the stovetop, ready to add at the right point. Cut vegetables into thin slices or fine shreds so that they will cook through fully. Usually, stir-fries include vegetables cooked until very hot and tender, but still crisp. Stir-fries lend themselves well to improvising, so you can add more vegetables or substitute one for another. Arrange your ingredients so it is easy to add them in the correct order: longest cooking to shortest.

➡ HEAT THE WOK AND THE OIL BEFORE YOU ADD THE AROMATIC INGREDIENTS

One of the biggest challenges when you stir-fry at home is to get the pan very hot and keep it hot throughout cooking. Preheat the pan over high heat for a few minutes before you add the oil, then add the oil to the hot pan in a swirl around the edge so that it coats the sides and runs down into the bottom of the wok. The first ingredients to add to the wok are the aromatic base: onions, shallots, garlic, or ginger, for instance. These ingredients will infuse the oil with flavor so that they are carried throughout the entire dish.

➡ ADD THE INGREDIENTS TO THE WOK IN SEQUENCE AND KEEP IN MOTION AS THEY COOK

To keep the wok as hot as possible, add ingredients a handful or two at a time. Use wide spoons or wok tools to keep the ingredients moving. As each ingredient is stirred into the wok and gets hot, push it up on the sides so the bottom can get very hot again before you add the next ingredient. Once all the ingredients are added, continue to stir and toss the ingredients until fully cooked.

➡ ADD THE FINAL SEASONINGS, FLAVORINGS, AND GARNISHES

In addition to the aromatic base you added to the wok at the start of the stir-fry, be sure to include seasonings. Salt and pepper are certainly important, but you will also want to add other pungent, flavorful ingredients, like soy or tamari sauce, or herbs such as chives or cilantro. Stir these final additions into the dish just enough to blend them evenly. Serve stir fried dishes very hot, straight from the wok.

See the step-by-step photographs accompanying the recipe for Stir-Fried Garden Vegetables with Marinated Tofu (page 248).

Vegetable Stew

MAKES 8 SERVINGS | PREPARATION TIME: 45 MINUTES

Vegetable Stew is shown here with Herbed Israeli Couscous (page 328).

$\mathcal{P}$acked with colorful vegetables, this hearty and warming stew is full of slightly sweet and spicy flavors. Serve the stew over a bed of couscous or rice.

1 tablespoon olive oil	1/2 cup fava beans, shelled	1/3 cup currants
2 leeks, cleaned, sliced	3 cups vegetable broth	3 tablespoons tomato puree, canned
2 tablespoons garlic, minced	2 cups zucchini, diced	2 teaspoons lemon juice
1 teaspoon red curry paste	2 1/2 cups eggplant, peeled, diced	1 1/2 teaspoons lemon zest, grated
1/2 pound butternut squash, peeled, diced	1 1/2 cups carrots, diced	1/4 teaspoon salt, or to taste
1 pound chickpeas, rinsed, drained	3/4 cup celery, diced	Freshly ground black pepper, to taste

Heat the oil in a large pot. Add the leeks and garlic and sauté until translucent, 3–5 minutes. Add the curry paste and sauté until fragrant.

Stir in the squash, chickpeas, and fava beans. Add enough broth to cover the vegetables and simmer for 10 minutes. Add the remaining broth, the zucchini, eggplant, carrots, celery, currants, and tomato puree. Simmer until the vegetables are tender, about 20 minutes.

Add the lemon juice and zest and season with salt and pepper. Serve the stew over rice or couscous.

Tofu
with Red Curry Paste, Peas, Scallions, and Cilantro

MAKES 8 SERVINGS | PREPARATION TIME: 45 MINUTES

Here tofu is complemented by the bold and exciting flavors of Thai cuisine. Curry pastes come in a broad variety of flavor intensities from mildly spicy to very hot. Prepared Thai red curry paste can be found in jars in the Asian foods section of many supermarkets or in specialty food shops and Asian markets.

2 cups brown rice

Grapeseed oil, as needed

1 package tofu, drained, cut into 1-inch cubes (14 ounces)

2 tablespoons lime juice

1 cup onion, diced

2 tablespoons garlic, minced

1 cup coconut milk

2 ounces red curry paste

1 tablespoon ground turmeric

Salt, to taste

Freshly ground black pepper, to taste

1$\frac{1}{2}$ cups peas, blanched

1 cup grape tomatoes, cut in half

$\frac{1}{3}$ bunch cilantro, chopped

$\frac{1}{2}$ bunch scallions, minced

1 cup pea shoots

18 oz brown rice, cooked

$\frac{1}{4}$ cup black sesame seeds

Bring 3½ cups of water and the rice to a boil and cover the pot tightly, turn the heat to low and cook for approximately 25 minutes, or until the rice is tender.

Heat a small amount of the oil in a medium nonstick sauté pan. Add the tofu and cook until the moisture is evaporated and the tofu is a light golden brown. Remove the tofu from the pan and sprinkle with the lime juice.

Heat more oil in the pan, add the onions and cook until translucent, about 5 minutes. Add the garlic and cook for an additional 2 minutes.

Add the coconut milk, curry paste, and turmeric. Season with salt and pepper. Reduce the heat and simmer until the sauce has slightly thickened, 10–12 minutes.

Add the peas, tomatoes, and tofu to the mixture and simmer just to combine. Adjust seasoning if necessary. Toss the mixture with the cilantro and scallions.

Serve the tofu mixture with the rice and 2 tablespoons of the peas shoots. Sprinkle the black sesame seeds on top of rice to garnish.

Goat Cheese and Red Onion Quesadilla

MAKES 8 SERVINGS | PREPARATION TIME: 40 MINUTES

*T*he combination of creamy goat cheese paired with Jack cheese, sour cream and tangy Tomatillo Salsa, make this a delicious snack or accompaniment for a light salad or cup of soup.

2 red onions, thinly sliced

5 tablespoons olive oil

1 teaspoon salt, or to taste

Freshly ground black pepper, to taste

1¹/₂ cups Jack cheese, grated

16 flour tortillas, 6-inch

¹/₂ cup goat cheese

1 cup cilantro leaves

¹/₂ cup sour cream

1 recipe Tomatillo Salsa (page 16)

Sauté the onion in 1 tablespoon of the olive oil until soft and translucent, about 7 minutes. Season with salt and pepper.

For each quesadilla, sprinkle 3 tablespoons of the Jack cheese on a flour tortilla. Crumble 1 tablespoon of the goat cheese over the Jack cheese. Spoon 2 tablespoons of the sautéed onions on top and lay 7 sprigs of cilantro over the onion. Cover with a second flour tortilla and press down.

Heat 1 tablespoon of the olive oil in a sauté pan over medium heat. Cook each quesadilla for approximately 2 minutes on each side, or until lightly browned and all the cheese is melted. Add more oil as needed to cook all 8 quesadillas.

Top each quesadilla with 1 tablespoon of sour cream and 3 tablespoons of the salsa. Serve immediately.

Vegetarian Refried Bean Quesadilla

MAKES 8 SERVINGS | PREPARATION TIME: 40 MINUTES

*T*he baby spinach provides an interesting element that adds both flavor and beauty to this quesadilla. You can substitute arugula for the spinach to add a spicy, nutty flavor to the quesadilla.

1¹/₂ cups Vegetarian Refried Beans (page 285)

16 flour tortillas, 6-inch

2 cups baby spinach

2 cups extra sharp cheddar cheese, grated

¹/₄ cup olive oil

¹/₂ cup sour cream

1 recipe Tomatillo Salsa (page 16)

For each quesadilla, spread 3 tablespoons of the refried beans on a flour tortilla. Lay 12 baby spinach leaves on the tortilla to cover the beans. Evenly sprinkle ¼ cup of the cheese over the spinach. Cover with a second flour tortilla and press down.

Heat 1 tablespoon of the olive oil in a sauté pan over medium heat. Cook each quesadilla for approximately 2 minutes on each side, or until lightly browned and all the cheese is melted. Add more oil as needed to cook all 8 quesadillas.

Top each quesadilla with 1 tablespoon of sour cream and 3 tablespoons of the salsa. Serve immediately.

Vegetable Fajitas

*C*utting this colorful mixture of vegetables into thin strips is the key to the quick cooking time and makes the vegetables an easy snack or light meal. Canned pinto beans, rinsed and drained, take the lengthy preparation element out of preparing the dried variety.

3 tablespoons olive oil

1¹/₂ cup red onion, cut into thin strips

1 tablespoon garlic, minced

1 pound red pepper, cut into
   thin strips

1 pound green pepper, cut into thin strips

1 pound yellow pepper, cut into thin strips

1 pound napa cabbage, chiffonade

15 ounces pinto beans, canned, rinsed,
   drained

3 tablespoons red chili sauce

16 flour tortillas, 12-inch diameter

2²/₃ cups grated cheddar cheese

1 tablespoon cilantro, chopped

Heat 2 tablespoons of the oil in a large sauté pan. Add the onions and garlic. Sweat until the onions are translucent, about 5–7 minutes.

Add the peppers and sauté for 5 minutes or just until they begin to soften. Add the cabbage and cook for another 5 minutes or until tender.

Stir in the beans and chili sauce. Heat just until warmed.

Cover the tortillas with a damp towel and warm in a 250°F oven before serving.

To assemble, wrap approximately ½ cup of the hot vegetable mixture with a few tablespoons of the grated cheese in a warmed tortilla. The traditional manner of serving fajitas is to bring the tortillas, filling, and garnishes to the table, to be assembled by each individual.

Vegetable Burgers

MAKES 8 SERVINGS | PREPARATION TIME: 45 MINUTES

Vegetable Burgers are shown here with Warm Potato Salad (page 306).

*V*eggie burgers have come a long way in recent years. Now readily available in most frozen food sections, this recipe will help you make your own, right at home. They freeze well, just like the commercial brands, so why not invest a bit of time for a healthy, homemade alternative to the usual variety?

4 carrots, peeled, grated

2 celery stalks, grated

1 onion, grated

1/4 cup red bell pepper, minced

3/4 cup mushrooms, minced

8 scallions, minced

2 eggs, lightly beaten

1/2 cup pecans, chopped

1 tablespoon fresh thyme, chopped

2 garlic cloves, minced

1 teaspoon salt, or to taste

1/2 teaspoon hot pepper sauce

2 teaspoons sesame oil

1/2 teaspoon ground pepper

3 cups matzo meal

2 tablespoons olive oil

Preheat the oven to 475 ° F.

Combine the carrots, celery, onion, bell pepper, mushrooms, scallions, eggs, pecans, thyme, garlic, salt, pepper sauce, sesame oil, and pepper in a large bowl and stir to thoroughly combine the mixture. Add 1 cup of the matzo meal, or more as needed, to make a firm, but still moist mixture. Form into 8 burgers. Dredge each burger in the remaining 2 cups of matzo meal.

Oil a baking sheet with the olive oil. Place the burgers on the sheet and bake, turning once, until browned and crisp at the edges, about 12 minutes.

Stir-Fried Garden Vegetables with Marinated Tofu

MAKES 6 SERVINGS | PREPARATION TIME: 35 MINUTES

Stir-Fried Garden Vegetables with Marinated Tofu is shown here with Asian Rice Pilaf (page 318).

Tofu is an excellent source of protein and a good medium to showcase brightly colored, well-seasoned garden vegetables. Because of the variety of textures available from silky to extra firm, tofu is now a delicious alternative for even die-hard meat lovers.

MARINATED TOFU

1¼ pounds tofu, firm, drained, cut into
    1-inch cubes

⅓ cup soy sauce

4 teaspoons ginger, peeled, minced

4 teaspoons garlic, minced

3 tablespoons all-purpose flour

1½ tablespoons peanut oil

STIR-FRIED VEGETABLES

1½ bunches scallions, thinly sliced

4 teaspoons ginger, peeled, minced

3 tablespoons garlic, minced

3 carrots, sliced on a bias

2 pounds broccoli florets

½ pound snow peas

5 tablespoons soy sauce

½ teaspoon sesame oil

5 tablespoons sesame seeds, toasted

To marinate the tofu, combine the tofu, soy sauce, ginger, and garlic in a zipper-lock plastic bag. Squeeze out the air and seal the bag; turn to coat the tofu. Refrigerate, turning the bag occasionally, about 20 minutes.

Drain the tofu and discard the marinade. Dry the tofu with paper towels and dust with flour, shaking off the excess.

Heat a nonstick wok or skillet over high heat until a drop of water skitters. Pour in the oil and swirl to coat the pan, then add the tofu, and stir-fry until lightly browned, about 2 minutes. Transfer the tofu to a plate.

Add the scallion, ginger, and garlic to the pan and toss briefly. Add the carrots, followed by the broccoli, then the snow peas (may be done in batches if necessary), and stir-fry until tender, about 4 minutes. Return all the vegetables to the pan (if cooking in batches). Add the tofu and soy sauce; toss to combine. Stir in the sesame oil. Sprinkle with the toasted sesame seeds.

ABOVE, LEFT TO RIGHT: Cut the vegetables into small pieces. Heat a small amount of fat in a pan/wok and add any aromatics. Add the prepared vegetables to the pan in sequence, beginning with those that take the longest to cook.

Risotto
with Peas and Scallions

MAKES 8 SERVINGS | PREPARATION TIME: 40 MINUTES

Creamy Arborio rice, cooked in broth, makes an excellent backdrop to showcase fresh, green spring vegetables. When spring is gone, substitute any variety

8¹/₄ cups vegetable broth, or as needed

2 tablespoons olive oil

1 onion, finely chopped

2³/₄ cups Arborio rice

2 cups green peas, frozen

8 scallions, sliced

1 tablespoon butter

2 teaspoons salt, or to taste

2 teaspoons freshly ground black pepper, or to taste

1 cup Parmesan cheese, grated, plus additional for garnish, or to taste

Bring the broth to a boil in a medium saucepan. Reduce the heat and simmer.

Heat 2 tablespoons of the oil in a large saucepan. Add the onion, reduce the heat, and sauté for 1 minute. Add the rice and cook, stirring to coat, about 2 minutes.

Add about one-third of the simmered vegetable broth to the rice and cook, stirring constantly, until the rice absorbs all the broth, about 6–8 minutes. Add the same amount of broth again and simmer, stirring, until the broth is absorbed, 6–8 minutes more. Add the remaining broth and simmer, stirring, until the risotto has a creamy consistency and the rice is tender, about 6–8 minutes more.

Before all of the liquid is absorbed, add the peas and 1 cup of the scallions. Stir in the butter, salt, pepper, and cheese. Garnish with additional grated cheese, if desired, and the remaining scallions.

Tempeh Club Sandwich

MAKES 8 SERVINGS | PREPARATION TIME: 30 MINUTES

*T*empeh is a soybean cake made from fermenting cooked soybeans and often times a rice or grain. It has a firm texture and a nutty flavor that will surprise your tastebuds. The cholesterol free tempeh will also help to round out a vegetarian diet because of its high protein and low fat content.

2 packages tempeh

4 tablespoons oil

Salt, to taste

Pepper, to taste

16 slices whole grain bread, toasted

1 cup Green Mayonnaise (page 34)

2 avocados, thinly sliced

1 jar sundried tomatoes, in oil, drained

2 cups sprouts (sunflower or alfalfa)

Slice each rectangular piece of tempeh in half lengthwise so that it is half its original thickness. Cut each piece in half again, making 2 smaller rectangles. There should be 8 pieces of tempeh (4 from each original piece), approximately the size of a slice of bread.

Heat a large nonstick pan on medium-high heat. Add 2 tablespoons of the oil and half of the tempeh. Sauté until golden on the first side, flip the tempeh and continue to cook until golden on the second side. Remove the tempeh from the pan, season with salt and pepper, and reserve. Repeat with the remaining tempeh.

To assemble the sandwiches, spread each half of the toasted bread with 1 tablespoon of the green mayonnaise. Top 8 slices of bread with the tempeh, the avocado slices, the sundried tomatoes, the sprouts, and a second piece of bread.

Slice the sandwich in half and serve immediately.

Spicy Vegetable Sauté

MAKES 8 SERVINGS | PREPARATION TIME: 35 MINUTES

Spicy Vegetable Sauté is shown here with Spicy Dill Rice (page 321),

and Cucumber Raita (page 23).

*T*he variety of spices in this extremely flavorful dish create a flavor profile that will have even the most discerning palette asking for the recipe. If you are looking for something out of the ordinary, you've found it. Serving the sauté with the recipes pictured in the photograph completes a truly spectacular meal.

1¹/₂ tablespoons vegetable oil

2 tablespoons mustard seeds

¹/₂ tablespoon cumin seeds

1 onion, diced

1 tablespoon ginger, peeled, minced

1 tablespoon garlic, minced

1 tablespoon jalapeño, seeded and diced

1 head broccoli florets

1 head cauliflower florets

4 turnips, diced

4 carrots, diced

¹/₂ teaspoon salt, or to taste

¹/₄ teaspoon freshly ground black pepper, or to taste

1 cup vegetable broth

8 chiles, dried

Heat the vegetable oil in a large sauté pan over medium heat. Add the mustard and cumin seeds and sauté until the seeds begin to brown, approximately 2–3 minutes. Add the onion and sauté until translucent, approximately 3 minutes. Add the ginger, garlic, and jalapeño and sauté for another minute. Add the remaining vegetables and season with salt and pepper. Add the vegetable broth and cover, letting the vegetables steam until they are cooked through (approximately 5–10 minutes, depending on the size of the cuts).

Serve the dried chiles on the side for those who prefer a spicier dish.

Moo Shu Vegetables

MAKES 8 SERVINGS | PREPARATION TIME: 45 MINUTES

Sweet and spicy crisp vegetables wrapped in paper-thin pancakes make a healthy and easy alternative to ordering in. Moo shu pancakes are available in Asian groceries and well-stocked supermarkets, but if you cannot find the pancakes, flour tortillas can be used as a substitute.

3 tablespoons peanut oil

1 tablespoon garlic, minced

1 tablespoon ginger, peeled, minced

1 tablespoon scallion, minced

1 red pepper, cut in 1–2 inch strips

4 celery stalks, cut in 1–2 inch strips

4 carrots, cut in 1–2 inch strips

½ head napa cabbage, chiffonade

2 tablespoons Hoisin sauce

3 tablespoons soy sauce

1 tablespoon sesame oil

1 egg, beaten

16 moo shu pancakes

Heat the oil in a wok or large sauté pan over high heat.

Add the garlic, ginger, and scallion. Stir-fry until aromatic.

Add the red pepper, celery, carrots, and cabbage. Stir-fry until tender, approximately 2 minutes.

Stir in the hoisin sauce, soy sauce, and sesame oil.

Make a well in the middle of the vegetable mixture, pour in the egg and let it set for 30 seconds, then break it up into the vegetables.

Serve with moo shu pancakes. The pancakes can be warmed before serving, in a stack with a damp cloth over them, in a 250°F oven for a few minutes or in a microwave for 30–45 seconds.

Chickpea and Vegetable Tagine

*T*agine, a Moroccan stew, is usually gently simmered in an earthenware vessel and served with couscous. This *tagine* of vegetables has the exotic fragrance of cumin, pepper, and cinnamon.

2 tablespoons olive oil

4 cups onions, chopped

3 garlic cloves, chopped

1 tablespoon ground cumin

1 teaspoon freshly ground black pepper, or to taste

Salt, to taste

$\frac{1}{4}$ teaspoon ground cinnamon

2 cups water

2 pounds butternut squash, peeled, seeded, cut into chunks

6 carrots, peeled, cut into chunks

2 pounds chickpeas, drained and rinsed

2 pounds diced tomatoes in juice (no salt added)

2 sweet potatoes, peeled, cut into chunks

4 parsnips, peeled, cut into chunks

1 bay leaf

$\frac{1}{4}$ cup parsley, chopped

Heat the oil in a large saucepan. Add the onions and sauté until softened and translucent, about 5 minutes. Add the garlic and sauté until golden, about 1 minute. Add the cumin, pepper, salt, and cinnamon. Cook, stirring for 1 minute.

Stir in the water, squash, carrots, chickpeas, tomatoes, sweet potatoes, parsnips, and the bay leaf; bring to a boil. Reduce the heat and simmer, partially covered, until the vegetables are tender, about 30 minutes. Discard the bay leaf, sprinkle with the parsley, and serve.

Pasta Quattro Formaggi

MAKES 6 SERVINGS | PREPARATION TIME: 25 MINUTES

*V*ery easy to make, this is nothing more than heavy cream carefully reduced with a selection of four (*quattro*) cheeses added. The selection of cheeses can vary, but generally includes a soft blue cheese, such as Gorgonzola, and Parmigiano-Reggiano, among others. Choose your favorites and enjoy.

2 cups heavy cream

1 cup Emmenthaler cheese

1 cup Gruyère cheese

1 cup Danish blue (Danablu) cheese

$3/4$ cup Parmesan cheese

$1^1/4$ pounds fusilli (corkscrew pasta)

2 teaspoons freshly ground black pepper, or to taste

Bring a large pot of well-salted water to a boil for the pasta.

Pour the cream into a large sauté pan and place it over medium heat, watching carefully to avoid scorching.

Bring the cream to a simmer and reduce it by one-quarter. Add the cheeses. Stir continuously while the cheese melts.

While the cheese is melting, cook the pasta until it is tender to the bite, about 8–10 minutes. Drain well.

Add the cooked pasta to the cream sauce mixture, toss to coat, and season with pepper. (Salt should not be needed due to the saltiness of the water used for cooking the pasta and the saltiness of the cheese.)

FOCUS ON | Cooking Pasta

Cook pasta in large amounts of boiling, well-salted water. Use a minimum of 4 quarts water and 1–2 tablespoons of salt for every pound of pasta.

Pasta is cooked until al dente, literally "to the tooth," or just yielding when bitten into. Cooking times depend on whether the pasta is dried or fresh, as well as the size and shape. Fresh pasta cooks very quickly, often needing only 60–90 seconds to cook.

To test dry pastas for doneness, break apart a piece of the pasta and check for a tiny, white chalky dot in the center. The pasta should be slightly chewy and firm. Fresh pasta should have an appealing, chewy texture, not too soft and not too pasty.

Drain the pasta well in a colander before combining it with a sauce. If you will not be using it immediately, rinse it with cold water to stop the cooking and prevent sticking.

Asparagus
with Shiitakes, Bowtie Pasta, and Spring Peas

MAKES 8 SERVINGS | PREPARATION TIME: 45 MINUTES

The appearance of peas at the farmer's market signifies the arrival of spring, and this dish takes advantage of three different varieties. Green peas quickly lose their freshness after being picked, so frozen green peas actually offer the best quality unless you are able to obtain them extremely fresh. Asparagus is best in the late spring, when the most flavorful and tender sprouts are readily available.

3 pounds asparagus, peeled, trimmed

3 tablespoons olive oil

2 teaspoons salt, or to taste

1 cup snow peas

1 cup sugar snap peas

2 cups green peas, frozen

1 pound bowtie pasta, dried

1 tablespoon butter

3 cups shiitakes, sliced

3 tablespoons shallots, minced

3 tablespoons marjoram, chopped

$1/4$ teaspoon freshly ground black pepper, or to taste

2 bunches scallions, split lengthwise, thinly sliced

Parmesan cheese, shaved, to taste

Bring a medium saucepan of salted water to a boil to blanch the peas and a large pot of salted water to boil to cook the pasta. Preheat the broiler.

Toss the asparagus with the oil and 1 teaspoon of the salt. Place in a baking pan under the broiler for 8 minutes, until tender. Slice the asparagus into 1-inch pieces.

Cook each type of pea separately in the boiling water until almost tender, about 2 minutes each. Remove them from the water using a slotted spoon or small strainer. Reserve.

Cook the pasta in boiling water until tender to the bite, about 10–12 minutes. Drain.

Heat the butter in a sauté pan until it begins to turn brown. Add the shiitakes and shallots. Sauté until the shallots and mushrooms are slighly brown.

Add the asparagus, green peas, snow peas, sugar snap peas, marjoram, pepper, and 1 teaspoon of salt. Heat the vegetables thoroughly.

Toss the pasta with the cooked vegetables and scallions.

Just before serving, place a few shavings of cheese on each portion.

Capellini
with Grilled Vegetables

MAKES 8 SERVINGS | PREPARATION TIME: 45 MINUTES

*T*he taste and texture of grilled vegetables with pasta are always a marvelous combination. You can use your broiler if you prefer. We offer a colorful mix of bell pepper, red onion, zucchini, yellow squash and fennel, plus a handful of fresh herbs tossed in. You can grill the vegetables ahead if you wish and let them stand at room temperature.

½ cup balsamic vinegar

⅔ cup olive oil, plus 1 tablespoon

2 teaspoons salt, or to taste

1 teaspoon freshly ground black pepper, or to taste

2 red onions, cut into ½-inch rings

2 zucchini, cut into ½-inch thick slices

2 yellow squash, cut into ½-inch thick slices

1 fennel bulb, cut into ½-inch rings

1 pound capellini

1 shallot, minced

2 garlic cloves, minced

2 pounds grape tomatoes, halved lengthwise

½ cup white wine

1 tablespoon parsley, chopped

1 tablespoon basil, chopped

½ cup vegetable broth

6 ounces Gorgonzola cheese, broken into small pieces

Preheat the grill and bring a large pot of salted water to a boil for the pasta.

Combine the vinegar, ⅔ cup olive oil, salt, and pepper. Toss the onion, zucchini, squash, and fennel with the vinaigrette and grill until tender. When the vegetables are cool enough to handle, cut them into 1½-inch dice.

Cook the capellini in the boiling water until al dente, about 6–8 minutes. Drain well. Heat the remaining tablespoon of oil in a sauté pan. Add the shallot and garlic. Sauté until aromatic. Add the grilled vegetables, tomatoes, and the wine. Heat thoroughly. Season with the herbs, salt, and pepper. Adjust the consistency with the broth if necessary.

Toss the capellini with about half of the gorgonzola cheese, and top with the vegetable mixture. Garnish with the remaining gorgonzola.

Eggplant and Havarti Sandwiches

MAKES 6 SERVINGS | PREPARATION TIME: 35 MINUTES

$\mathcal{B}$roiling the eggplant for this sandwich gives it a crisp texture on the outside while the inside stays smooth and creamy. The red onion adds a crisp bite to the sandwich and a slightly sweet flavor. All of the ingredients come together to make a sandwich that pairs well with the Cream of Tomato Soup with Rice and Basil found on page 60.

$\frac{1}{4}$ cup olive oil

$\frac{1}{2}$ cup balsamic vinegar

1 teaspoon garlic, minced

Salt, to taste

$\frac{1}{4}$ teaspoon freshly ground black pepper, or to taste

1 eggplant, cut into six $\frac{1}{2}$-inch slices

6 hard rolls, sliced in half

1 roasted red pepper (page 113)

1 red onion, cut into six $\frac{1}{4}$-inch slices

12 slices Havarti cheese, 1 ounce each

Heat the broiler.

In a medium bowl, mix the olive oil, balsamic vinegar, garlic, salt, and black pepper together until thoroughly incorporated.

Dip the eggplant slices into the oil and vinegar mixture to coat, and reserve the extra.

Place the slices on a broiling rack. Broil the eggplant for 6–7 minutes per side, or until lightly golden. Reserve.

Spoon the remaining oil and vinegar mixture generously on both sides of the rolls.

Toast rolls under the broiler until lightly golden, about 45 seconds.

Top one half of each roll with a slice of eggplant, a piece of roasted red pepper, and 1 slice of cheese, and the other half with a slice of red onion and 1 slice of cheese.

Season with salt and pepper as needed.

Return to the broiler and heat until the cheese is melted, roughly 1–1½ minutes.

Assemble the sandwiches, cut in half, and serve.

Madeira-Glazed Portobello Sandwiches

MAKES 8 SERVINGS | PREPARATION TIME: 30 MINUTES

Portobello mushrooms are actually mature cremini mushrooms, and have a dense, meaty texture when cooked. They can easily be prepared for this recipe a day ahead; cool the broiled mushroom caps completely and refrigerate until needed. Slice the mushrooms and allow them to return to room temperature prior to assembling the sandwiches.

8 portobello mushrooms

¼ cup Madeira

3 tablespoons olive oil

2 garlic cloves, bruised

½ teaspoon oregano, dried

2 teaspoons salt, or to taste

1 teaspoon freshly ground black pepper, or to taste

3 cups onion, sliced

8 hard rolls, split

8 slices Swiss cheese

4 cups mixed baby greens

Preheat the broiler and place the oven rack in the upper third of the oven.

Remove the stems from the mushrooms and using a sharp paring knife, cut away the gills. Combine the Madeira, 2 tablespoons of the olive oil, the garlic cloves, oregano, 1 teaspoon of the salt, and ½ teaspoon of the pepper in a large bowl; add the mushrooms and toss to coat. Set aside for 10 minutes to marinate.

Heat the remaining tablespoon of olive oil in a sauté pan set over medium-high heat. Add the onions and sauté until soft and translucent, about 5–6 minutes. Season with the remaining 1 teaspoon of salt and ½ teaspoon of pepper.

Place the mushrooms on a baking sheet, brush with the marinade, and broil until browned and tender, about 4 minutes on each side. When cool enough to handle, thinly slice each mushroom and place one entire sliced mushroom on the bottom half of each roll. Place 1 slice of cheese on top of each mushroom.

Place the bottom half of each roll with the mushroom and cheese on a baking pan and place under the broiler until the cheese is melted, about 2 minutes.

Top each sandwich with ¼ cup of the onions, ½ cup of the greens, and the top half of the roll.

Orechiette
with Cannellini Beans & Spinach

MAKES 8 SERVINGS | PREPARATION TIME: 35 MINUTES

*O*rechiette is a pasta shape that lends itself well to a simple sauce like the one made here. You can choose to serve this family style or as a side dish to a serving of grilled, marinated chicken.

1 tablespoon olive oil

2¹/₂ cups onion, thinly sliced

3 garlic cloves, chopped

2 15-ounce cans cannellini beans,
   drained and rinsed

1 cup vegetable broth

¹/₄ teaspoon crushed red pepper flakes

¹/₂ teaspoon salt, or to taste

1 pound orechiette pasta

2 10-ounce bags spinach, stems removed

¹/₂ cup Parmesan cheese, grated

Bring a large pot of salted water to a boil for the pasta.

Meanwhile, in a large nonstick skillet over medium-high heat, heat the olive oil. Add the onion and sauté over medium-high heat until golden brown, about 10–12 minutes, stirring occasionally. Add the garlic and cook an additional 2 minutes.

Add the cannellini beans, vegetable broth, crushed red pepper flakes, and ½ teaspoon salt to the pan. Simmer over medium-high heat until the sauce thickens slightly, about 15 minutes.

Cook the pasta in the boiling water until tender to the bite, about 8–10 minutes. Just before draining pasta, stir the spinach into the pasta pot until it wilts. Drain the pasta and spinach and return them to pot. Add the cannellini bean mixture and mix well.

Serve in large, heated pasta bowls and top with grated Parmesan cheese.

Fettuccine
with Corn, Squash, Chiles, Crème Fraîche, and Cilantro

MAKES 8 SERVINGS | PREPARATION TIME: 45 MINUTES

Creamy, sweet and spicy, this dish is a fresh alternative to the more commonly found pasta dishes of Italian origin. Crème fraîche is a cultured cream very similar in flavor to sour cream. Its rich texture softens the spiciness of the chiles and provides a velvety sauce for this luscious dish.

1 pound fettuccine noodles	4 cups corn kernels, frozen or fresh	1 tablespoon salt, or to taste
2 tablespoons olive oil	2 jalapeños, diced	1/4 teaspoon freshly ground black pepper
2 onions, diced	2 teaspoons garlic, minced	1/2 cup crème fraîche
2 zucchini, diced	2 cups vegetable broth	1/4 cup cilantro, chopped

Bring a large pot of salted water to a boil for pasta. Heat the olive oil in a large saucepan or Dutch oven. Sauté the onions and zucchini until the onions are translucent and the zucchini is tender, approximately 8–10 minutes. Add the corn, jalapeños, and garlic. Cook for another 5 minutes.

Add the vegetable broth and season with the remaining salt and pepper. Cook the pasta until tender to the bite, about 8–10 minutes. Drain the pasta, add it to the sauté pan, and mix with the sauce.

Portion into pasta bowls and add a dollop of crème fraîche to each serving. Garnish with the cilantro.

CHAPTER NINE

Side Dishes

S IDE DISHES AND ACCOMPANIMENTS INCLUDE ANY OF A NUMBER OF SMALL DISHES MADE FROM VEGETABLES, GRAINS, PASTA, OR POTATOES THAT ARE MEANT TO ENHANCE A MEAL BY ADDING FLA- VORS, TEXTURES, COLORS, AND SHAPES. THESE VEGETABLE, PASTA, potato, and grain dishes do more than simply fill up the empty space on a plate. The combination of foods you prepare serves to enhance and complement the entrée, add excitement to the meal, and leave your family and guests fulfilled. When you move beyond basic boiled carrots, rice, or potatoes, you can use side dishes to add excitement, color, and nutrition to any meal. Pilafs, salads, stir fries, braises, and stews let you stretch your repertoire and increase the appeal of every meal.

While it is easy to fall into a pattern when selecting and preparing sides to serve with your main dish, the wide variety of high quality ingredients available to cooks today can be a powerful enticement to try something new, or enjoy an old favorite in a new way. This chapter includes everything from old time favorites, such as Roasted Potatoes (page 304), to Sweet Potato Cakes (page 307), a more unusual preparation.

Once you understand the basics of preparing vegetables, grains, pasta, and potatoes, you can make interesting substitutions, for example, preparing bulgur using the same method you might use for rice (Bulgur and Lentil Pilaf, page 302), or perhaps broccoli rabe instead of broccoli (Sautéed Broccoli Rabe with Toasted Pine Nuts, page 278).

Serve a room temperature salad of legumes (Black Bean Salad, page 282) or grains (Tabbouleh Salad, page 300) instead of a hot dish, or a hearty cold salad of rice, diced meat, cheese, and vegetables (Rice Salad, page 323).

Another quick and easy method of adding more interest to your meals is to try new seasonings and flavorings. The spices, herbs, oils, or aromatics you choose can extend the flavors of the main dish, or perhaps add something new and unexpected. Add a glaze of mustard or honey, introduce some wine or exotic mushrooms, or use a spice blend.

Use of the most appropriate, efficient cooking technique for each type of food encountered is perhaps the most essential ingredient for success in the quick kitchen. Foods that are well-cooked will develop their best flavor, as well as retain their nutritional value and an appealing color and texture. Use these recipes to become acquainted with new foods and cooking techniques, and reacquainted with familiar favorites.

The flavorful side dishes featured in this chapter represent such a variety of ingredients and cuisines, you and your family can enjoy delicious and interesting new side dishes at any meal, whether for an ordinary weekday meal, a formal dinner party, or a special celebration.

AT A GLANCE | Cooking Vegetables

	TECHNIQUE	REASON
ORANGE AND YELLOW VEGETABLES	Cook in water	Minimizes loss of fat-soluble pigments
	Cook covered or uncovered	Maintains color
	Longer cooking methods	Maintains color
	Avoid overcooking	Loses structure and color
WHITE VEGETABLES	Keep covered	Contains beneficial acids
	Add acidic ingredients (lemon juice, vinegar, wine)	Helps maintain color
	Avoid too much acid	Toughens the vegetables
	Avoid overcooking	Loses color, creates undesirable smell and taste

Vegetables

As vegetables cook, their flavors and textures change dramatically. Their nutritional value also changes. To keep these changes working for you to create a well-balanced and appealing dish, it helps to know that the color of the vegetable has a role in what you can expect the vegetable to behave like and how different cooking techniques can enhance its attributes.

Pasta

This internationally loved dish, which gets its name from the Italian word meaning *paste,* is made from a stiff dough that includes wheat or other flours and water. Fresh pasta typically includes eggs for added flavor and a good texture. While pasta is often served as a main dish in this country, its versatility and speed of preparation makes it a good choice for delicious and satisfying side dishes as well.

Preparing pasta from scratch is a time-consuming, labor-intensive task. Thankfully, home cooks can find a wide variety of high-quality fresh and dried pastas in different shapes, textures, sizes, and flavors at their local markets.

Pasta Beyond the Traditional

Orzo is a small durum wheat pasta, resembling rice, used in pilafs as well as on its own as a side dish.

	TECHNIQUE	REASON
GREEN VEGETABLES	Cook in a large amount of water	Dilutes acids
	Salt the water	Cooks slightly faster and adds flavor
	Bring to a rolling boil	Minimizes loss of vitamin C
	Keep uncovered	Acids evaporate
	Cook quickly	Color lost after 5–7 minutes
	Avoid aluminum, iron or tin	Dulls color
RED VEGETABLES	Cook in a small amount of water	Minimizes loss of color
	Keep covered	Contains beneficial acids
	Add acidic ingredients (lemon juice, vinegar, wine)	Helps maintain color
	Keep beets unpeeled and uncut	Minimizes loss of color
	Prepare and cook red cabbage in non-reactive containers	Iron or aluminum will discolor

Couscous, a staple of North African and Middle Eastern cooking, was originally an Arab dish. Light in texture, couscous may be used in salads, pilafs, or combined with sautéed vegetables

Asian noodles include cellophane or bean thread noodles made from mung-bean starch, popular in China. Some Japanese favorites include soba noodles, made from buckwheat and wheat, with a shape like spaghetti; somen noodles, very thin straight wheat noodles; and udon noodles, made from buckwheat, brown rice, or whole wheat with a thick, flat shape, similar to fettuccine.

Legumes

Dried beans and peas are delicious, satisfying, nutritious, and economical. There are more than 13,000 varieties of legumes grown in the world. Of these, approximately, 40 are consumed. Black-eyed peas and red lentils cook quickly, but other beans require longer cooking times. You can fit them into your schedule by purchasing canned beans. It is important to rinse and drain canned beans when a recipes instructs you to, as they often contain large amounts salt.

Potatoes

Slice or cube potatoes so that they have a shorter cooking time, whether you are planning to make a salad or a puree. Buy baby red potatoes to cut back on both preparation and cooking time.

Whole Grains

Whole grains are a great way to add new flavors and textures to your meals. Cuisines around the world feature these wholesome, nutritious foods in a variety of guises.

Long-, short-, and medium-grain rice is a familiar and popular dish the world over. Choose long grain varieties for a fluffy finished texture. Short grain rices cook up moist and slightly sticky, perfect for picking up with chopsticks. Medium grain rice is creamy and porridge-like when you cook it into risotto. Quick cooking wild rice blends, such as Wild Rice Pilaf, page 320, make it easy to feature the nutty flavor as well as adding a healthful boost to your meals.

Pilaf made from long grain rice is a perfect quick meal recipe. Even considering the prep time to mince some onions and measure the rice, you can go from start to finish in less than twenty minutes.

Pilafs are incredibly adaptable. Although rice is the most familiar grain prepared by the pilaf technique, this is an excellent method for other grains such as quinoa and bulgur.

Onions, shallots, or leeks provide essential flavor, while herbs and spices such as bay leaves, thyme sprigs, saffron, curry powder, and parsley, to name just a few of the options you might choose, add various notes.

You can add more vegetables, dried fruits, nuts, and a host of flavorings to custom-fit the pilaf to the meal. With enough additions, a pilaf can actually be the meal, if you like. An initial step known as "parching" toasts the grains before you add the liquid to give them their wonderful fluffy texture and imbue them with a distinctive, nutty flavor.

➡ COOK THE AROMATICS

Heat a bit of oil or butter in a flat-bottomed, ovenproof pan. (It is best to choose a pot with a tight-fitting lid, but you can improvise by covering the pan with foil.)

Add minced onion and other aromatic vegetables (celery, mushrooms, carrots, or leeks, for example), and cook, stirring from time to time, until the vegetables are tender and translucent.

➡ PARCH THE GRAIN

Add the grain and sauté them, stirring frequently, until the individual grains are coated with oil and heated through. There will be a subtle color change as they parch. You'll know they've cooked long enough when you smell a rich, toasted aroma.

➡ ADD THE BROTH AND FINISH THE PILAF

Add the broth and bring it to a simmer, stirring the grains once or twice to prevent them from sticking to the bottom of the pan. (To shorten the amount of time it takes for the pilaf to return to a boil, you can heat the broth while you prep and sauté the vegetables and parch the grain. A microwave is helpful, since you can simply measure the broth into a glass measuring cup and warm it directly in the cup.)

Stir in any herbs and spices you want to include at the correct point; consult your recipe for specific guidance. Ground or whole spices are often added along with the aromatic vegetables. Dried herbs, bay leaves, and thyme sprigs are generally added to the simmering pilaf just before you cover the pot.

Cover the pot and finish the pilaf in the oven, or over very low heat. Cook until the grains are tender but still slightly firm, not soft or mushy. They should separate easily when you pour them from a spoon onto a plate.

➡ ALLOW THE PILAF TO REST BEFORE SERVING

For the best texture, let the pilaf rest out of the oven or off the heat, still covered, for 5–10 minutes. Then, use a fork to gently separate and fluff the grains and fold in any final flavorings or garnishes just before serving.

See the step-by-step photographs accompanying the recipe for Basic Rice Pilaf (page 318).

Roasted Carrots and Parsnips with Herbs

MAKES 6 SERVINGS | PREPARATION TIME: 45 MINUTES

Root vegetables like carrots and parsnips develop a mellow, sweet flavor when slowly oven-roasted. By keeping the cuts relatively similar in size, the pieces will all cook in the same amount of time. This side is delicious with roasted meats and poultry, particularly in the fall and winter when root vegetables are more prevalent.

4 parsnips

5 carrots

3 tablespoons olive oil

1 teaspoon salt, or to taste

1/2 teaspoon freshly ground black pepper, or to taste

2 teaspoons rosemary, chopped

2 teaspoons sage, chopped

Preheat the oven to 350°F.

Peel the parsnips and carrots. Cut them into chunky pieces roughly 2 inches long and ¾-inch thick. All the pieces should be of uniform size and shape

Toss the parsnips and carrots with the oil, salt, pepper, rosemary, and sage in a large bowl.

Spread in a large shallow baking pan. Roast the vegetables in the lower third of the oven until tender, about 30–35 minutes.

Tarragon Green Beans

MAKES 8 SERVINGS | PREPARATION TIME: 10 MINUTES

*T*he light and delicate anise-flavor of tarragon offers a delicious complement to this simple combination of green beans, shallots, and butter.

2 pounds green beans, trimmed	1 tablespoon shallots, minced	Salt, to taste
1 tablespoon butter	1 tablespoon tarragon, roughly chopped	Freshly ground black pepper, to taste

Parboil the beans in salted water until tender to the bite, about 5 minutes. Drain.

Sauté the shallots in butter until tender, add the beans, and sauté for 2–3 minutes, until warm.

Stir in the chopped tarragon, season with salt and pepper, and serve.

Coleslaw

See photograph on page 137.

There are about as many varieties of coleslaw as there are people that love it. Typically, however, coleslaw is a combination of red and green cabbages, sweet onions, and carrots, tossed with a mayonnaise-style dressing that is usually slightly sweet.

3 cups green cabbage, chiffonade

1 cup red cabbage, chiffonade

2 carrots, thinly sliced into 1–2 inch strips

1 red pepper, thinly sliced into 1–2 inch strips

1/2 red onion, thinly sliced

DRESSING

3 tablespoons sugar

1 teaspoon Dijon mustard

1 teaspoon celery seed

1/2 cup mayonnaise

1/2 cup sour cream

2 tablespoons cider vinegar

1 tablespoon horseradish

Salt, to taste

1–2 teaspoons ground white pepper

4 shakes Tabasco sauce

Combine the cabbages, carrots, peppers, and onions. Reserve.

Stir together the sugar, mustard, and celery seed until well blended. Add the remaining dressing ingredients and stir to combine.

Fold the vegetables into the dressing. The salad is ready to serve now, or it may be chilled before serving.

Warm Vegetable Slaw

The variety of vegetables give this slaw its tantalizing flavor and its warm temperature makes it a distinctive side dish.

1/4 cup white wine

1 1/2 cups red bell pepper, thinly sliced into 1–2 inch strips

1 1/2 cups yellow bell pepper, thinly sliced into 1–2 inch strips

1 cup carrot, thinly sliced into 1–2 inch strips

1 cup red onion, thinly sliced

1 1/2 pounds napa cabbage, chiffonade

5 tablespoons Dijon mustard

1/4 cup vegetable stock

1/4 teaspoon salt, or to taste

Freshly ground black pepper, to taste

Bring the wine to a simmer in a large sauté pan. Add the peppers, carrots, and onions and sweat until the vegetables are slightly tender, about 5 minutes.

Add the cabbage, mustard, and vegetable stock. Simmer until the cabbage is tender, about 5–7 minutes.

Season with salt and pepper, and serve warm.

Ratatouille

MAKES 8 SERVINGS | PREPARATION TIME: 45 MINUTES

*T*he word *ratatouille* is a French term referring to a ragout of summer vegetables and herbs that originated in France's Provençe region. Common to most *ratatouille* recipes are tomatoes, eggplant, sweet bell peppers, yellow squash, zucchini, and onions. Simmered together with herbs and olive oil, the vegetables release natural juices that provide outstanding flavor. This is a terrific dish that improves if allowed to sit overnight.

1 teaspoon olive oil

$^2/_3$ cup red onion, diced

1$^1/_2$ tablespoons garlic, minced

1 tablespoon shallots, minced

1 tablespoon tomato paste

5 plum tomatoes, seeded, sliced $^1/_4$-inch thick

1 cup zucchini, diced

1 cup red bell pepper, diced

1$^1/_2$ cups eggplant, diced

1 cup yellow squash

1 cup vegetable stock

1 tablespoon basil, chiffonade

Dried oregano, to taste

$^1/_2$ teaspoon salt, or to taste

$^1/_4$ teaspoon freshly ground black pepper, or to taste

Heat the oil in a medium saucepot. Add the onions, garlic, and shallots. Sauté until the onions are translucent, about 5–7 minutes.

Add the tomato paste and sauté until brown, about 3–4 minutes.

Add the remaining vegetables and the stock. Bring to a gentle simmer and stew, stirring occasionally, until the vegetables are tender, about 15 minutes.

Season with the basil, oregano, salt, and pepper.

Sautéed Broccoli Rabe
with Toasted Pine Nuts

MAKES 6 SERVINGS | PREPARATION TIME: 25 MINUTES

See photograph on page 194.

*T*he bitter and pungent flavor of broccoli rabe is made more delicate by blanching it first. If a stronger flavor is desired, the trimmed broccoli rabe can be added raw to the sauté pan after the shallots have been sweated and cooked in the same pan. Simply add a small amount of water to steam it through.

3 pounds broccoli rabe

¼ cup pine nuts

¼ cup olive oil

1 teaspoon garlic, chopped

1 tablespoon shallots, chopped

1 teaspoon salt, or to taste

1 teaspoon freshly ground black pepper, or to taste

Bring a large pot of salted water to a boil.

Wash the broccoli rabe and remove any tough stems and very large leaves.

Toast the pine nuts in a small dry skillet over medium heat, stirring frequently, about 3–4 minutes.

Blanch the broccoli rabe in the boiling water until just wilted, about 2–4 minutes. Drain.

Heat the olive oil in a large sauté pan over medium-high heat. Sweat the garlic and shallots in the oil just until translucent, about 3–4 minutes.

Add the broccoli rabe to the sauté pan. Quickly sauté all the ingredients. Add the pine nuts and adjust the seasoning.

Sautéed Swiss Chard

*S*wiss chard can be found in the produce aisle near other leafy greens. Although white and red chard are typically found in most grocery stores, rainbow chard makes this dish truly beautiful.

1/2 cup pine nuts

3 tablespoons olive oil

6 tablespoons shallots, minced

2 tablespoons garlic, minced

2 bunches Swiss chard, torn into pieces

1 teaspoon salt, or to taste

1/2 teaspoon freshly ground black pepper, or to taste

1/4 cup white wine

Toast the pine nuts in a small dry skillet over medium heat, stirring frequently, about 3–4 minutes.

Heat the olive oil in a large sauté pan over medium-high heat. Add the shallots to the pan and sweat until translucent, about 5 minutes. Add the garlic and sweat until aromatic, another 2 minutes.

Add the chard to the pan, and season with salt and pepper. Sauté until just barely wilted, about 5–7 minutes. Sauté in batches if necessary.

Add the white wine to the pan and cover. Steam the chard until the spines are tender and the liquid has almost evaporated, about 5 minutes.

Summer Squash Sauté

MAKES 8 SERVINGS | PREPARATION TIME: 30 MINUTES

See photograph on page 165.

This versatile side adds a refreshing element to almost any dish and using seasonal vegetables eliminates the need for heavy garnishes.

1 tablespoon olive oil

1 onion, sliced

1 pound zucchini, cut into $^1/_4$-inch slices

1 pound yellow squash, cut into $^1/_4$-inch slices

2 tomatoes, chopped

Salt, to taste

Freshly ground black pepper, to taste

Heat the olive oil in a large sauté pan over medium-high heat.

Add the onions, zucchini, and yellow squash, and sauté until light brown and tender, about 5–7 minutes.

Season with salt and pepper.

Stir in the chopped tomato, cook for an additional 2 minutes, and serve.

Pan-Steamed Lemon Asparagus

MAKES 8 SERVINGS | PREPARATION TIME: 20 MINUTES

See photograph on page 143.

Spring and early summer is the optimal time for asparagus as delicate, pencil-thin stems are more readily available. This very easy recipe maximizes the unique flavor of fresh asparagus, by using simple seasoning agents for this seasonal favorite.

2 bunches asparagus

2 tablespoons olive oil

$^1/_4$ cup shallots, minced

4 teaspoons garlic, minced

$^1/_4$ cup lemon juice

$^1/_4$ cup white wine

Trim the bottoms off the asparagus spears so that the asparagus are equal in length.

Heat the oil in a large sauté pan over medium heat. Sweat the shallots and garlic until translucent, about 2 minutes. Add the asparagus and cook for 4–5 minutes.

Add the lemon juice and white wine to the pan and cover. Steam the asparagus for 3 minutes, or until cooked through. Serve immediately.

Pan-Steamed Zucchini
and Yellow Squash Noodles

MAKES 8 SERVINGS | PREPARATION TIME: 30 MINUTES

See photograph on page 147.

A mandoline is a manual slicer, with a long rectangular shape and adjustable blade settings, that makes long, narrow, even slicing a snap. It is the ideal tool with which to accomplish the long thin "noodle-like" cuts called for in this dish. Otherwise, use a chef's knife or cleaver to carefully cut the squashes into long, thin julienne strips.

1¹/₂ pounds zucchini	1 tablespoon garlic, minced	1 teaspoon lemon juice
1¹/₂ pounds yellow squash	¹/₄ cup vegetable broth	¹/₂ teaspoon salt, or to taste
1 tablespoon butter	1 tablespoon chives, minced	¹/₄ teaspoon freshly ground black pepper
3 tablespoons shallots, minced	1 tablespoon tarragon, minced	

Cut the zucchini and yellow squash lengthwise into ¼-inch thick noodles using a mandoline. Discard the center of the squashes. Heat the butter in a large sauté pan over medium heat. Add the shallots and garlic. Sweat until the shallots are translucent, about 3–4 minutes.

Add the squash noodles and broth. Cover the pan and steam the squash until tender, about 5 minutes. Drain any excess liquid.

Season with the herbs, lemon juice, salt, and pepper.

Black Bean Salad
with Lime-Cilantro Vinaigrette

MAKES 8 SERVINGS | PREPARATION TIME: 10 MINUTES

*B*lack beans are commonly found in Southwestern-style and Mexican cuisines. Also known as "turtle beans," they are available dried or canned in most supermarketa.

3 cups canned black beans, drained
   and rinsed

3 cups assorted bell peppers, diced

5 tablespoons red onion, diced

3 tablespoons jalapeño, minced

3 tablespoons garlic, minced

1 tablespoon cilantro, chopped

3 tablespoons Lime-Cilantro Vinaigrette
   (page 127)

Combine all the ingredients for the salad and toss thoroughly with the vinaigrette.

Allow the salad ingredients to marry in the vinaigrette for 5 minutes before serving.

Grilled Vegetables

MAKES 8 SERVINGS | PREPARATION TIME: 45 MINUTES

See photograph on page 184.

*T*his dish is excellent when grilling is the favored cooking method and the abundant summer harvest is at its peak. No need to complicate the delicious flavor of grilled vegetables with anything other than a bit of garlic, olive oil, and parsley; just the right side for any of your favorite grilled meats.

- 1 pound yellow squash, sliced ¼-inch thick on a bias
- 1 pound zucchini, sliced ¼-inch thick on a bias
- 2 pounds Vidalia onion, sliced ¼-inch thick
- 3 pounds eggplant, sliced ¼-inch thick
- 3 tablespoons salt, or to taste
- 1 cup extra-virgin olive oil, or as needed
- 2 garlic cloves, minced
- 3 tablespoons parsley, chopped
- 1 teaspoon freshly ground black pepper, or to taste

Preheat the grill on the highest setting

Lay the sliced vegetables on baking sheets and sprinkle them lightly with salt. Allow the vegetables to rest for 15 minutes to begin extracting water. Gently blot the vegetables dry to remove excess water before grilling.

Toss the vegetables with the olive oil and garlic.

Grill the vegetables until lightly charred and tender, about 1–2 minutes per side. Transfer to a platter, season to taste with salt and pepper, and garnish with parsley.

Vegetarian Refried Beans

MAKES 8 SERVINGS | PREPARATION TIME: 30 MINUTES

*T*he brown-and-pink pinto bean is the standard bean used in *frijoles refritos,* or refried beans. Refried beans are typically made with lard; this vegetarian version uses corn oil and spices for flavor. As they cook, some of the beans will break down to a puree and some of the beans will remain whole, giving the mixture a creamy, yet slightly chunky texture.

1 tablespoon corn oil

2 cups onion, diced

2 tablespoons garlic, minced

$^{1}/_{2}$ teaspoon salt, or to taste

1 cup tomatoes, diced

4 15$^{1}/_{2}$-ounce cans pinto beans, rinsed
and drained

1 teaspoon cumin seeds, toasted, cracked

1 teaspoon chili powder

Tabasco sauce, to taste

Heat the oil in a large sauté pan. Add the onions and garlic and sweat until the onions are translucent, about 5 minutes.

Add the tomatoes, salt, and beans. Mash the beans using a potato masher until only some of the beans still remain whole. Cook over low heat, stirring constantly, until the flavor is well developed, about 10 minutes.

Season with the cumin, chili powder, and Tabasco.

Sweet and Sour Green Beans

See photograph on page 187.

These tasty, stir-fried green beans are easy to prepare, and have a refreshing flavor that will complement your favorite Asian-inspired entrées.

1 pound green beans, trimmed, cut into
    2-inch lengths

2 tablespoons soy sauce

2 tablespoons hoisin sauce

2 tablespoons rice wine vinegar

2 teaspoons peanut oil

1 teaspoon (or to taste) hot pepper sauce

1 garlic clove, minced

1 8-ounce can water chestnuts, sliced,
    drained

1 teaspoon dark sesame oil

Place the green beans in a steamer basket and set in a saucepan over 1 inch of boiling water. Cover and steam until just tender, about 5 minutes; drain.

Combine the soy sauce, hoisin sauce, vinegar, and the hot pepper sauce in a small bowl.

Put 2 teaspoons of peanut oil in a wok or large skillet, and set over high heat. Add the green beans and garlic. Stir-fry the beans for 2 minutes; add the soy sauce mixture and cook, stirring, about 2 minutes. Stir in the water chestnuts and drizzle with the sesame oil. Serve at once.

Haricots Verts
with Walnuts

MAKES 8 SERVINGS | PREPARATION TIME: 20 MINUTES

See photograph on page 154.

*H*aricot vert is the French term for extra-thin, delicate green beans. Tossed with toasted walnuts, shallots, and garlic, they make an elegant side dish for cuts of beef and various chicken dishes. Regular green beans may be substituted if *haricots verts* are unavailable.

2 pounds haricots verts, trimmed

1 teaspoon olive oil

2 tablespoons shallots, minced

2 garlic cloves, minced

$^1/_4$ cup walnuts, toasted, chopped

$^1/_4$ teaspoon salt, or to taste

Freshly ground black pepper, to taste

2 tablespoons butter

Cook the haricots verts in simmering water until barely tender to the bite, about 3–5 minutes.

Heat the oil in a small sauté pan. Add the shallots and garlic. Sweat until the shallots are translucent, about 3–4 minutes.

Combine the haricots verts with the shallots, garlic, walnuts, salt, pepper, and butter. Toss to coat. Reserve warm.

Haricots Verts
with Prosciutto and Gruyère

MAKES 8 SERVINGS | PREPARATION TIME: 30 MINUTES

This is a stunning addition to any meal and it requires minimal preparation. This side dish can be served in individual portions or on a large platter for a beautiful presentation.

1 pound haricots verts, trimmed

DRESSING
3 tablespoons lemon juice, or to taste
1 tablespoon white wine vinegar

$1/2$ teaspoon salt, or to taste
$1/4$ teaspoon freshly ground black pepper, or to taste
2 tablespoons shallots, minced
6 tablespoons olive oil

$1/4$ pound prosciutto, thinly sliced
$1/4$ pound Gruyère cheese
1 teaspoon cracked black peppercorns

Combine the lemon juice, vinegar, salt, pepper, and shallots. Gradually whisk in the oil to make a dressing.

Cook the haricots verts in salted boiling water until barely tender to the bite, about 3–5 minutes. Rinse the haricots verts under cold water, drain, and blot dry.

Toss the haricots verts with the dressing and let marinate at room temperature for 10 minutes.

Twist the prosciutto into spirals so that they look like roses.

Serve the haricots verts alongside the prosciutto roses. Using a vegetable peeler, shave curls of the Gruyère on top and garnish with cracked black peppercorns.

Braised Belgian Endive

*B*elgian endive are deliberately protected from light as they grow to produce pale, satiny heads. Choose tight heads that show no scars or blemishes. The leaves should be closed into a tight point and should be pale ivory to light yellowish green in color.

1¹/₂ teaspoons vegetable oil

²/₃ cup onion, diced

¹/₄ cup carrot, diced

¹/₄ cup celery, diced

8 Belgian endive

1 quart water

¹/₂ cup white wine

¹/₄ cup lemon juice

1 teaspoon salt, or to taste

2 thyme sprigs

1 bay leaf

Heat the vegetable oil in a large saucepan. Add the onions, carrots, and celery. Sweat until the onions are translucent, about 5 minutes. Add the remaining ingredients. If necessary, add more water to completely cover the endive. Keep the endive submerged during cooking to avoid browning. Simmer the endive until they are tender, about 20–25 minutes. Drain before serving.

Sautéed Apples

*T*hese spicy-sweet sautéed apples provide the perfect balance to a savory dish. Eliminate the cayenne pepper and this can be served on top of your favorite ice cream.

4 Granny Smith apples, cut into wedges

¹/₂ cup brown sugar, packed

¹/₄ teaspoon ground cloves

¹/₄ teaspoon cinnamon

¹/₂ teaspoon salt, or to taste

Pinch cayenne pepper (optional)

¹/₄ cup butter

6 tablespoons Calvados

Toss the apples with the brown sugar, cloves, cinnamon, salt, and cayenne, if using.

Heat 2 tablespoons of the butter over high heat in a large sauté pan. Sauté half of the apples, stirring only occasionally, until the sugar has caramelized and the apples are golden brown, about 10 minutes. Deglaze with 3 tablespoons Calvados and allow the liquid to reduce by half.

Repeat with the remaining butter, apples, and Calvados.

Broccoli
with Orange-Sesame Sauce

MAKES 8 SERVINGS | PREPARATION TIME: 15 MINUTES

See photograph on page 207.

Complement one of your many favorite Asian dishes with a side of this lightly steamed broccoli, seasoned with orange, honey and ginger and topped with crunchy sesame seeds.

2 pounds broccoli florets

1 cup orange juice

2 tablespoons honey

1 tablespoon ginger, peeled and grated

1 tablespoon lemon juice

2 teaspoons sesame oil

2 tablespoons sesame seeds, toasted

Place the broccoli in a steamer basket and set in a saucepan over 1 inch of boiling water. Cover tightly and steam until just tender, 3–5 minutes

To make the sauce, combine the orange juice, honey, and ginger in a small nonstick saucepan and bring to a boil. Cook until the sauce thickens, about 3 minutes. Remove the pan from the heat; stir in the lemon juice and sesame oil, and cook an additional 2 minutes.

Arrange the broccoli in a serving bowl, top with the sauce, sprinkle with the sesame seeds and serve immediately.

Steamed Broccoli and Red Peppers

MAKES 6 SERVINGS | PREPARATION TIME: 15 MINUTES

Steaming is great for quick-cooking vegetables. Seasoned with butter, lemon juice, and salt, this easy side dish results in a delicious, brightly colored accompaniment to just about any meat or poultry item.

3 tablespoons lemon juice

6 tablespoons butter, softened

1½ pounds broccoli florets

1 cup red bell pepper, cut into thin strips

½ teaspoon salt, or to taste

¼ teaspoon freshly ground black pepper, or to taste

Reduce the lemon juice by half and stir it into the softened butter. Refrigerate until needed.

Bring water to a full boil in the bottom of the steamer.

Arrange the broccoli and peppers on a steamer rack so that the pieces are not crowded. Place the steamer rack on top of the boiling water, and cover. Steam the vegetables for 3–5 minutes, or until just tender.

Season with salt, pepper, and lemon butter.

Sautéed Brussels Sprouts
with Pancetta

MAKES 8 SERVINGS | PREPARATION TIME: 35 MINUTES

The majority of the preparation work comes in removing the core and pulling the brussel sprout layers apart. This is well worth the effort, as the tender leaves cook quickly and evenly to a beautiful bright green color, lightly glazed with olive oil and bits of crisp pancetta.

6 cups Brussels sprouts, trimmed

2¹/₂ ounces pancetta, roughly chopped

¹/₄ cup extra-virgin olive oil

¹/₂ cup onion, chopped

1 tablespoon butter

2 tablespoons water

1 teaspoon salt, or to taste

¹/₂ teaspoon freshly ground black pepper, or to taste

Slice each Brussels sprout in half and remove the core. Gently pull the layers of leaves apart.

Heat a large sauté pan and add the olive oil and pancetta. Render the fat from the pancetta, until it is lightly crispy. Remove the pancetta and reserve.

Add the onions and cook until translucent, about 5 minutes.

Add the butter and swirl to melt.

Add the Brussels sprouts and 2 tablespoons of water.

Sauté over medium heat, tossing to coat. Cook until leaves are tender and bright green, about 6–8 minutes. Season to taste with salt and freshly ground black pepper. Fold in the reserved pancetta and serve immediately.

Stewed Chickpeas
with Tomato, Zucchini, and Cilantro

MAKES 8 SERVINGS | PREPARATION TIME: 30 MINUTES

Native to the Mediterranean region, chickpeas are commonly found in the cuisines surrounding the Mediterranean Sea and those of the Middle East. Here chickpeas are combined with tomato and zucchini for a hearty and delicious side dish that can be made in a snap and only improves with time.

3 tablespoons olive oil

3 tablespoons garlic, minced

3 cups zucchini, small dice

1 cup tomato, seeded, diced

3 cups canned chickpeas, drained
  and rinsed

2 tablespoons chicken or vegetable broth

$\frac{1}{4}$ cup cilantro, chopped

1 teaspoon salt, or to taste

$\frac{1}{2}$ teaspoon freshly ground black pepper,
  or to taste

$\frac{1}{4}$ cup lime juice

Heat the olive oil in a large sauté pan over medium heat. Add the garlic and cook until aromatic, about 1 minute. Add the zucchini and tomato and sauté until the zucchini is tender, about 8 minutes.

Add the chickpeas and enough broth to keep them moist. Stew until heated through, about 6–7 minutes.

Add the cilantro and season to taste with salt, pepper, and lime juice.

Artichokes and Mushrooms
in White Wine Sauce

MAKES 8 SERVINGS | PREPARATION TIME: 30 MINUTES

*U*sing canned artichoke hearts speeds both the preparation and cooking time of this delicious side dish. It's delicate flavors are an ideal complement to chicken or fish dishes.

2 tablespoons olive oil

3 cups white mushrooms, halved

1 tablespoon garlic, minced

3 cups canned artichoke hearts, drained and rinsed, halved

1$\frac{1}{2}$ cups water

1 cup dry white wine

$\frac{1}{4}$ cup lemon juice

$\frac{1}{4}$ teaspoon dried thyme

1 tablespoon tomato paste

$\frac{1}{2}$ teaspoon salt, or to taste

$\frac{1}{4}$ teaspoon freshly ground black pepper, or to taste

Heat the oil in a medium saucepan. Add the mushrooms. Cook over medium heat for 4 minutes, stirring occasionally. Add the garlic and sweat until aromatic, about 1 minute.

Add the remaining ingredients and mix well. Cover and continue to cook over low heat until the artichokes are tender and the flavors have blended together, about 10 minutes.

Drain the vegetables and reduce the cooking liquid to a sauce consistency, about 10 minutes. Return the vegetables to the sauce and serve.

Asparagus with Morels

MAKES 8 SERVINGS | PREPARATION TIME: 30 MINUTES

*C*elebrate spring with this delectable combination of fresh morels and asparagus. Morels have an intense smoky, earthy, nutty flavor that is prized among wild mushrooms. Although morels are expensive, a little goes a long way, so they're well worth the cost. If they are not available, substitute portobello mushrooms; scrape the gills off with a spoon, then cut into chunks.

2 pounds asparagus

$^1/_2$ cup water

1 tablespoon vegetable oil

2 tablespoons shallots, minced

4 ounces morel mushrooms

1 tablespoon chives, minced

$^1/_2$ teaspoon salt, or to taste

$^1/_4$ teaspoon freshly ground black pepper, or to taste

2 tablespoons butter

1 teaspoon lemon juice

Trim the ends of the asparagus, then cut on the bias into 1-inch long pieces. Wipe the mushrooms clean, trim the stems, and cut into quarters or slice thin.

Heat the oil in a large skillet over medium heat. Add the shallots and cook until aromatic, about 1 minute. Add the morels and a pinch of salt; sauté, stirring frequently, until the morels are very hot, about 4–5 minutes. Remove the mushroom mixture from the skillet and fold in the chives.

Heat the water in the same skillet over high heat. Add the asparagus, salt, and pepper. Cover the skillet and pan-steam over high heat until the asparagus are tender and bright green, about 6–7 minutes. (There should be about ⅓ of a cup of liquid in bottom of the pan; pour off if excessive or add a bit of water if dry.)

Add the mushroom mixture to the asparagus and sauté, stirring until evenly blended and very hot. Add the butter and continue to cook, swirling the pan over the heat, just until the butter melts and thickens the liquid enough to cling to the vegetables. Taste and adjust the seasoning with salt and pepper if needed. Drizzle the lemon juice over the asparagus. Serve at once.

Asian Vegetable Slaw

MAKES 8 SERVINGS | PREPARATION TIME: 30 MINUTES

*S*weet and tangy, this recipe combines the delicious texture of thinly sliced vegetables with a quick and easy vinaigrette, and is sure to be the perfect accompaniment to your favorite Asian entrée.

1 head savoy cabbage,
   chiffonade

5 carrots, thinly sliced

1/2 cup cilantro, chopped

1 head red cabbage, chiffonade

5 scallions, sliced thin on bias

DRESSING

1 cup peanut oil

1/2 cup rice wine vinegar

2 tablespoons soy sauce

Cayenne pepper, to taste

1/2 cup peanuts, toasted, chopped

1/4 cup sesame seeds, toasted

Toss together the cabbage, carrots, cilantro, and scallions.

Mix the ingredients for the dressing together and pour them over the cabbage mixture. Adjust the seasoning as necessary with the cayenne pepper.

Toss in the peanuts and 3 tablespoons of the sesame seeds.

Sprinkle the remaining sesame seeds on the top of the dish to garnish.

Tabbouleh Salad

Tabbouleh Salad is shown here with Hummus and Pita Chips, page 21.

*T*his recipe offers a faithful rendition of a healthful Middle Eastern favorite that is, according to some, more a parsley salad with some bulgur than the other way around.

3 cups bulgur

6 cups boiling water

1¹/₂ cups parsley, chopped

6 cups tomatoes, diced

1 cup scallions, finely sliced

¹/₄ cup mint, chopped

DRESSING

1 cup extra-virgin olive oil

¹/₂ cup lemon juice

2 teaspoons salt, or to taste

2 teaspoons freshly ground black pepper, or to taste

Place the bulgur in a bowl. Add the boiling water, cover, and allow to soak for 30 minutes, or until the bulgur is tender. Drain any excess water, if necessary.

In a large bowl, combine the bulgur with the parsley, tomatoes, scallions, and mint.

Whisk together the dressing ingredients, pour over the salad, and toss to coat evenly.

The salad is ready to serve now, or it may be held under refrigeration.

Bulgur and Lentil Pilaf
with Caramelized Onions

MAKES 8 SERVINGS | PREPARATION TIME: 45 MINUTES

*T*his healthy and delicious combination of bulgur wheat and lentils makes for an appealing grain-based side dish, packed with the flavor of sweet caramelized onions and spicy crushed red pepper flakes.

1 cup lentils, washed

6½ cups chicken broth, or water

3 tablespoons butter

3 tablespoons olive oil

5 onions, peeled, halved, thinly sliced

2 cups bulgur, coarse grain

Salt, to taste

Freshly ground black pepper, to taste

1 tablespoon tomato paste

¼ teaspoon crushed red pepper flakes

Boil the lentils in 3 cups of chicken broth or water until tender, about 20 minutes. Reserve any residual cooking liquid.

While the lentils are cooking, heat the butter and olive oil in a medium sauté pan over medium heat. Slowly sauté onions until caramelized, about 15 minutes. Reserve in pan.

Bring the remaining 3½ cups chicken stock or water to a boil, adding bulgur, residual cooking liquid, salt and tomato paste. Reduce the heat to low and cook, covered, for 20 minutes.

Add the black pepper and red pepper flakes to the caramelized onions. Pour the mixture over the bulgur and add the lentils, stirring gently. Season with salt and pepper, as needed.

Potato Gratin

MAKES 6 SERVINGS | PREPARATION TIME: 45 MINUTES

See photograph on page 143.

Gruyère is the cheese classically used in a potato gratin. This cow's milk cheese, produced in Switzerland and France, has a nutty, rich flavor and melts beautifully.

1 pound russet potatoes, peeled, cut into
  $1/4$-inch slices
1 cup whole milk
1 cup heavy cream

1 garlic clove, minced
$1/2$ teaspoon salt, or to taste
$1/4$ teaspoon freshly ground black pepper,
  or to taste

$1/2$ cup Gruyère cheese, grated
3 tablespoons breadcrumbs
3 tablespoons Parmesan cheese

Combine the potatoes, milk, heavy cream, garlic, salt, and pepper in a large saucepan. Simmer until the potatoes are three-quarters cooked, about 8–10 minutes.

Remove the potatoes from the heat and stir in the Gruyère.

Pour the potatoes into a small, shallow pan. Combine the breadcrumbs and Parmesan and scatter evenly over the potatoes. Bake in a 350°F oven until golden brown, about 30 minutes. Allow the potatoes to set for 5–7 minutes before slicing.

Oven-Roasted Potatoes

MAKES 6 SERVINGS | PREPARATION TIME: 45 MINUTES

See photograph on page 138.

Never underestimate a simple, proven favorite. Potato wedges tossed with a bit of oil and fresh herbs provide an excellent accompaniment to roasted meats or fowl.

2 pounds russet potatoes, sliced into
  $1^1/2$-inch × $1/2$-inch wedges
$1^1/2$ tablespoons olive oil

2 teaspoons rosemary, chopped
4 garlic cloves, minced

$1/2$ teaspoon black peppercorns, crushed
1 teaspoon salt, or to taste

Preheat a baking sheet or roasting pan in a 400°F oven.

Toss the potatoes with the oil, rosemary, garlic, pepper, and salt. Spread the potatoes in a single layer on the preheated pan.

Roast the potatoes in the oven until browned on one side, about 15 minutes. Flip the potatoes and continue roasting until they are golden brown on the second side and tender, about 15 minutes.

Potato Puree

MAKES 6 SERVINGS | PREPARATION TIME: 35 MINUTES

See photograph on page 194.

This basic recipe lends itself to a myriad of variations, including the two that are listed below. Leaving the skins on makes for a more rustic presentation that is just as tasty.

2¹/₄ pounds russet potatoes, peeled and quartered

2 tablespoons salt

³/₄ cup butter

1 cup milk

1 cup heavy cream

1¹/₂ teaspoons salt, or to taste

³/₄ teaspoon freshly ground black pepper, or to taste

Place the potatoes in a pot with enough cold water to cover by about 2 inches with 2 tablespoons salt. Simmer the potatoes until cooked through, about 20–25 minutes.

While the potatoes are boiling, melt the butter and add the milk and cream. Keep warm.

Drain the potatoes and return them to the heat. Add the cream mixture and mash the potatoes using a potato masher, mixer, or handheld blender. Season the potatoes with salt and pepper. Serve immediately.

VARIATIONS:

Fried Garlic and Asiago Cheese Mashed Potatoes: While the potatoes are boiling, melt the butter over medium-high heat. Add 6 tablespoons roughly chopped garlic and fry until light golden brown, about 5 minutes. Add the cream and milk and allow the flavors to blend together. Add the mixture to the potatoes and mash. Stir in ¹/₂ cup Asiago cheese and season with salt and pepper.

Herbed Mashed Potatoes: Add 2 tablespoons of chopped rosemary and 2 tablespoons chopped sage to the cream-butter mixture and allow to steep while the potatoes are boiling. Add the herb mixture to the potatoes and mash. Season with salt and pepper.

Mediterranean Potato Salad

MAKES 8 SERVINGS | PREPARATION TIME: 45 MINUTES

*P*ut a new spin on potato salad. The pungent flavors of anchovy, capers and garlic come together with two delicious vinegars for a refreshing new version of an old favorite.

2³/₄ pounds waxy potatoes (such as Yukon Gold), peeled and quartered

1 cup extra-virgin olive oil

3 ounces red wine vinegar

2 tablespoons balsamic vinegar

¹/₂ cup parsley, chopped

¹/₄ cup capers

1 tablespoon anchovies, chopped

1 teaspoon garlic, minced

1 teaspoon salt, to taste

¹/₄ teaspoon ground white pepper, ground

Simmer the potatoes in salted water until just tender, about 15–18 minutes.

While the potatoes are cooking, mix the dressing ingredients.

Drain the potatoes and dry briefly to remove any excess moisture. Dice the potatoes while still hot and place them in a bowl.

Mix the dressing to recombine, and pour over the potatoes.

Serve the salad warm, or chill and serve at room temperature.

Warm Potato Salad

MAKES 8 SERVINGS | PREPARATION TIME: 30 MINUTES

See photograph on page 247.

*W*hile the potatoes are simmering and cooling, prepare the rest of the ingredients for this simple and satisfying potato salad.

3 pounds baby red potatoes

6 tablespoons olive oil

¹/₄ cup cider vinegar

3¹/₂ tablespoons parsley, chopped

2 tablespoons shallots, minced

1¹/₂ tablespoons Dijon mustard

1¹/₂ tablespoons tarragon, chopped

1¹/₂ teaspoons sugar

¹/₂ teaspoon salt, or to taste

¹/₄ teaspoon freshly ground black pepper, or to taste

Simmer the potatoes in salted water until just tender, about 15–18 minutes. When cool enough to handle, slice ¼-inch thick.

In a large bowl, whisk together the remaining ingredients. Gently toss the potatoes in the dressing and serve warm.

Sweet Potato Cakes

MAKES 8 SERVINGS | PREPARATION TIME: 40 MINUTES

See photograph on page 154.

*R*usset potato, chives, and sage balance the flavor of sweet potato in these creamy cakes. To save on cleanup, cook both types of potato in the same pan-but keep an eye on them because sweet potatoes tend to cook faster than russets.

3 russet potatoes, peeled, quartered

2 sweet potatoes, peeled, quartered

$^2/_3$ cup breadcrumbs

$^1/_3$ cup milk

2 tablespoons mayonnaise

2 tablespoons chives, chopped

1 tablespoon sage, chopped

$^1/_2$ teaspoon salt, or to taste

$^1/_4$ teaspoon freshly ground black pepper, or to taste

Preheat the oven to 250°F.

Combine the russet and sweet potatoes and enough water to cover in a large saucepan. Bring to a boil; reduce the heat and simmer, covered, until the sweet potatoes are tender, about 15 minutes.

Using tongs, transfer the sweet potatoes to a baking sheet and continue to simmer the russet potatoes until tender, 5–10 minutes more.

Drain the russet potatoes and place on the baking sheet. Place the potatoes in the oven to steam-dry, about 5 minutes.

Remove from the oven and increase the oven temperature to 475°F.

Pass the hot potatoes through a food mill or ricer set over a large bowl. Let stand until slightly cooled. Stir in the breadcrumbs, milk, mayonnaise, chives, sage, salt, and pepper. Form into 16 small cakes, about ½-inch thick. Spray a baking sheet with cooking spray and arrange the cakes on the baking sheet.

Bake until the cakes are golden on both sides, turning if necessary as they bake (use a gentle touch so they don't fall apart), about 12 minutes total.

Steak Fries

MAKES 6 SERVINGS | PREPARATION TIME: 35 MINUTES

See photograph on page 196.

*T*he secret to this recipe is the temperature of the oil. Be sure that the oil is not too hot in the beginning or the fries will be undercooked on the inside and golden brown on the outside. If possible, do a test run with a couple of fries to make sure that the oil is at the correct temperature. As a bonus, you can eat what you test!

3 pounds yukon gold potatoes	2 cups olive oil, or as needed	1 teaspoon sea salt, or to taste

Slice potatoes skin on, to ½-inch × ½-inch thick fries.

Place olive oil in a large frying pan or Dutch oven over medium-high heat and carefully heat oil, just until the surface of the oil shimmers slightly without reaching smoke point.

Reduce heat to medium and gently place steak fries into hot oil. Cook the fries for 10–15 minutes without color, but allow the exterior to begin crisping, while moving pan gently to prevent sticking.

When fries are almost fully cooked, increase heat slightly and allow fries to crisp to light golden brown.

Remove the fries from the oil to a plate or a baking sheet lined with clean paper toweling and drain slightly.

Place in a large bowl and toss gently with sea salt.

Serve immediately.

German Potato Salad

MAKES 8 SERVINGS | PREPARATION TIME: 35 MINUTES

*T*his hearty potato salad is typically made from sliced potatoes, bacon, onions, and celery. A small amount of bacon fat is used to flavor the vinaigrette that seasons this dish. It is most often served warm or at room temperature for the very best flavor.

2 $\frac{1}{4}$ pounds potatoes (waxy variety, such as Yukon Gold)

4 slices bacon

2$\frac{1}{2}$ cups chicken broth

$\frac{1}{4}$ cup white wine vinegar

1 cup onions, diced

1 teaspoon salt, or to taste

1 teaspoon sugar, or to taste

$\frac{1}{4}$ teaspoon ground white pepper

$\frac{1}{4}$ cup vegetable oil

2 tablespoons mild brown mustard

$\frac{1}{2}$ bunch chives, snipped

Cook the potatoes in simmering salted water until just tender, about 15–18 minutes. Drain and dry. While the potatoes are still hot, remove the skins and slice the potatoes ½-inch thick.

While the potatoes are cooking, prepare the dressing. Cook the bacon over medium-high heat until the fat has rendered and the bacon is crisp. Remove the bacon to a plate with a slotted spoon, reserving the bacon fat in the pan; crumble the bacon into small pieces, and reserve.

Bring the chicken broth, vinegar, onions, salt, sugar, and pepper to a boil.

Combine the oil, rendered bacon fat, and mustard with the warm potatoes. Pour the boiling broth-vinegar mixture over the potatoes. Toss in the crumbled bacon and chives.

The salad may be served warm, at room temperature, or chilled.

Boiled Potatoes
with Saffron and Parsley

See photograph on page 181.

Boiled new potatoes, flecked with saffron and fresh green herbs, are a simple and appealing accompaniment to a variety of entrées, from grilled meats and poultry to more subtly flavored seafood dishes.

1½ pounds baby red potatoes

Pinch saffron

2 tablespoons salt

3 tablespoons butter

3 tablespoons parsley, chopped

Salt, to taste

Freshly ground black pepper, to taste

Place the potatoes in a pot with enough cold water to cover by about 2 inches. Add the saffron and salt.

Simmer the potatoes until just tender, about 15–18 minutes.

Drain the potatoes. Return them to the pot and dry briefly over very low heat until the steam evaporates from the potatoes.

Heat the butter in a large sauté pan, and add the parsley and potatoes. Toss gently and season with salt and pepper as needed.

Jalapeño Jack Polenta

MAKES 8 SERVINGS | PREPARATION TIME: 35 MINUTES

See photograph on page 145.

This hearty, warm side dish can be made with the cheese incorporated into the polenta or the polenta can be spooned atop a portion of the cheeses, so that as they melt they form a liquid center.

4 cups water

3/4 cup yellow cornmeal

1/4 cup Parmesan cheese, grated

1/2 pound Jalapeño Jack cheese, grated

Salt, to taste

1/4 teaspoon ground white pepper

Heat the water to a simmer in a medium saucepan. Gradually pour the cornmeal into the water while stirring constantly. Cook over low heat, stirring frequently with a wooden spoon, until the polenta pulls away from the sides of the pan, 25–30 minutes.

Remove the pan from the heat and stir in the Parmesan and Jack cheeses, salt, and pepper.

Serve the polenta immediately.

Corn, Pepper, and Jicama Salad

MAKES 8 SERVINGS | PREPARATION TIME: 35 MINUTES

*T*his colorful, crunchy salad is best served at room temperature. Jicama (HEE-kah-mah), also know as the Mexican potato, is a root vegetable with a sweet flavor and a texture like an apple. Use a sharp paring knife to trim its thin skin just before using.

2¹/₂ cups corn kernels, fresh or frozen

1 jicama, peeled and cut into thin strips

1 red onion, thinly sliced

1 red bell pepper, cut into thin strips

1 green bell pepper, cut into thin strips

1 jalapeño, seeded, minced

4 tablespoons red wine vinegar

4 tablespoons olive oil

2 tablespoons water

1 teaspoon dry mustard

1 teaspoon salt, or to taste

1 tablespoon garlic clove, minced

Freshly ground black pepper, to taste

Put the corn and 2 inches of water in a saucepan and bring to a boil. Reduce the heat and simmer, covered, until tender, 3–5 minutes. Drain well.

Combine the corn, jicama, onion, bell peppers, and the jalapeño in a large bowl.

Whisk together the vinegar, oil, water, mustard, salt, garlic, and pepper in a small bowl. Add the dressing to the vegetables and toss to coat.

Lima Bean and Roasted Corn Succotash

MAKES 8 SERVINGS | PREPARATION TIME: 35 MINUTES

*T*his recipe can be made year round using frozen lima beans, but the fresh beans have a creamy texture and appealing flavor that is unmistakably better. You are most likely to find fresh lima beans at your local farmers' market in the early summer.

1½ pounds lima beans, frozen

4 cups corn kernels, fresh or frozen

⅓ cup chives, minced

1 tablespoon tarragon, chopped

1 tablespoon butter

1 teaspoon salt, or to taste

1 teaspoon freshly ground black pepper, or to taste

Bring the lima beans and 1 inch of water to a boil in a saucepan. Reduce the heat and simmer, covered, until tender, about 3 minutes for fresh or 5 minutes for frozen beans. Drain and set aside.

While the lima beans are simmering, put the 4 cups of corn and 2 inches of water in a saucepan and bring to a boil. Re-duce the heat and simmer, covered, until tender, 3–5 minutes. Drain well and roast the corn in a large, dry cast iron skillet, stirring occasionally, until golden brown, about 3 minutes. Stir in the lima beans, chives, tarragon, butter, salt, and pepper. Cook until the flavors are blended, about 5 minutes. Serve at once.

Cornbread

*T*his recipe has been used in the school for a number of years and produces a moist cornbread with a delicate crumb. It is quite versatile and can be made into cornbread muffins as well.

½ cup sugar

2 tablespoons milk powder

1 teaspoon salt

1¼ cups bread flour

½ cup cornmeal

3½ teaspoons baking powder

2 eggs

5 ounces water

¼ teaspoon vanilla extract

6 tablespoons corn oil

Preheat the oven to 350°F.

Combine all of the dry ingredients in a bowl and mix thoroughly.

Combine the wet ingredients and mix thoroughly. Add the wet ingredients to the dry ingredients and mix together.

Grease a 10½-inch long, 7-inch wide, and 1-inch deep baking pan.

Pour the batter in the pan and bake at 350°F for 22–25 minutes, or until a knife inserted in the center comes out clean and the top of the cornbread springs back lightly to the touch.

Allow the cornbread to cool slightly before cutting. Cut the cornbread into twelve rectangular pieces and serve two per person.

Vegetarian Dirty Rice

MAKES 8 SERVINGS | PREPARATION TIME: 30 MINUTES

*A*lthough traditional dirty rice is decidedly not vegetarian, this variation might have purists ready to convert. It combines a variety of robust flavors into a dish that would enhance any item that it is served with.

6 ounces pinto beans, canned

$^1/_2$ cup onion, diced

$^1/_2$ tablespoon garlic, minced

1 tablespoon peanut oil

$^3/_4$ cup long grain rice

$1^1/_2$ cups vegetable broth

1 tablespoon tomato paste

1 tablespoon white balsamic vinegar

2 teaspoons chipotle peppers, chopped

1 teaspoon cumin seeds

Salt, to taste

1 teaspoon freshly ground black pepper, or to taste

1 teaspoon paprika

$^1/_4$ teaspoon cayenne pepper

$^1/_2$ cup aged cheddar cheese, grated

$^1/_2$ cup corn kernels, fresh or frozen, cooked

2 tablespoons cilantro, chopped

Rinse the beans under cold water and drain. Mash the beans with a fork and reserve. In a medium saucepan over medium-high heat, sweat the onions and garlic in the oil until translucent, about 3–4 minutes.

Add the rice and sauté briefly, about 1 minute.

Add the broth, tomato paste, vinegar, chipotle pepper, cumin, pepper, paprika, and cayenne. Bring the broth to a boil and cover the pot tightly, turn the heat to low and cook for approximately 15 minutes until rice is tender.

Fold the mashed beans, cheese, and corn into the rice, and garnish with cilantro.

Basic Rice Pilaf

MAKES 8 SERVINGS | PREPARATION TIME: 25 MINUTES

The Asian Variation of Basic Rice Pilaf is shown here.

Pilafs—in their simplest form, a grain, usually rice or bulgur, sautéed in butter or oil, then cooked in broth—are typically started on the stovetop but finished in the oven, leaving you free to finish other preparation tasks in the meantime.

2 tablespoons olive oil

1/3 cup onions, diced

1 clove garlic, minced

1 1/2 cups long-grain white rice

3 cups chicken or vegetable broth

1 teaspoon salt, or to taste

1/2 teaspoon freshly ground black pepper,
   or to taste

1 bay leaf

1 sprig thyme

Preheat the oven to 350°F. Simmer the broth and reserve.

Heat the olive oil in a 2-quart saucepan over medium heat. Add the onions and garlic and sweat until translucent, about 3–4 minutes. Add the rice and sauté, stirring constantly, until the grains are well coated and aromatic, about 2–3 minutes.

Add the warm broth, salt, pepper, bay leaf, and thyme, and bring to a boil, stirring constantly. Cover the pot and cook in a 350°F oven until the rice is tender and has absorbed all the liq-uid, about 20 minutes. Let the pilaf stand for 5 minutes, remove and discard the bay leaf and thyme, then fluff with a fork to separate the grains and release steam before serving.

VARIATION: *Asian Rice Pilaf*

Substitute a 1-inch piece of ginger for the bay leaf and thyme. Leave the ginger in the mixture through the cooking process and remove just before serving. Garnish the finished pilaf with 2 tablespoons of chopped cilantro and 1 tablespoon of toasted sesame seeds.

ABOVE, LEFT TO RIGHT: Sweat the aromatic vegetables in oil until softened; add the grains and sauté until they are well coated with fat and smell slightly toasted. Add the seasonings and warm broth to the grains, bring to a boil, cover the pot, and cook in a 350°F oven for about 20 minutes. Let the pilaf stand for 5 minutes, uncover, and fluff with a fork. Adjust the seasoning and serve.

Wild Rice Pilaf

MAKES 6 SERVINGS | PREPARATION TIME: 45 MINUTES

See photograph on page 184.

*T*his simple dish of wild rice, shallots and garlic is cooked pilaf-style for an easy "hands-free" side that takes care of itself. Any combination of garnishes can be added at the end to the cooked pilaf, including sliced toasted almonds, sliced scallions or a favorite dried fruit that has been diced and re-hydrated slightly in a touch of juice, white wine or warm water.

3 tablespoons olive oil	1^1/$_2$ cups wild rice blend	^{1}/$_2$ teaspoon freshly ground black pepper, or to taste
6 tablespoons shallots, minced	4^1/$_2$ cups chicken or vegetable broth	
2 tablespoons garlic, minced	1 teaspoon salt, or to taste	

Preheat the oven to 350°F. Simmer the broth and reserve.

Heat the olive oil in a 2-quart saucepan over medium heat. Add the shallots and garlic and sweat until translucent, about 3–4 minutes. Add the rice and sauté until the grains are well coated and aromatic, about 2–3 minutes.

Add the warm broth, salt, and pepper, and bring to a boil. Cover the pot and cook in a 350°F oven until the rice is tender and has absorbed all the liquid, about 20 minutes. Let the pilaf stand for 5 minutes, then fluff with a fork to separate the grains and release steam before serving. Season with additional salt and pepper before serving, if desired.

Spicy Dill Rice

MAKES 8 SERVINGS | PREPARATION TIME: 35 MINUTES

*D*ill, cardamom, and jalapeño come together to lend an interesting twist to basmati rice. Packed with flavor, this rice is terrific with poultry or seafood entrees.

2 tablespoons peanut oil

1 cup onions, chopped

1 teaspoon ground cardamom

1 jalapeño, chopped

1 1/2 cups basmati rice

1/2 cup dill, chopped

1 teaspoon salt, or to taste

3 cups chicken or vegetable broth

Heat the oil in a 2-quart saucepan over medium heat. Add the onions, cardamom, and jalapeño, and sauté for one minute. Add the rice and sauté, stirring constantly, until the grains are well coated, about 1 minute. Add the dill and the salt and sauté over low heat for 2 minutes.

Add the broth, cover, and cook over low heat until the rice is tender and has absorbed all the liquid, about 25 minutes. Let the rice stand for 5 minutes, then fluff with a fork to separate the grains and release steam before serving.

Rice Salad

MAKES 8 SERVINGS | PREPARATION TIME: 45 MINUTES

*R*ice salads are commonly served in the north of Italy as a hearty cold side dish. Garnishes of seasonal vegetables, olives, and corn are often added.

1 cup long-grain white rice

8 marinated artichoke hearts,
    sliced in eighths

¹/₂ cup Gruyère cheese, diced

¹/₂ cup ham, diced

¹/₄ cup Nicoise olives, pitted,

¹/₄ cup green olives, small, pitted

3 tablespoons extra-virgin olive oil

Juice of ¹/₂ lemon

2 teaspoons salt, or to taste

¹/₂ teaspoon freshly ground black pepper,
    or to taste

2 scallions, trimmed, sliced thinly on a bias

Bring the rice to a boil in salted water. Cover, and cook over low heat until the rice is tender and has absorbed all the liquid, about 25 minutes. Spread the cooked rice on a baking sheet to cool rapidly.

Place the cooled rice into a large mixing bowl and add the artichoke hearts, Gruyère, ham, and olives.

Add the olive oil, lemon juice, salt, and pepper, and toss well to coat. Adjust the seasoning as needed and garnish with the sliced scallions.

Coconut Rice with Ginger

MAKES 8 SERVINGS | PREPARATION TIME: 30 MINUTES

Coconut Rice with Ginger can be made with many different variations. At the point when you fluff the rice prior to serving, try stirring in one of the following: 2 cups raisins, 2 cups sliced almonds, 1¾ cups pistachios, 8 seeded and chopped jalapeños, or 2 cups shredded coconut.

¼ cup butter	1½ cups long-grain white rice	1 tablespoon salt, or to taste
4 garlic cloves, minced	1 cup coconut milk	1 teaspoon freshly ground black pepper, or to taste
2½ tablespoons ginger, minced	2 cups water	

Heat the butter in a 2-quart saucepan over medium heat. Add the garlic and ginger and sauté until aromatic, about 2–3 minutes. Add the rice and sauté, stirring constantly, until the grains are well coated with butter, about 1 minute.

Add the coconut milk, water, salt, and pepper, and bring the mixture to a boil. Reduce the heat, cover, and cook the rice until tender, about 25 minutes.

Let the rice stand for 5 minutes, then fluff with a fork to separate the grains and release steam before serving.

Curried Rice Salad

MAKES 8 SERVINGS | PREPARATION TIME: 40 MINUTES

*B*asmati rice, raisins, pumpkin seeds and curry come together in this unique rice salad. Served at room temperature or lightly chilled, this dish is an excellent alternative to typical rice or potato salad.

2^1/$_2$ cups chicken or vegetable broth

1^1/$_2$ cups basmati rice

1 tablespoon curry powder

^{1}/$_4$ cup peanut oil

^{1}/$_4$ cup pumpkin seeds, toasted

2 tablespoons rice wine vinegar

3 tablespoons golden raisins

^{1}/$_2$ cup onions, chopped

1 cup Granny Smith apple, diced

Salt, to taste

^{1}/$_4$ teaspoon freshly ground black pepper, or to taste

^{1}/$_2$ cup peas, frozen

Bring the broth to a boil in a 2-quart saucepan. Add the rice and cover, cooking over low heat until the rice is tender and has absorbed all the liquid, about 25 minutes.

Lightly toast the curry powder in a small sauté pan over low heat, about 30 seconds.

Add the oil and toast the pumpkin seeds over medium heat until golden brown, about 3 minutes.

Remove the pan from the heat and add the vinegar, raisins, onions, apple, salt, and pepper.

Place the pan back on low heat and sauté for one minute. Add the peas and cook for an additional minute.

Place the contents in a large bowl and allow to cool in the refrigerator as the rice continues to cook.

Remove the rice from the heat, toss it in the bowl with the curry mixture, and allow the mixture to cool in the refrigerator for an additional 10 minutes before serving.

Herbed Basmati Rice

MAKES 8 SERVINGS | PREPARATION TIME: 30 MINUTES

See photograph on page 175.

Basmati is an aromatic, long-grain rice with a sweet and nutty flavor, commonly paired with dishes boasting the bold flavor profiles of the Far East.

1/4 cup canola oil	3 cups water	1 tablespoon mint, chopped
1 garlic clove, minced	1/2 bay leaf	1 tablespoon cilantro, chopped
1 1/2 cups basmati rice	2 thyme sprigs	

Heat the oil in a 2-quart saucepan over medium heat. Add the garlic and cook, stirring frequently, until translucent, about 2 minutes.

Add the rice and sauté, stirring constantly, until the grains are well coated with oil, about 1 minute. Add the water, bay leaf, and thyme, cover, and cook over low heat until the rice is tender and has absorbed all the liquid, about 25 minutes.

Let the pilaf stand for 5 minutes, remove and discard the bay leaf and thyme, then fluff with a fork to separate the grains and release steam. Fold in the mint and cilantro and serve.

Quick Couscous

Gaining in popularity more pervasively, couscous originated in the cuisines of North Africa. This quick couscous recipe can be tailored with a number of variations; some are listed below.

3 cups water

2 tablespoons butter

2 tablespoons salt, or to taste

2 cups couscous

Bring the water to a boil in a 2 quart saucepan. Add the butter and salt. Stir in the couscous, making sure that all of it is wet.

Cover, and set the saucepan aside in a warm place for 15–20 minutes, or until the couscous is tender.

VARIATIONS:

Pine Nut and Raisin Couscous: After the couscous and water are combined, stir in $1/2$ a cup of golden raisins and $1/2$ cup of toasted pine nuts.

Curry Couscous: Add 2 tablespoons of curry powder with the butter.

Herbed Israeli Couscous

MAKES 8 SERVINGS | PREPARATION TIME: 25 MINUTES

See photograph on page 238

Many people might not know about Israeli couscous and would be surprised to find out that it is pasta. It can be used in a variety of ways and has even been used as "vegetarian caviar." Here, it is paired beautifully with a variety of savory herbs.

2 tablespoons olive oil

2 cups Israeli couscous

4 cups chicken or vegetable broth

$1/4$ cup parsley, chopped

1 tablespoon tarragon, chopped

1 tablespoon rosemary, chopped

$1/4$ cup lemon juice

1 teaspoon salt, or to taste

$1/2$ teaspoon freshly ground black pepper, or to taste

Heat the olive oil in a 2-quart saucepan over medium heat. Add the couscous and sauté, stirring constantly, until well coated and aromatic, about 2–3 minutes.

Add the broth and bring to a boil. Reduce the heat to medium-low and simmer until just tender, about 10–12 minutes.

Add the herbs and lemon juice. Season with salt and pepper.

Red Pepper Orzo

MAKES 8 SERVINGS | PREPARATION TIME: 35 MINUTES

*I*n Italian, *orzo* literally means barley, but most commonly it refers to little pasta that have a rice- or diamond-like shape. This quick-cooking pasta makes for a hearty dish combining red pepper, herbs, fennel, and feta cheese.

$\frac{1}{2}$ pound orzo

2 teaspoons salt, or to taste

$\frac{1}{4}$ cup olive oil

1 red onion, diced

1 red pepper, diced

1 green pepper, diced

1 fennel bulb, finely diced

1 tablespoon garlic, chopped

1 tablespoon thyme, chopped

$\frac{1}{2}$ cup tomato juice

$\frac{1}{4}$ cup parsley, chopped

1 teaspoon freshly ground black pepper, or to taste

1 cup feta cheese, crumbled

Boil the orzo in salted water until tender, about 8–10 minutes. Drain and rinse under cold water. Toss the orzo with 3 tablespoons of the olive oil, cover, and refrigerate.

In a large saucepan, sauté the onions, peppers, and fennel in the remaining 1 tablespoon of olive oil until just tender, about

4 minutes. Add the garlic and thyme and cook an additional 2 minutes.

Toss the sautéed vegetables with the reserved orzo. Add the tomato juice. Toss in the parsley, pepper, feta cheese, and remaining 1 teaspoon of salt.

CHAPTER TEN

Desserts

Serving something sweet is the perfect way to end any meal. You don't have to spend hours to make great desserts. This chapter is full of helpful tips to facilitate your dessert-making experience. A key element is to utilize a variety of high-quality prepared items to make your own specialty—strudel dough wrapped around sliced and seasoned fruits (Apple Strudel, page 348), a crisp shell (classically known as Vol-au-Vent, page 339) made from puff pastry, or sheets of puff pastry topped with fruit and crimped around a filling for a rustic galette (Fresh Fruit Galette, page 350) are some of the options available to the busy cook with a well-stocked freezer.

Sweets aren't just for dessert, of course. Freshly baked cookies are a perfect afternoon treat, with a glass of milk or a cup of tea or coffee. The cookie recipes featured in this chapter are not only delicious, they are also quick and easy to prepare. Rather than buying slice-and-bake cookie dough at the store, you can make your own dough, then store it in the refrigerator or freezer, ready to slice and bake. Freshly baked cookies are just minutes away, perfect for when an unexpected guest stops by or your sweet tooth kicks in (page 344).

Dessert sauces are an easy way to make a dessert memorable. Something as simple as Rice Pudding (page 357) is brought to another level when accompanied by Apple Cider and Raisin Sauce (page 335). There is a great variety of dessert

sauce recipes included in this chapter, all of which can take a bowl of ice cream from ordinary to extraordinary.

Selection

Frozen pastry doughs are perfect to have on hand for last-minute desserts. You can choose from puff pastry sheets (often sold in a 17-ounce box that contains two 8-inch square sheets), or pre-shaped shells (or vol-au-vents). See pages 333 and 339.

Another extremely versatile frozen dough is phyllo. Phyllo is rolled into paper-thin sheets, available in two different sizes: 11 × 16 inches or 8 × 12 inches. See pages 348–349.

In addition to these purchased frozen doughs, you can prepare crêpes to have on hand. To freeze your own crêpes (page 362), stack them with wax or parchment paper in between, wrap well, and freeze for up to 8 weeks.

Preparation

Look for prepared doughs in the freezer case at the grocery store. Keep them frozen until you are ready to use them.

Most doughs thaw adequately in 3 or 4 hours in the refrigerator. If you are in a rush, most will thaw well at room temperature in about 20 minutes.

To use puff pastry sheets, unfold the sheet carefully and put it on a floured surface. Roll it with a lightly floured rolling pin to even out the thickness.

Since phyllo sheets are so thin and delicate, you need to set up your work area to keep them from drying out. Before you unwrap the dough, have the filling prepared (and cooled, if necessary), the butter melted, and all the tools you need, including baking sheets, ready.

Unwrap the phyllo sheets and lay them flat on a work surface. Cover the sheets with plastic and then with lightly dampened paper or flatweave towels. Lift up this covering and slide a sheet of phyllo onto the work surface. Replace the covering to keep the phyllo you aren't working with from drying out. Brush the phyllo evenly with butter, and then repeat to make a stack with as many sheets as called for in your recipe.

STEP-BY-STEP | Working with Cookie and Pastry Doughs

By making a few advance preparations, and keeping time-saving ingredients like frozen puff pastry sheets and dessert shells on hand, it is possible to produce delicious, homemade baked goods in the quick kitchen. The following tips will help simplify the process:

➥ WRAPPING COOKIE DOUGHS TO REFRIGERATE OR FREEZE

To make later shaping and baking easy, freeze the dough in a log. First lay a piece of plastic wrap, parchment, wax, or freezer paper on a work surface. Cut the paper 16–18 inches long with the long edge parallel to the edge of the work surface.

Roll the dough into a relatively even log. Place the log on the plastic wrap or paper and roll, while pushing against the paper-encased dough to give the cylinder an even diameter. Once the dough is the correct diameter, twist the ends of the plastic wrap or paper and fold them inwards to seal.

➥ ROLLING OUT TART DOUGH TO CHILL OR FREEZE

When working with tart dough you have more than one option. You can simply shape the dough into a flat disk, wrap it well in plastic wrap, put it in a zipper-lock bag, and refrigerate (up to 4 days) or freeze (up to 8 weeks). Let refrigerated dough rest at room temperature for a few minutes before rolling it out. Thaw frozen dough in the refrigerator for 4–8 hours before rolling.

Another option, if time permits, is to roll out the dough, fit it into a disposable pie or tart pan, and crimp or flute the edges. To protect the dough, you can set a second pie pan inside the lined pan.

Wrap the assembly well and freeze it for up to 8 weeks before par-baking and adding a filling.

➥ SLICING COOKIE DOUGH TO BAKE

Unwrap the dough and use a sharp knife to make even slices of a consistent thickness. Set the sliced cookies onto a lightly greased cookie sheet and bake. Leave about 2 inches between most cookies so that they have enough room to spread while they bake without running into each other.

➥ BAKING AND FILLING PUFF PASTRY SHELLS

Keep pre-shaped puff pastry refrigerated until you are ready to put it into the oven. The oven should be preheated properly before you start to bake the shells for the best height and appearance. Bake them until they are crisp and light (follow the timing instructions on the package). Pastry shells are already docked and crimped so that the sides puff up and leave behind a hollow that you can fill with berries and whipped cream.

➥ MAKING GALETTES FROM PUFF PASTRY

A galette is a rustic pie baked without a pie or tart pan. Using a 6-inch saucer as a guide, cut dough circles out of a sheet of puff pastry. Mound the filling in the center of each, leaving a border around the edge. Fold this edge up to keep the filling and any juices from running off the side of the pastry and crimp slightly so that it stays in place.

See the step-by-step photographs accompanying the recipes for Sand Cookies (page 344) and the Fresh Fruit Galette (page 350).

Classic Caramel Sauce

MAKES 2 CUPS | PREPARATION TIME: 15 MINUTES

See photograph on page 358.

Sugar burns easily, so be sure to use a heavy-bottomed pot to prevent the caramel from scorching. When adding the warm cream, take the pot off the heat as the hot caramel will foam up, and possibly spatter, when the liquid is added. Serve this delicious caramel sauce either hot or cold, over ice cream, or with Apple Strudel (page 348).

1½ cups heavy cream
1 cup sugar

½ cup corn syrup

2 tablespoons butter, soft, cubed

Pour the cream into a saucepan and bring to a boil over medium heat. Reduce the temperature and keep the cream warm over very low heat.

Prepare an ice bath large enough to accommodate the pan that the caramel will be cooked in. Combine the sugar and corn syrup in a heavy-bottomed saucepan and slowly cook over moderate heat, stirring constantly until all of the sugar has dissolved. Stop stirring and continue to cook to a golden caramel.

Remove the caramel from the heat and shock the saucepan in the ice bath for about 10 seconds to stop the cooking.

Remove from the ice bath and stir in the butter. Carefully stir in the hot cream with a wooden spoon, mixing until fully blended. Serve immediately, or allow to cool to room temperature, transfer to a sealed container, and store, refrigerated, up to 3 weeks. Warm the refrigerated sauce briefly in the microwave or in a small saucepan on low heat before serving.

Cider and Raisin Sauce

MAKES 2 CUPS | PREPARATION TIME: 45 MINUTES

See photograph on page 356.

*B*ourbon, raisins, and apple cider lend a deep, complex flavor to this simple sauce, perfect for a winter dessert.

1¹/₂ cups raisins or dried currants

¹/₂ cup plus 1 tablespoon bourbon

3¹/₄ cups apple cider

3 tablespoons arrowroot

1¹/₂ teaspoons lemon juice

Combine the raisins, 6 tablespoons of the bourbon, and enough cider (about 1½ cups) to cover the raisins in a small saucepan. Bring to a simmer and remove from the heat. Plump the raisins for 25 minutes. Drain the raisins, reserving the liquid.

While the raisins are plumping, reduce the remaining cider by half. After the raisins are plumped, add the reserved liquid and continue to simmer until the liquid is reduced by half. Lower the heat to a simmer.

Mix the arrowroot with the remaining bourbon to form a slurry. Add the slurry, lemon juice, and plumped raisins to the cider. Simmer until the sauce thickens, about 1 minute.

The sauce may be stored under refrigeration for 5–8 days.

Vanilla Sauce

MAKES 2 CUPS | PREPARATION TIME: 20 MINUTES

*T*his basic vanilla custard sauce is very versatile, excellent with bread pudding, fruit tarts, or chocolate desserts.

1 cup heavy cream

1 cup whole milk

¹/₂ vanilla bean

¹/₂ cup sugar

9 egg yolks

Bring the milk, vanilla bean, and half of the sugar to a boil. Be sure to watch for scorching.

Combine the egg yolks with the remaining sugar and pour ¼ cup of the hot milk into the egg mixture to temper it. Whisk to combine.

Add the tempered egg mixture back into the hot milk, whisk to combine, and return to a low heat.

Stirring constantly with a wooden spoon, heat the mixture to 165°F. Remove immediately from the stove. Strain through a fine-mesh sieve into a container that is set into an ice bath.

Hot Fudge Sauce

MAKES 2 CUPS | PREPARATION TIME: 10 MINUTES

No ice cream sundae would be complete without this decadent dark-chocolate fudge sauce. Use good-quality chocolate and cocoa powder for a sauce with superior fudge taste and texture.

$^2/_3$ cup dark chocolate, melted

6 tablespoons cocoa powder

$^1/_2$ cup plus 3 tablespoons water

$^1/_2$ cup butter

$^3/_4$ cup plus 2 tablespoons sugar

3 tablespoons light corn syrup

$^1/_4$ teaspoon salt

$^1/_2$ tablespoon vanilla extract

Place the melted chocolate, cocoa, and water in a saucepan over low heat and stir gently until fully combined. Add the butter, sugar, corn syrup, and salt and simmer over medium heat until thick, about 5 minutes.

Remove from the heat and stir in the vanilla extract.

Strain the sauce if there are any lumps. Serve immediately, or allow to cool to room temperature, transfer to a sealed container, and store, refrigerated, up to 2 weeks. Warm the refrigerated sauce briefly in the microwave or in a small saucepan on low heat before serving.

Raspberry Coulis

MAKES 2 CUPS | PREPARATION TIME: 15 MINUTES

See photograph on page 338.

A coulis is simply a term used to refer to a thick puree or sauce. It is easy to create variations of this sauce by substituting fresh or frozen strawberries, kiwi puree, or chopped mango for the raspberries.

2 cups raspberries, fresh or frozen   1 cup, plus 2 tablespoons sugar   2 tablespoons lemon juice

Combine the raspberries, 1 cup of the sugar, and the lemon juice in a saucepan over medium heat. Simmer, stirring, until the sugar has dissolved, about 10 minutes.

Strain the coulis through a fine-mesh sieve.

Add more sugar and/or lemon juice to taste, if necessary.

FOCUS ON | Fresh Fruits for Dessert

Fruits make a great dessert, whether you intend to serve them fresh, baked into a pastry, or made into a sauce to drizzle over other desserts or ice cream.

Pick the freshest fruits possible. Look for a good color with no obvious bruises, scars, nicks, or gouges. Most ripe fruits have a good aroma. Avoid fruits that have either no smell or a bitter or sour smell.

Berries should be plump and firm, not shriveled. Avoid packages that have moldy berries or juice-stained cartons.

If you are making a coulis or a fruit filling, perfectly-shaped fruit is not so important, though the flavor remains as important as ever.

Store fruits at the right temperature. Bananas, and fruits that you want to soften a bit, like peaches or apricots, keep best at room temperature; otherwise, in general, store fruits in the refrigerator, away from strongly-flavored foods.

Vol au Vents
with Fresh Berries and Whipped Cream

MAKES 8 SERVINGS | PREPARATION TIME: 45 MINUTES

Vol au Vents with Fresh Berries are shown here with Raspberry Coulis, page 337.

*F*rozen puff pastry shells are readily available in the frozen food section of most supermarkets. They provide a quick, easy, and delicious shell for seasonal berries and fresh whipped cream.

8 frozen, prepared puff pastry shells

3 pints assorted berries (raspberries, blueberries, blackberries, etc.)

2½ cups heavy cream, whipped

8 mint sprigs

1 cup Raspberry Coulis (page 337)

Bake the puff pastry shells according to the manufacturers' instructions. Cool completely.

Spoon 2 tablespoons of the whipped cream into each baked shell. Arrange 5 berries on top of the whipped cream. Layer with another 3 tablespoons of the whipped cream and arrange 9 more berries on top.

Garnish with a sprig of mint.

Serve with 2 tablespoons of Raspberry Coulis.

Tiramisu

MAKES 8 SERVINGS | PREPARATION TIME: 45 MINUTES

*I*n Italian, *tiramisu* literally means "pick me up." After one bite of the espresso-and-Kahlua-soaked ladyfingers, creamy mascarpone cheese, and grated chocolate, you will understand why this dessert is a classic. For a contemporary twist on the original, make the tiramisu in individual glasses.

1 egg	3¹/₄ cups mascarpone cheese	48 ladyfingers
6 egg yolks	3 egg whites	¹/₄ cup cocoa powder
1¹/₂ cups sugar	1 cup espresso	2 tablespoons powdered sugar
1 teaspoon vanilla extract	¹/₂ cup Kahlua	

Whip the egg, egg yolks, 1 cup of the sugar, and the vanilla together in a large stainless steel bowl over simmering water for about 3–4 minutes, or until the volume nearly doubles and the mixture becomes a light lemon yellow.

Transfer the egg and sugar mixture to the bowl of an electric mixer and beat on high speed until the mixture has cooled to room temperature, about 8–10 minutes. Add the mascarpone and blend on low speed until very smooth, about 2–3 minutes. Scrape the sides and bottom of the bowl to blend evenly.

Beat the egg whites with the remaining sugar in a clean bowl to medium-stiff peaks, about 5–6 minutes. Fold the beaten egg whites into the mascarpone mixture in two additions. Refrigerate until needed.

Combine the espresso and Kahlua to make a syrup. Place a layer of ladyfingers in a 2½-quart bowl. Moisten the ladyfingers well with the syrup and dust evenly with cocoa powder. Top with a 1-inch thick layer of the mascarpone filling. Repeat layering in this sequence until the bowl is full, ending with a layer of filling.

Dust the entire surface of the cake with cocoa power and powdered sugar. Chill thoroughly before serving.

Swedish Oatmeal Cookies

MAKES 36 COOKIES | PREPARATION TIME: 40 MINUTES

See photograph on page 356.

*T*hese delicate oatmeal cookies are made with cake flour and without eggs. Though the cookie looks the same as the traditional, its texture will amaze you.

1³/₄ cups cake flour

1 teaspoon baking soda

1¹/₄ cups butter, room temperature

³/₄ cup, plus 2 tablespoons sugar

1³/₄ cups rolled oats

¹/₂ cup raisins

¹/₂ cup golden raisins

Preheat the oven to 375°F.

Line 4 cookie sheets with parchment paper.

Sift together the cake flour and the baking soda.

Cream the butter and sugar together on medium speed with the paddle attachment, scraping down the bowl periodically, until the mixture is smooth and light in color, about 5 minutes. On low speed, mix in the sifted dry ingredients and oats until they are just combined. Mix in the raisins until they are just incorporated.

Drop rounded tablespoons of the dough onto the parchment-lined sheets and bake at 375°F for 10–12 minutes or until golden brown.

Alternately, the dough may be divided into 2 equal portions and rolled into cylinders, wrapped in plastic wrap, and frozen for up to 3 months. The dough may then be sliced frozen (about ¾-inch wide), laid on cookie sheets lined with parchment, and baked at 375°F for 12–14 minutes.

Chocolate Chunk Cookies

MAKES 16 COOKIES | PREPARATION TIME: 45 MINUTES

See photograph on page 345.

*F*or a delicious twist on a classic, add ¾ cup chopped dried cherries along with the chocolate chunks.

1½ cups all-purpose flour

½ teaspoon baking soda

¾ teaspoon salt

½ cup butter, softened

½ cup sugar

⅓ cup light brown sugar

½ tablespoon vanilla extract

1 egg

1 cup semi-sweet chocolate chunks

Preheat the oven to 375°F.

Line 2 cookie sheets with parchment paper.

Sift together the flour, baking soda, and salt.

Cream the butter and sugars on medium speed with the paddle attachment, scraping down the bowl periodically, until the mixture is smooth and light in color, about 5 minutes.

Combine the eggs and vanilla. Add to the butter-sugar mixture and mix until fully incorporated, scraping down the bowl as needed. On low speed, mix in the sifted dry ingredients and the chocolate chunks until just incorporated.

Scale the dough into 2-tablespoon portions and place onto prepared cookie sheets. Alternately, the dough may be shaped into a 16-inch long log, rolled tightly in plastic wrap, and refrigerated until firm enough to slice. The chilled log may be sliced into 16 pieces and arranged on the prepared cookie sheets in even rows.

Bake at 375°F until golden brown around the edges, about 12–14 minutes. Cool completely on cookie sheets.

Sand Cookies

MAKES 42 COOKIES | PREPARATION TIME: 35 MINUTES

Sand Cookies are shown here with the Chocolate Chunk Cookies (page 345).

Named for the slightly "gritty" texture that coarse sugar lends to this short dough, these cookies are simple and straightforward. Perfect with coffee or tea, these cookies are sure to satisfy your sweet tooth.

¹/₂ cup confectioners' sugar, sifted

¹/₂ cup butter, softened

¹/₂ teaspoon vanilla extract

2 tablespoons lemon zest, grated

2 cups cake flour

¹/₄ cup milk

¹/₂ cup coarse sugar

Using an electric mixer with the paddle attachment, cream together the sugar, butter, vanilla extract, and lemon zest on high speed until smooth and light, about 3 minutes.

Add the flour all at once and mix on low speed until combined.

Divide the dough in half and roll into 6-inch long cylinders (they should be 1 ¼-inch in diameter). At this point the cookies may be tightly wrapped in plastic wrap and frozen or refrigerated for later use or they may be prepared for baking.

To bake the cookies preheat the oven to 350° F. Brush the cylinders of cookie dough with milk and roll them in the coarse sugar.

Cut the logs into ¼-inch thick slices and place them on parchment-lined cookie sheets.

Bake for 12 minutes or until light golden brown.

ABOVE, LEFT TO RIGHT: Wrapping finished cookie-dough cylinders of Chocolate Chunk Cookies (page 343) and Sand Cookies in plastic wrap, to be refrigerated or frozen; rolling a cylinder of Sand Cookie dough in coarse sugar; slicing Sand Cookie dough to bake.

Grand Marnier-Honey Chocolate Fondue

MAKES 6 SERVINGS | PREPARATION TIME: 15 MINUTES

*F*ondue is a concept that originated in Switzerland, though its popularity has spread throughout the world. Originally intended as a savory preparation of melted cheeses, the concept of a sweet preparation, using chocolate, has become equally as popular. Grand Marnier, a brandy-based liqueur flavored with orange peel, adds a distinctive flavor.

1 cup bittersweet chocolate, melted

1 cup semi-sweet chocolate, melted

$1/2$ cup heavy cream

2 teaspoons orange zest

Pinch salt

2 tablespoons honey

$1/4$ cup Grand Marnier

Assorted fresh fruit, cut into bite-sized pieces, as needed

Ladyfingers or pound cake, cut into bite-sized pieces, as needed

Combine the melted chocolates and keep warm.

Bring the heavy cream, orange zest, salt, and honey to a simmer. Remove from heat and allow the zest to steep for 5 minutes. Strain the mixture into the chocolate and whisk together.

Add the Grand Marnier and mix thoroughly. Serve warm in a fondue pot with a variety of foods to dip (e.g. strawberries with the stems on, pitted cherries, sponge cake pieces, apricots, ladyfingers, orange segments, etc.).

NOTE: If you prefer, omit the Grand Marnier and substitute an additional $1/4$ cup of heavy cream.

VARIATION: For white chocolate fondue, substitute 2 cups melted white chocolate for the bitterweet and semi-sweet chocolate.

Apple Strudel

MAKES 8 SERVINGS | PREPARATION TIME: 45 MINUTES

A traditional favorite is made easy using layers of phyllo dough. Varieties of pears, stone fruits, and berries may be substituted for the apples, depending on the season.

3½ pounds Granny Smith apples, peeled, cored, thinly sliced

¾ cup brown sugar, packed

4 teaspoons ground cinnamon

½ teaspoon ground nutmeg

⅔ cup golden raisins, plumped in warm brandy or water

1½ cups butter, melted

¼ cup breadcrumbs, plain

8 sheets phyllo dough, thawed

Preheat the oven to 425°F.

Combine the apples with ½ cup brown sugar, cinnamon, nutmeg, and raisins in a mixing bowl.

Heat 2 tablespoons butter in a large sauté pan over high heat. Add half of the apples and sauté until golden brown, about 10 minutes. Repeat with 2 more tablespoons of butter and the remaining apples.

Combine the remaining brown sugar with the breadcrumbs.

To assemble each strudel, lay a sheet of phyllo dough on your work surface with the longer edge of the dough parallel to the edge of the work surface. As you work, keep the unused sheets of phyllo covered with plastic wrap to keep them from drying out.

Brush the dough with melted butter and sprinkle with 1 tablespoon of the breadcrumb mixture. Top with another sheet of phyllo dough and repeat this process until a stack of 4 buttered phyllo sheets is formed.

Mound half of the apple filling (about 3½ cups) along the bottom of the phyllo, leaving a 2-inch border at the edges. Beginning with the bottom edge, carefully roll up the dough and filling, and seal. Repeat with the remaining dough and filling to make a second strudel. Transfer the strudels seam-side down to a parchment paper-lined baking sheet. Brush with the remaining melted butter, and score the dough on a bias to indicate 4 portions.

Bake in a 425°F oven until golden brown, about 15 minutes. Slice the jagged ends off of each strudel. Slice each strudel into 4 portions and serve warm.

Baklava

Baklava, popular in Greece and Turkey, consists of phyllo layered with nuts and spices. After the dessert is baked to a beautiful golden brown, a honey syrup is poured on top, making a sweet and flaky pastry.

3¹/₂ cups walnuts, chopped

¹/₂ cup sugar

1 teaspoon ground cinnamon

¹/₂ teaspoon ground cardamom

¹/₄ teaspoon ground cloves

1 pound package phyllo sheets, thawed

1¹/₂ cups butter, melted

SYRUP

2 cups, plus 2 tablespoons sugar

1¹/₂ cups water

¹/₂ cup honey

¹/₄ lemon, peel only

1 clove

Preheat the oven to 375°F.

Mix together the walnuts, sugar, and spices and set aside.

As you work, keep the sheets of phyllo covered with plastic wrap to keep them from drying out. Place 1 sheet of phyllo on the bottom of a jelly roll pan (12-inch × 16-inch). Brush the dough lightly with melted butter. Repeat this process until there are 8 sheets of phyllo in the pan.

Sprinkle one-third of the nut mixture onto the phyllo sheets.

Place 4 more sheets of phyllo on top of the nuts, brushing melted butter between each sheet.

Place another one-third of the nut mixture on the dough.

Layer the remaining sheets of phyllo on top of the nuts, brushing melted butter in between each sheet. Brush the top sheet with butter as well.

Trim the edges so that they do not stand above the level of the dough.

Cut the pastry into 2-inch squares, making sure not to slice through the bottom layer of phyllo dough. Leaving the bottom layer uncut will allow the syrup to soak in more efficiently.

Bake at 375°F for 25–30 minutes or until the top layer of the phyllo takes on a light golden brown color.

While the dough bakes, prepare the syrup. Combine all of the ingredients and bring to a boil. Remove the clove and lemon peel.

Remove the baklava from the oven and immediately pour hot syrup over the top.

Before serving allow the baklava to stand at room temperature until cooled. Slice through the bottom layer of phyllo dough and serve.

Fresh Fruit Galette

MAKES 8 SERVINGS | PREPARATION TIME: 45 MINUTES

*E*legantly rustic, these tantalizing fruit tarts are simple to prepare. Use fresh seasonal fruits at their peak of sweetness.

1 quart fruit, firm-fleshed (pears, apples, peaches, apricots, cherries, etc.)

1 package puff pastry dough, thawed

6 tablespoons apricot jam, strained, warm

1 egg

1 teaspoon water

½ cup coarse sugar

Preheat the oven to 350°F.

Wash, peel, trim, core, and slice the fruit as needed.

Let the dough relax just a few minutes, but work quickly enough that it does not get too soft and pliable.

Roll the dough slightly until it is 12-inches square and of a uniform thickness.

Cut four 6-inch round circles out of each sheet of dough.

Lay the pastry circles onto baking sheets that have been lined with parchment.

Refrigerate the dough for 5–10 minutes if it is too soft.

Spread ½ teaspoon of the apricot jam in the center of the circle, leaving a ¼-inch border around the edge of the dough.

Place ½ cup of prepared fruit on top of the jam, leaving a 1-inch border around the edge of the dough.

Fold a ½-inch section of dough up onto the fruit, pressing gently so that it adheres slightly. Crimp another ½-inch section of dough over the fruit and lightly press the dough that overlaps together. Crimp the remaining dough around the fruit. The fruit should be barely encased inside the dough. Repeat with the remaining galettes.

Mix the egg with the water to make an egg wash.

Lightly brush the dough and the crimped seams with the egg wash. Sprinkle coarse sugar on the egg wash. Bake at 350°F for about 30 minutes or until golden brown and baked through.

FROM LEFT: Cutting rounds from prepared puff pastry dough using a 6-inch saucer; crimping the puff pastry dough around the fresh fruit.

OPPOSITE: The finished fruit galettes.

Fresh Berry Napoleon

MAKES 8 SERVINGS | PREPARATION TIME: 45 MINUTES

*T*his elegant French dessert is usually made with puff pastry; however, this version uses phyllo dough. Napoleons should be assembled just prior to serving so that the phyllo layers remain crispy.

8 sheets phyllo dough, thawed

1/4 cup breadcrumbs, plain

1/4 cup butter, melted

1/4 cup sugar

1 egg white

1/2 cup sour cream

1 tablespoon light brown sugar, packed

1/2 teaspoon vanilla extract

1/4 cup heavy cream, whipped to medium peaks

2 cups fresh berries (sliced strawberries, blueberries, raspberries, etc.)

2 tablespoons confectioners' sugar

Preheat the oven to 350°F. Spray a nonstick baking sheet with nonstick spray, or line with parchment paper.

As you work, keep the sheets of phyllo covered with plastic wrap to keep them from drying out. Place one phyllo sheet on a clean, dry cutting board; lightly brush the dough with a little of the melted butter and sprinkle with 2 teaspoons of breadcrumbs. Continue layering the remaining sheets, brushing with butter and sprinkling with the crumbs in between each layer. With a pizza wheel or sharp knife, cut the phyllo into twenty-four 3-inch squares. Transfer to the baking sheet. Sprinkle each of the rectangles with sugar (use about 1–2 tablespoons for all of the pieces) and bake until crisp and golden brown, about 6–8 minutes. Transfer to a wire rack and cool completely.

With an electric mixer (or a hand-held mixer) beat the egg white until thick and foamy. Gradually add the remaining sugar while beating the white. Beat on high speed to stiff peaks.

Combine the sour cream, brown sugar and vanilla extract. Fold in the whipped cream, followed by the beaten egg white.

To assemble the napoleons, place a small dollop of the filling mixture on the plate to secure the napoleon. Top with a phyllo square. Add 2 tablespoons of the filling mixture and 2 tablespoons of the fruit. Add another phyllo square and top with another 2 tablespoons of filling and fruit. Add the final layer of phyllo and dust lightly with confectioner's sugar. Repeat to complete all of the remaining napoleons.

Molten Chocolate Cake

MAKES 6 SERVINGS | PREPARATION TIME: 45 MINUTES

$\mathcal{D}$ecadent and delicious, these individual cakes are irresistible for true chocolate lovers. Serve the cakes directly from the oven, so that the molten center remains liquid as you take your first bite.

GANACHE FILLING

$^1/_4$ cup heavy cream

2 teaspoons light corn syrup

$^1/_3$ cup semi-sweet chocolate, chopped finely

CAKE BATTER

$^1/_2$ cup butter, softened

$^1/_4$ cup semi-sweet chocolate, melted

$1^1/_2$ tablespoons unsweetened chocolate, melted

2 eggs

2 egg yolks

6 tablespoons all-purpose flour

$^1/_2$ cup confectioners' sugar

Preheat the oven to 375°F.

Bring the cream and the corn syrup to a simmer and pour over the chopped chocolate. Let sit for 5 minutes and mix until smooth. Place in the freezer until just firm enough to scoop, about 20 minutes. Stir the ganache occasionally while it is in the freezer.

While the ganache is cooling, whisk the butter and the two chocolates together and add to the eggs.

Sift the flour and sugar together and fold into the chocolate mixture.

Butter and flour six 4-fluid-ounce ramekins. Fill the ramekins with 3 tablespoons batter and make a small well in the center by pushing the batter up slightly on the sides. However, the bottom of the ramekin should not be visible.

Scoop 1 tablespoon of the ganache and place it in the center of each ramekin.

Spoon another 2 tablespoons of cake batter on top of the ganache, making sure to seal it between the two layers of batter. The batter should come up to ¼-inch from the top of the ramekin.

Bake the cakes in a 375°F oven for 15–20 minutes or until the top of the cake springs back lightly to the touch.

Loosen the edges of the cakes before unmolding, and place on a small dessert plate. Serve with a dollop of whipped cream and Classic Caramel Sauce (page 334) or Raspberry Coulis (page 337).

Individual Pecan Pies

MAKES EIGHT 3-INCH TARTLETS | PREPARATION TIME: 45 MINUTES

Making mini versions of the traditional pecan pie dramatically reduces baking time, allowing you to enjoy these sweet and nutty pies in no time at all.

1½ pounds Tart Dough (page 361)

1 tablespoon sugar

2 tablespoons bread flour

1 cup dark corn syrup

2 eggs, beaten

1 teaspoon vanilla extract

1 teaspoon salt

2 tablespoons butter, melted

2 cups pecan halves, toasted

Preheat the oven to 350°F.

Lightly grease eight tartlet pans. Roll out the dough to ⅛-inch thick. Cut out eight 4½-inch diameter circles and line each of the tartlet pans. Generously prick the dough with a fork. Allow the tart shells to rest in the refrigerator while preparing the filling, at least 10 minutes.

Parbake the tart shells for 10 mintues, or until light golden brown on the edges.

Combine the sugar and flour in a bowl and whisk together. Add the corn syrup and blend thoroughly. Add the eggs, vanilla, and salt and mix until incorporated. Stir in the melted butter.

Spread about ¼ cup of the pecans evenly in the prebaked tart shell, and pour the corn syrup mixture over the pecans until it comes to just below the rim of the dough.

Bake at 350°F until the filling is just firm, about 18 minutes.

VARIATION:

Pecan Cranberry Pie: Add 2 tablespoons of fresh or frozen cranberries to each tart shell along with the pecans before adding the corn syrup mixture.

Cheesecake

MAKES 8 MINIATURE CHEESECAKES | PREPARATION TIME: 45 MINUTES

Prepared graham cracker shells, available at most supermarkets, save time needed to grind, mix, and press whole graham crackers. To create a marbled cheesecake, chill the Classic Caramel Sauce (page 334), Hot Fudge Sauce (page 336), or the Raspberry Coulis (page 337). Once the batter has been scaled into the individual shells, swirl about 1 teaspoon of sauce into each one.

1¹/₂ cups cream cheese

¹/₂ cup sugar

¹/₄ teaspoon salt

2 eggs

6 tablespoons heavy cream, chilled

1 teaspoon vanilla extract

8 individual-sized prepared graham cracker dessert shells

Preheat the oven to 325°F.

Combine the cream cheese, sugar, and salt. Mix on medium speed with the paddle attachment, occasionally scraping down the bowl, until the mixture is completely smooth, approximately 3 minutes.

Whisk the eggs together. Add the eggs to the cream cheese in two additions, mixing until fully incorporated after each addition, and scraping down the bowl as needed.

Add the heavy cream and the vanilla and mix until just incorporated.

Scale ¼ cup of the batter into each graham cracker shell. Gently tap the pans to release any air bubbles.

Place the cheesecakes on a baking sheet. Bake at 325°F until the centers of the cakes are set, about 15–20 minutes.

Place the cheesecakes on wire racks until completely cool. Cover the cheesecakes with plastic wrap, and refrigerate for 1–1½ hours to allow them to set properly.

To serve, unmold the cheesecakes from their aluminum pans onto individual serving plates. Serve plain, or with a pool of caramel or fudge sauce or fresh fruit coulis.

Rice Pudding

Rice Pudding is shown here with Swedish Oatmeal Cookies (page 342)
and Cider and Raisin Sauce (page 335).

*R*insing the rice helps wash excess starch from the grains, which in turn will keep the rice from forming clumps in the finished pudding.

1 quart milk	1 teaspoon ground cinnamon	24 raspberries, for garnish
1/2 cup long-grain white rice	2 teaspoons cornstarch	8 mint sprigs, for garnish
1/2 cup sugar	2 eggs	

Combine 3½ cups of the milk with the rice, sugar, and cinnamon in a medium saucepan. Cover and simmer until the rice is tender, about 25 minutes.

Combine the remaining milk with the cornstarch and eggs.

Remove the pan from the heat and add approximately 2 cups of the hot liquid to the cornstarch mixture, whisking constantly. Add the warmed cornstarch mixture to the remaining milk mixture in the pan. Return the pan to the heat and while stirring constantly, bring the pudding to a boil and cook for 1 minute.

Portion the pudding into dessert dishes. The pudding can be served warm at this point, or cooled completely and refrigerated, covered with plastic wrap to keep a skin from forming.

Garnish each serving with 3 raspberries and a sprig of mint.

Bread Pudding

MAKES 6–8 SERVINGS | PREPARATION TIME: 45 MINUTES

Bread Pudding is shown here with Classic Caramel Sauce (page 334).

*S*oft, egg-enriched challah bread makes a wonderful addition to this homey dessert. Similar to French toast, this pudding also makes a great brunch dish.

CUSTARD

1 pint milk, hot

4 eggs, large, beaten

2 egg yolks, large, beaten

½ cup sugar

¼ teaspoon vanilla extract

3 cups challah bread, preferably 1–2 days old, cubed

⅓ cup raisins

Preheat the oven to 325°F.

Combine the milk, eggs and egg yolks, sugar, and vanilla and whisk thoroughly.

Add the bread cubes and the raisins to the custard, and gently mix to combine.

Butter 4-fluid-ounce ramekins and fill to ¼ inch below the rim with the pudding mixture. Place the filled ramekins in a paper towel-lined baking dish, large enough to accommo-date the ramekins with moderate space in between. Prepare a water bath by carefully pouring very hot water into the baking dish until it reaches about halfway up the sides of the ramekins.

Bake at 325°F for 30 minutes, or until the custard is slightly firm. Remove the baking dish from the oven, but allow the bread pudding to sit in the waterbath for 5 minutes. Unmold the puddings and serve warm or cool to room temperature.

Fresh Fruit Sabayon

Sabayon (or *zabaglione* as it's known in Italy, from whence it originated) is a delicate, frothy dessert sauce of egg yolks whisked and cooked with sugar and a bit of wine or liqueur. It should be made just before serving, as it does not hold well.

10 egg yolks

1 cup sugar

½ cup dessert wine or liqueur

3 pounds fruit, ripe, trimmed, and cleaned, (seasonal stone fruit or berries)

Combine the egg yolks, sugar and wine in a mixing bowl. Whisk over a pot of barely simmering water until the eggs become frothy and begin to thicken. Continue to whisk vigorously until the eggs reach the "ribbon stage" or approximately 165°F.

Portion the fruit into dessert bowls or parfait glasses, allowing about 1 cup of fruit per serving. Top the fruit with about ¼ cup of the sabayon.

Serve immediately.

Broiled Pineapple with Coconut

The rich tropical flavors of rum, pineapple, and coconut come together in this simple satisfying dessert. Canned pineapple makes this recipe a breeze to prepare, but if time allows, consider using fresh. Pineapple, trimmed and sliced into rings, is now available in the produce section of most supermarkets.

3½–4 pound pineapple, trimmed, cored, sliced in half lengthwise

¼ cup dark rum

1½ tablespoons dark brown sugar

1 cup pineapple juice

⅓ cup shredded coconut

Slice each half of the pineapple into 8 pieces. Each slice should be about 2 ounces and each portion will contain two slices.

Preheat the broiler. Line a shallow baking dish with foil. Combine the rum, brown sugar, and pineapple juice in a small bowl; stir until the sugar is dissolved.

Arrange the pineapple slices in a single layer in the baking dish; drizzle evenly with the rum mixture. Broil the pineapple 5 inches from the heat until the slices are lightly browned, about 5–8 minutes. Sprinkle with the coconut and continue broiling until the coconut is lightly browned, about 3–4 minutes more.

Place two slices on each plate and drizzle the pineapple with the juices from the dish. Serve immediately.

NOTE: This would also be suitable as a topping for ice cream.

Clafouti

Clafouti originated in the Limousin region in central France, a simple country dessert of fresh fruit baked in a custard-like batter. Though traditionally made with cherries, other seasonal fruits, such as apples or pears, may be easily substituted. If you replace the cherries with apples or pears, replace the kirsch with Calvados or pear brandy, respectively.

1 pint milk	³/₄ cup sugar	¹/₂ cup all-purpose flour
1 vanilla bean, split	4 eggs	3 cups cherries, tart, pitted
¹/₄ teaspoon salt		

Preheat the oven to 350°F.

Combine the milk, vanilla bean, salt, and half of the sugar in a saucepan. Bring to a boil.

Combine the eggs, flour, and the remaining half of the sugar in a stainless steel bowl. Fully whisk the mixture together. Add half of the hot milk to the egg mixture and whisk thoroughly to temper.

Add the egg mixture to the remaining hot milk and mix well.

Strain the mixture and skim any impurities off of the top.

Divide the cherries equally between 8 buttered and sugared shallow ramekins.

Pour the custard evenly over the cherries and bake at 350°F for approximately 16–18 minutes or until custard is firm.

Tart Dough

For a delicious variation on the regular tart dough, add 1 tablespoon of finely grated lemon zest when creaming the butter.

1 cup butter, softened	1 teaspoon vanilla extract	3 cups cake flour, sifted
¹/₂ cup sugar	1 egg	

Cream together the butter, sugar, and vanilla extract in an electric mixer on medium speed using a paddle attachment, scraping down the bowl periodically, until smooth and light in color.

Add the egg and blend until smooth. Add the flour all at once and mix on low speed until just blended.

Turn the dough out onto a lightly floured work surface. Wrap tightly and refrigerate for at least 30 minutes before rolling.

For information on storing the finished tart dough, see page 333, Rolling Out Tart Dough to Chill or Freeze.

Chocolate Crêpes
with Brandied Cherry Filling

MAKES 6 SERVINGS | PREPARATION TIME: 45 MINUTES

*F*or a dessert that is as elegant as it is delectable, serve these crêpes with Vanilla Sauce (page 335).

CHOCOLATE CRÊPES

1½ cups whole milk

4 eggs

⅔ cup all-purpose flour

⅔ cup Dutch-process cocoa powder

1½ tablespoons sugar

2 tablespoon butter, melted

1 teaspoon salt

1 recipe Brandied Cherry Filling
(recipe follows)

Confectioners' sugar, as needed

Blend all of the ingredients for the crêpes in a food processor for 1 minute. Scrape down the sides and blend for an additional 30 seconds. Allow the batter to rest for 15 minutes.

Heat a 5-inch nonstick skillet or crêpe pan over medium heat. Ladle about 2 tablespoons of the batter into the pan and cook the first side until the edges start to look dry. Turn the crêpe once and cook the second side briefly. Repeat until the batter is finished, stirring occasionally to prevent the flour

from settling. This should yield 24 crêpes. Keep the crêpes warm until needed.

Prepare the Brandied Cherry Filling.

Place 2–3 tablespoons of the filling in each crêpe, roll, and garnish with confectioners' sugar before serving.

NOTE: Put the confectioners' sugar in a cheesecloth pouch to dust the crêpes.

Brandied Cherry Filling

MAKES 6 SERVINGS | PREPARATION TIME: 15 MINUTES

3½ cups pitted frozen cherries and juice,
thawed, at room temperature

6 tablespoons water

¼ cup sugar

1 lemon, juice only

½ cup brandy

½ cup kirsch

¼ cup butter, unsalted

Place the cherries in a sauté pan with their juice and the water. Sprinkle with sugar and add the lemon juice. Heat gently and swirl to allow the sugar to dissolve. Reduce the mixture for 5–7 minutes, or until it becomes a light syrup.

Remove the pan from the heat source, add the brandy, and ig-

nite. When the flame extinguishes, the alcohol will have burned off. Alternately, bring the mixture to a simmer for 30 seconds to 1 minute to burn off the alcohol.

Add the kirsch and, while still warm, swirl in the butter to thicken the filling.

Chocolate Mousse

*C*hoose a good bittersweet chocolate for this luscious dessert. Taste-test a few brands to find your favorite. This recipe calls for raw egg whites; if you are concerned about possible health risks associated with raw eggs, substitute pasteurized egg whites.

2 egg whites

6 tablespoons sugar

1 cup heavy cream, plus extra for garnish

4 egg yolks

3 tablespoons brandy

1 cup bittersweet chocolate chips, melted

1 recipe Espresso-Hazelnut Brittle
(recipe follows)

Beat the egg whites and 2 tablespoons sugar in the bowl of an electric mixer until the meringue forms medium peaks, about 8–10 minutes. Reserve under refrigeration until needed.

Whip the heavy cream with 2 tablespoons sugar until the mixture forms soft peaks. Reserve under refrigeration until needed.

Combine the egg yolks with the brandy and the remaining sugar. Whisk over a hot water bath until mixture reaches 110°F, about 6–8 minutes. Add the melted chocolate and blend together over the hot water bath. Whip the mixture to room temperature in the bowl of an electric mixer, about 5 minutes.

Fold the meringue into the chocolate mixture in two additions. Fold in the whipped cream. Spoon into serving dishes and refrigerate until needed. Garnish with whipped cream and Espresso-Hazelnut Brittle.

Espresso-Hazelnut Brittle

1 cup hazelnuts, coarsely chopped

1 cup plus 2 tablespoons sugar

$^1/_2$ teaspoon brandy

$^1/_4$ cup heavy cream

3 tablespoons espresso roast coffee beans, coarsely ground

$2^1/_2$ fluid ounces water

2 tablespoons light corn syrup

Coat the hazelnuts in ½ tablespoon of the sugar and the brandy. Toast in a 350°F oven until golden brown, about 7–8 minutes. Remove from the oven and reserve.

Bring the cream and the espresso to a simmer. Remove from the heat, cover and allow to steep for 10 minutes. Strain the mixture and keep warm.

Prepare an ice bath.

Combine the remaining sugar, water and corn syrup, and bring to a boil, stirring constantly. Skim off any scum that floats to the top. Continue to boil the sugar syrup, brushing the sides of the pan occasionally with water, until it turns a light golden brown. Shock the caramel in the ice bath for about 10 seconds.

Carefully stir in the cream and the chopped hazelnuts. Pour the brittle onto a lightly greased piece of parchment paper or a silicone baking mat and spread as thin as possible.

Allow to cool to room temperature. Break into medium-sized pieces for use as garnish or into smaller pieces to use as a topping.

Index

aïoli, grilled chicken sandwich with pancetta, arugula, and, 172

almonds
    chicken curry with, 183
    goat cheese with mesclun, pears, and toasted, baked, 106

anchovies, broiled swordfish with tomatoes, garlic, and, 231

appetizers, 13–47
    presenting, principles for, 25
    selection to suit your menu, 14

apples
    chutney, sautéed pork medallions with, 157
    salad:
        frisée with walnuts, grapes, blue cheese, and, 105
        Waldorf, 103
    sautéed, 290
    squash soup with lime gremolata, curried, 55
    strudel, 348

apricot-Armagnac compote, roasted pork loin with, 160

artichokes
    chicken breast with, and mustard sauce, 170
    Mediterranean salad, 94
    and mushrooms in white wine sauce, 296
    rice salad, 323

arugula, grilled chicken sandwich with pancetta, aïoli, and, 172

Asiago cheese for Mediterranean salad, 94

Asian grilled shrimp, spicy, 206

Asian noodles, 270

Asian vegetable slaw, 299

asparagus
    and morels, 297
    pan-steamed lemon, 280
    risotto with scallops and, 221
    with shiitakes, bowtie pasta, and spring peas, 259

avocados
    crostini, black bean and, 27
    guacamole, 18
    salad, crab and, 42
    soup, chilled cream of, 57

bacon
    German potato salad, 309
    turkey club sandwich, 196

baklava, 349

balsamic vinaigrette, 128

basil, cream of tomato soup with rice and, 60

beans, 270
    salad, mixed bean and grain, 97
    see also specific types of beans

beef
    brisket for Reuben sandwich, 137
    cuts of, and quick cooking methods, 129–31
    removing the silverskin, 131–32
    Satay of, with peanut sauce, 141
    steak:
        grilled flank, 139
        salad with horseradish dressing, grilled, 115
        Satay of beef with peanut sauce, 141
    stir-fry citrus, 135
    tenderloin of:
        with blue cheese and herb crust, 142
        with Southwestern-style sauce, 144
    testing for doneness, 132–33
    trimming before cooking, 129–31

beets
    borscht, 74
    salad, roasted, 98

Belgian endives, braised, 290

berries
    Napoleon, fresh, 352
    and whipped cream, vol au vents with fresh, 339

black beans
    and avocado crostini, 27
    salad with lime-cilantro vinaigrette, 282
    salsa, papaya and, 24
    soup, traditional, 56

blue cheese
    Cobb salad, traditional, 122
    salad:
        frisée with walnuts, apples, grapes, and, 105
        mixed green, with pears, walnuts, and, 103
    tenderloin of beef with, and herb crust, 142

borscht, 74

brandied cherry filling, chocolate crêpes with, 362

bread
    cornbread, 316
    croutons, homemade, 121
    panzanella (bread salad with fresh tomatoes), 91
    pudding, 358

breading technique, standard, 11

broccoli
    and orange-sesame sauce, 291
    and red peppers, steamed, 291

broccoli rabe with toasted pine nuts, sautéed, 278

Brussels sprouts with pancetta, sautéed, 293
bulgur
    and lentil pilaf with caramelized onions, 302
    salad, mixed bean and grain, 97
    tabbouleh salad, 300
bulgur wheat, *see* bulgur
burgers, vegetable, 246
burritos, grilled chicken, 176
butter, garlic and parsley, 36
butternut squash
    chickpea and vegetable tagine, 256
    soup with lime gremolata, curried apple, 55

cabbage
    Asian vegetable slaw, 299
    coleslaw, 276
Caesar salad, grilled chicken, 121
cake
    cheesecake, 355
    molten chocolate, 353
Camembert crisps, 44
canapés
    making, 15
    prosciutto and melon, 28
cannellini beans
    puree, 17
    and rosemary ragout, broiled lamb chops and, 164
    salmon with Southwest white bean stew, grilled herbed, 222
    and spinach, orechiette with, 264
cantaloupe canapé, prosciutto and, 28
capers, veal scallopine with lemon and, 146
caramel sauce, classic, 334
carrots
    Asian vegetable slaw, 299
    coleslaw, 276
    and parsnips with herbs, roasted, 273
cashews, spicy roasted, 45
catfish, peanut-crusted, with Creole rémoulade sauce, 211
cheddar cheese for vegetarian refried beans quesadillas, vegetarian, 243
cheese
    pasta quattro formaggi, 257
    see also specific types of cheese
cheesecake, 355

cherries
    chili-roasted peanuts with dried, 47
    clafouti, 361
    filling, brandied, 362
        chocolate crêpes with, 362
chicken
    breasts:
        with artichokes and mustard sauce, 170
        grilled, with pancetta, arugula, and aïoli, 172
        herb-breaded, with creamy mustard sauce, 182
        pesto-stuffed, with tomato relish, 185
        stir-fry, spicy Szechuan, 188
        walnut, 186
    broth with shiitakes, scallions and tofu, double, 69
    burritos, grilled, 176
    butterflying boneless cuts, 169
    cooking techniques, best, 168
    curry with almonds, 183
    doneness temperature and tests, 169
    herb-breaded, with creamy mustard sauce, 182
    jerk, 177
    lemon-ginger grilled, 180
    Moroccan lemon, and mango chutney, 174
    quesadillas, roasted chicken with Jalapeño Jack and mango salsa, 179
    salad:
        Caesar, grilled, 121
        Cobb salad, traditional, 122
        pecan and, grilled, 124
    soup:
        broth with shiitakes, scallions and tofu, double, 69
        and corn, Amish-style, 71
chickpeas
    hlelem (Tunisian vegetable and bean soup), 79
    hummus with pita chips, 21
    salad, mixed bean and grain, 97
    with tomato, zucchini, and cilantro, stewed, 294
    and vegetable tagine, 256
chiles, corn chowder with, and Monterey Jack, 62
chili-roasted peanuts with dried cherries, 47
chipotles, salsa de, 25

chocolate
    cake, molten, 353
    chunk cookies, 343
    crêpes with brandied cherry filling, 362
    fondue, Grand Marnier-honey, 347
    mousse, 363
chorizo
    soup, vegetable and, 76
    strudels, fennel and, 158
chowder
    corn, with chiles and Monterey Jack, 62
    crab and mushroom, 63
    Manhattan clam, 65
    New England clam, 66
chutney
    apple, sautéed pork medallions with, 157
    mango:
        Moroccan lemon chicken and, 174
        spicy, 176
cider
    -braised pork medallions, 152
    and raisin sauce, 335
cilantro
    Asian vegetable slaw, 299
    chickpeas with tomato, zucchini, and, stewed, 294
    fettuccine with corn, squash, chiles, crème fraîche, and, 266
    tofu with red curry paste, peas, scallions, and, 240
    vinaigrette, lime-, 127
        black bean salad with, 282
clafouti, 361
clam chowder
    Manhattan, 65
    New England, 66
Cobb salad
    traditional, 122
    vinaigrette, 126
coconut
    broiled pineapple with, 360
    rice with ginger, 324
cod in a rich broth with fall vegetables, seared, 229
coleslaw, 276
cookie doughs, working with, 333
cookies
    chocolate chunk, 343
    sand, 344

cookies (*continued*)

    Swedish oatmeal, 342

cooking techniques, 9

    en papillote, 202

    grilling, 171

    for pasta, 257

    sautéing, 134

    stir-frying, 237

corn

    chowder with chiles and Monterey Jack, 62

    fettuccine with squash, chiles, crème

        fraîche, cilantro and, 266

    salad, pepper, jicama, and, 313

    soup, Amish-style chicken and, 71

    succotash, lima bean and roasted, 314

Cornish game hens

    cooking techniques, best, 169

    doneness temperature and tests, 169

cornmeal

    cornbread, 316

    for Jalapeño Jack polenta, 311

couscous, 270

    Israeli, herbed, 328

    quick, 328

    salad, mixed bean and grain, 97

crabmeat

    chowder, mushroom and, 63

    salad, avocado and, 42

    and shrimp sandwich, 227

crème fraîche, fettuccine with corn, squash,

    chiles, cilantro, and, 266

crêpes with brandied cherry filling, chocolate,

    362

crostini

    black bean and avocado, 27

    goat cheese and sweet onion, 31

    lobster and prosciutto, 30

    making, 15

    mussel, 33

croutons, homemade, 121

cucumber

    raita, 23

    salad, tomato, feta, and, 94

curry(ied)

    chicken, with almonds, 183

    rice salad, 326

    soup:

        apple squash, with lime gremolata, 55

        Thai fresh pea, 54

tofu with red curry paste, peas, scallions,

    and cilantro, 240

desserts, 331–63

    frozen pastry doughs, 332

    preparation, 332

    working with cookie and pastry doughs, 333

dill rice, spicy, 321

dry rubs, 10

duckling

    breast with Pinot Noir sauce, sautéed, 195

    cooking techniques, best, 168

    shrimp, and andouille gumbo, 193

eggplant

    and Havarti sandwiches, 262

    panini, prosciutto and, 163

    ratatouille, 277

eggs

    fresh fruit sabayon, 360

    soup, egg drop, 70

        stracciatella alla Romana (Roman egg

        drop soup), 70

egg wash, 11

endive, braised Belgian, 290

en papillote, cooking, 202

    bass and scallops, 223–24

    salmon, 216

equipment, 5, 8

espresso-hazelnut brittle, 363

fajitas, vegetable, 245

fennel

    and chorizo strudels, 158

    salad, orange and, 95

feta cheese salad, cucumber, tomato, and, 94

fish, *see* seafood; *specific types of fish*

flounder sauté à la Meunière, 203

freezing, 6

French lentil salad, 89

frisée with walnuts, apples, grapes, and blue

    cheese, 105

fruit, 6–7

    fresh:

        for dessert, 337

        galette, 350

        sabayon, 360

    salad with orange-blossom syrup, 100

    see also specific types of fruit

garlic

    butter, parsley and, 36

    broiled swordfish with tomatoes, anchovies,

        and, 231

gazpacho, chilled, 73

German potato salad, 309

ginger

    coconut rice with, 324

    lemon-, grilled chicken, 180

    sea bass with gingered broth, 205

goat cheese

    baked, with mesclun, pears, and toasted

        almonds, 106

    crostini, sweet onion and, 31

    marinated, with fresh herbs, 37

    and red onion quesadilla, 242

grains, 270

    salad, mixed bean and, 97

    see also specific grains

Grand Marnier-honey chocolate fondue,

    347

grapefruit salad with walnuts and Stilton,

    romaine and, 110

grape leaves, Greek salad with, lemon-infused,

    108

grapes, frisée with walnuts, apples, blue cheese,

    and, 105

Greek salad with grape leaves, lemon-infused,

    108

green beans

    haricots verts, *see* haricots verts

    sweet and sour, 286

    tarragon, 274

grilling, 171

Gruyère

    haricots verts with prosciutto, 289

    potato gratin, 304

    rice salad, 323

guacamole, 18

gumbo, duck, shrimp, and andouille,

    193

halibut with roasted red and yellow pepper

    salad, grilled, 226

ham for turkey club sandwich, 196

haricots verts

    Niçoise-style grilled tuna, 116

    with prosciutto and Gruyère, 289

    with walnuts, 287

Havarti sandwiches, eggplant and, 262
hazelnut-espresso brittle, 363
herbs
    -breaded chicken with creamy mustard
        sauce, 182
      marinated goat cheese with fresh, 37
      salad, spring, 111
        and marinated tomatoes, grilled tuna
          with, 118
honey-mustard sauce, roasted pork tenderloin
    with, 155
hot fudge sauce, 336
hummus with pita chips, 21

Israeli couscous, herbed, 328

Jalapeño Jack
    polenta, 311
    whole wheat quesadillas with roasted
      chicken, mango salsa, and, 179
jalapeños
    fettuccine with corn, squash, crème fraîche,
      cilantro, and, 266
    salsa de chipotles, 25
jerk chicken, 177
jerk pork kebabs, 153
jicama salad, corn, pepper, and, 313

lamb
    chops with white bean and rosemary
      ragout, 164
    removing the silverskin, 131–32
    testing for doneness, 132–33
    trimming before cooking, 129–31
leeks for vichyssoise, 52
legumes, see beans; peas
lemon
    asparagus, pan-steamed, 280
    -ginger grilled chicken, 180
    veal scallopine with capers and,
      146
    vinaigrette, parsley-, 126
lentils
    bulgur and, pilaf with caramelized onions,
      302
    ragout, grilled swordfish with, 219
    salad:
      French lentil, 89
      mixed bean and grain, 97

lima beans
    hlelem (Tunisian vegetable and bean
      soup), 79
    succotash, roasted corn and, 314
lime
    gremolata, curried apple squash soup with,
      55
    vinaigrette, cilantro-, 127
      black bean salad with, 282
lobster
    classic boiled, 230
    crostini, prosciutto and, 30
    salad, roasted red pepper and, 113

mango
    chutney:
      Moroccan lemon chicken with, 174
      spicy, 176
    salsa:
      fiery fruit, 22, 214
      whole wheat quesadillas with roasted
        chicken, Jalapeño Jack, and, 179
    spinach salad with tangerines and, 95
Manhattan clam chowder, 65
marinades, 10
mascarpone cheese for tiramisu, 340
mayonnaise, green, 34
    shrimp open-faced sandwich, 34
meat, 129–65
    beef, see beef
    cuts of, and quick cooking methods, 129–31
    lamb, see lamb
    pork, see pork
    removing the silverskin, 131–32
    testing for doneness, 132–33
    trimming before cooking, 129–31
    veal, see veal
Mediterranean potato salad, 306
Mediterranean salad, 94
melon
    salad, prosciutto and summer, 40
    see also specific types of melon
mesclun
    herb salad, spring, 111
    pears, and toasted almonds, baked goat
      cheese with, 106
minestrone, 77
Monterey Jack, corn chowder with chiles
    and, 62

moo shu vegetables, 254
morels and asparagus, 297
Moroccan lemon chicken and mango chutney,
    174
Moroccan spice crust, seared salmon with a,
    208
mousse, chocolate, 363
mushrooms
    artichokes and, in white wine sauce, 296
    asparagus and morels, 297
    chowder, crab and, 63
    gratin, scallop and, 209
    portobello, Madeira-glazed, 263
    shiitakes, see shiitakes
    soup, cream of, 59
mussels
    cleaning, 218
    crostini, 33
    debearding, 80, 218
    in saffron and white wine broth, 218
    soup, 80
mustard
    chicken breast with artichokes and, sauce,
      170
    -honey sauce, roasted pork tenderloin with,
      155
    sauce, herb-breaded chicken with creamy,
      182
    Thai-spiced loin chops with hot-sweet, 161

New England clam chowder, 66
nuts
    spiced mixed, 45
    see also specific types of nuts

oatmeal cookies, Swedish, 342
olives
    Greek salad with grape leaves, lemon-in-
      fused, 108
    Mediterranean salad, 94
    Niçoise-style grilled tuna, 116
    rice salad, 323
    tapenade, 22
onions
    bulgur and lentil pilaf with caramelized, 302
    goat cheese crostini, sweet onion and, 31
    red, spinach salad with marinated shiitakes
      and, 119
orange-blossom syrup, fruit salad with, 100

oranges
    beef, stir-fry citrus, 135
    blood, warm salad of hearty greens and,
        with tangerine-pineapple vinaigrette,
        102
    salad, fennel and, 95
orechiette with cannellini beans & spinach, 264
orzo, 269
    red pepper, 329
oyster po' boy with rémoulade, 217

pancetta
    Brussels sprouts and, sautéed, 293
    grilled chicken sandwich with arugula, aïoli,
        and, 172
panini, eggplant and prosciutto, 163
pantry, stocking the, 2–4
panzanella (bread salad with fresh tomatoes),
    91
papaya
    and black bean salsa, 24
    salsa, fiery fruit, 22, 214
parchment paper, 202
parsley
    boiled potatoes with saffron and, 310
    butter, garlic and, 36
    vinaigrette, lemon-, 126
parsnips and carrots with herbs, roasted, 273
pasta, 269–70
    bowtie, asparagus with shiitakes, spring
        peas, and, 259
    cooking, 257
    fettuccine:
        with corn, squash, chiles, crème fraîche,
            and cilantro, 266
        veal saltimbocca with, 149–50
    with grilled vegetables, capellini, 260
    orechiette with cannellini beans & spinach,
        264
    puttanesca sauce, sautéed shrimp with
        penne, 210
    quattro formaggi, 257
    swordfish with peppered, grilled, 232
pastry doughs
    frozen, 332
    phyllo dough, see phyllo dough
    preparation of, 332
    tart dough, 361
    working with cookie and, 333

peanuts
    chili-roasted, with dried cherries, 47
    -crusted catfish with Creole rémoulade
        sauce, 211
peanut sauce, Satay of beef with, 141
pears
    baked goat cheese with mesclun, toasted al-
        monds, and, 106
    mixed green salad with walnuts, blue cheese
        and, 103
peas, 270
    Mediterranean salad, 94
    risotto with scallions and, 250
    soup, Thai fresh, 54
    spring, asparagus with shiitakes, bowtie
        pasta, and, 259
    tofu with red curry paste, green onions,
        cilantro, and, 240
pecan
    pies, individual, 354
    salad, grilled chicken and, 124
pesto-stuffed chicken breasts with tomato
    relish, 185
phyllo dough, 332
    apple strudel, 348
    baklava, 349
    berry Napoleon, fresh, 352
    Camembert crisps, 44
    fennel and chorizo strudels, 158
pies, individual pecan, 354
pilaf
    basic rice, 318
    cooking a, 271
    wild rice, 320
pineapple
    with coconut, broiled, 360
    -tangerine vinaigrette, warm salad of
        hearty greens with blood oranges
        and, 102
    vinaigrette, tangerine-, 127
pine nuts, sautéed broccoli rabe with toasted,
    278
pinto beans
    refried beans, vegetarian, 285
        quesadilles, 243
    vegetable fajitas, 245
    vegetarian dirty rice, 317
pita chips, hummus with, 21
polenta, Jalapeño Jack, 311

pork
    bacon, see bacon
    chorizo, see chorizo
    kebabs, jerk, 153
    loin chops with hot-sweet mustard, Thai-
        spiced, 161
    loin with apricot-Armagnac compote,
        roasted, 160
    medallions:
        with apple chutney, sautéed, 157
        cider-braised, 152
        sautéed, with Southwestern-style sauce,
            156
    prosciutto, see prosciutto
    removing the silverskin, 131–32
    tenderloin with honey-mustard sauce, 155
    testing for doneness, 132–33
    trimming before cooking, 129–31
port wine vinaigrette, 128
potato(es), 270
    cakes, sweet, 307
    gratin, 304
    Niçoise-style grilled tuna, 116
    oven-roasted, 304
    puree, 305
    with saffron and parsley, boiled, 310
    salad:
        German, 309
        Mediterranean, 306
        warm, 306
    steak fries, 308
    vichyssoise, 52
poultry, 167–98
    butterflying boneless cuts, 169
    cooking techniques, best quick, 168
    doneness and temperature tests, 168
    safety, 168
    white and dark meat, 167–68
    see also specific types of poultry
prosciutto
    crostini, lobster and, 30
    haricots verts with prosciutto and, 289
    and melon canapé, 28
    panini, eggplant and, 163
    and summer melon salad, 40
    veal saltimbocca with fettuccine, 149–50
pudding
    bread, 358
    rice, 357

puff pastry shells
    baking and filling, 333
    fresh fruit galette, 350
    frozen, 332
    vol au vents with fresh berries and whipped
        cream, 339
puttanesca sauce, sautéed shrimp with penne
    pasta and, 210

quesadillas
    goat cheese and red onion, 242
    with roasted chicken, Jalapeño Jack, and
        mango salsa, whole wheat, 179
    vegetarian refried bean, 243

raisin and cider sauce, 335
raspberry(ies)
    berry Napoleon, fresh, 352
    coulis, 337
    vol au vents with fresh berries and whipped
        cream, 339
ratatouille, 277
red bell peppers
    broccoli and, steamed, 291
    orzo, 329
    ratatouille, 277
    salad:
        corn, jicama, and, 313
        lobster and roasted, 113
    smoked turkey and roasted, sandwich, 190
    and yellow pepper salad, grilled halibut, 226
red onion quesadilla, goat cheese and, 242
refried beans, vegetarian, 285
    quesadillas, 243
relish, pesto-stuffed chicken breasts with
    tomato, 185
remoulade, oyster po' boy with, 217
Reuben sandwich, 137
rice
    coconut, with ginger, 324
    herbed basmati, 327
    pilaf:
        basic, 318
        cooking a, 273
        wild rice, 320
    pudding, 357
    salad, 323
        curried, 326
    spicy dill, 321

tomato soup with basil and, cream of, 60
vegetarian dirty, 317
risotto
    with peas and scallions, 250
    with scallops and asparagus, 221
romaine and grapefruit salad with walnuts and
    Stilton, 110
rosemary and white bean ragout, broiled lamb
    chops with, 164
Russian dressing, 137

saffron
    boiled potatoes with parsley and, 310
    mussels in, with white wine broth, 218
salads, 85–125
    about, 85
    bean and grain, mixed, 97
    beet, roasted, 98
    black bean, with lime-cilantro vinaigrette,
        282
    chicken:
        Caesar, grilled, 121
        Cobb salad, traditional, 122
        and pecan, grilled, 124
    Cobb, traditional, 122
    composed, 102
    corn, pepper, and jicama, 313
    of crab and avocado, 42
    cucumber, tomato, and feta, 94
    frisée with walnuts, apples, grapes, and blue
        cheese, 105
    fruit, with orange-blossom syrup, 100
    goat cheese with mesclun, pears, and
        toasted almonds, baked, 106
    grain and bean, mixed, 97
    Greek salad with grape leaves, lemon-in-
        fused, 108
    herb, spring, 111
    lentil, French, 89
    lobster and roasted red pepper, 113
    Mediterranean, 94
    mixed green, with pears, walnuts, and blue
        cheese, 103
    orange and fennel, 95
    panzanella (bread salad with fresh toma-
        toes), 91
    potato:
        Mediterranean, 306
        warm, 306

preparation, 86–87
prosciutto and summer melon, 40
rice, 323
    curried, 326
romaine and grapefruit, with walnuts and
    Stilton, 110
selection of salad greens, 85–86
soba noodle, 92
spinach:
    with marinated shiitakes and red
        onions, 119
    with tangerines and mango, 95
steak, with horseradish dressing, grilled, 115
tuna:
    Niçoise-style grilled, 116
    with spring herb salad and marinated
        tomatoes, grilled, 118
vinaigrettes, see vinaigrettes
Waldorf, 103
warm, of hearty greens and blood oranges
    with tangerine-pineapple vinaigrette,
    102
washing greens, 86–87
salmon
    en papillote, 216
    grilled herbed, with Southwest white bean
        stew, 222
    seared, with a Moroccan spice crust, 208
salsa
    de chipotle, 25
    fiery fruit, 22, 214
    mango, whole wheat quesadillas with
        roasted chicken, Jalapeño Jack, and, 179
    papaya and black bean, 24
    tomatillo, 16
    tomato, 24
    verde, seared tuna with, 213
salt and pepper, 8
sand cookies, 344
sandwiches
    chicken grilled, with pancetta, arugula, and
        aïoli, 172
    eggplant and Havarti, 262
    Madeira-glazed portobello, 263
    panini, eggplant and prosciutto, 163
    shrimp:
        crabmeat and, 227
        open-faced, 34
    tempeh club, 251

sandwiches (*continued*)
   turkey:
      club, 196
      and roasted red pepper, smoked, 190
Satay of beef with peanut sauce, 141
sausage
   andouille gumbo, duck, shrimp, and, 193
   chorizo, *see* chorizo
sautéing, 134
scallions and peas, risotto with, 250
scallops
   bass and, en papillote, 223–24
   with fiery fruit salsa, seared, 214
   and mushroom gratin, 209
   risotto with asparagus and, 221
sea bass
   with gingered broth, 205
   and scallops en papillote, 223–24
seafood, 199–234
   cooking en papillote, 202
   cooking methods for, best, 200–201
   cutting up a whole fillet into individual
      servings, 203
   shopping for, 199–201
seasonings, about, 9–10
seeds, toasting, 9
sesame sauce, broccoli and orange-, 291
shellfish, *see* seafood; *specific types of fish*
shiitakes
   asparagus with, bowtie pasta, and spring
      peas, 259
   chicken broth with scallions, tofu, and,
      double, 69
   spinach salad with marinated, and red
      onions, 119
shrimp
   bisque with fresh tarragon, 68
   cocktail, 44
   duck, and andouille gumbo, 193
   sandwich:
      crabmeat and, 227
      open-faced, 34
   sautéed, with penne pasta and puttanesca
      sauce, 210
   soup, Thai hot and sour, 82
   spicy Asian grilled, 206
side dishes, 267–329
soba noodles, 270
   salad, 92

soups, 49–84
   about, 49
   avocado, chilled cream of, 57
   black bean, traditional, 56
   borscht, 74
   chicken:
      broth with shiitakes, scallions and tofu,
         double, 69
      and corn, Amish-style, 71
   chorizo and vegetable, 76
   chowder:
      corn, with chiles and Monterey Jack, 62
      crab and mushroom, 63
      Manhattan clam, 65
      New England clam, 66
   corn chowder with chiles and Monterey
      Jack, 62
   cream:
      of avocado, chilled, 57
      corn chowder with chiles and Monterey
         Jack, 62
      evaluating the quality of, 56
      of mushroom, 59
      New England clam chowder, 66
      preparation of, 51
      shrimp bisque with fresh tarragon, 68
      of tomato, with rice and basil, 60
   curried:
      apple squash soup with lime gremolata,
         55
      Thai fresh pea soup, 54
   egg drop, 70
      stracciatella alla Romana (Roman egg
         drop soup), 70
   evaluating the quality of puree and cream, 56
   gazpacho, chilled, 73
   ingredients, 49–50
   minestrone, 77
   mussel, 80
   pea, Thai fresh, 54
   preparing and serving, 50–51
   Thai hot and sour, 82
   tomato, with rice and basil, cream of, 60
   tortilla, 84
   vegetable:
      chorizo and, 76
      hlelem (Tunisian vegetable and bean
         soup), 79
      minestrone, 77

spices, toasting, 9
spinach
   orechiette with cannellini beans &, 264
   salad:
      with marinated shiitakes and red
         onions, 119
      with tangerines and mango, 95
   stracciatella alla Romana (Roman egg drop
      soup), 70
steak, *see* beef
stew
   chickpeas:
      with tomato, zucchini, and cilantro, 294
      and vegetable tagine, 256
   vegetable, 239
Stilton cheese, romaine and grapefruit salad
      with walnuts and, 110
stir-frying, 237
   garden vegetables with marinated tofu, 248
   spicy Szechuan chicken, 188
storage tips, 6–8
strudel, apple, 348
Swedish oatmeal cookies, 342
Swiss chard, sautéed, 279
Swiss cheese for Reuben sandwich, 137
swordfish
   with lentil ragout, grilled, 219
   with peppered pasta, grilled, 232
   with tomatoes, anchovies, and garlic,
      broiled, 231
Szechuan chicken stir-fry, spicy, 188

tabbouleh salad, 300
tagine, chickpea and vegetable, 256
tangerines
   -pineapple vinaigrette, warm salad of hearty
      greens and blood oranges with, 102
   spinach salad with mango and, 95
   vinaigrette, pineapple-, 127
tapenade, 22
tarragon
   green beans, 274
   shrimp bisque with fresh, 68
tart dough, 361
tempeh club sandwich, 251
Thai fresh pea soup, 54
Thai hot and sour soup, 82
Thai-spiced loin chops with hot-sweet mus-
      tard, 161

time-saving tips, 6–9
tiramisu, 340
toasting seeds or spices, 9
tofu
 chicken broth with shiitakes, scallions and, double, 69
 with red curry paste, peas, scallions, and cilantro, 240
 stir-fried garden vegetables with marinated, 248
tomatillo salsa, 16
 verde, seared tuna with, 213
tomato(es)
 chickpeas with zucchini, cilantro, and, stewed, 294
 gazpacho, chilled, 73
 marinated, grilled tuna with spring herb salad and, 118
 panzanella (bread salad with fresh tomatoes), 91
 ratatouille, 277
 relish, pesto-stuffed chicken breasts with, 185
 salad, cucumber, feta, and, 94
 salsa, 24
  de chipotle, 25
 soup:
  Manhattan clam chowder, 65
  with rice and basil, cream of, 60
 swordfish with anchovies, garlic, and, broiled, 231
 tabbouleh salad, 300
tortillas for quesadillas, see quesadillas
truffle oil, spring herb salad, 111
tuna
 Niçoise-style grilled, 116
 seared, with salsa verde, 213
 with spring herb salad and marinated tomatoes, grilled, 118
turkey
 burger, 191
 club sandwich, 196
 smoked, and roasted red pepper sandwich, 190

vanilla sauce, 335
veal
 cutlets, pan-fried, 148
 removing the silverskin, 131–32
 saltimbocca with fettuccine, 149–50
 scallopine with lemon and capers, 146
 testing for doneness, 132–33
 trimming before cooking, 129–31
vegetables, 7
 burgers, 246
 capellini with grilled, 260
 cooking, 268–69
 fall, seared cod in a rich broth with, 229
 grilled, 284
  appetizer, 39
 moo shu, 254
 ratatouille, 277
 sauté, spicy, 253
 slaw, warm, 276
 soups, see soups, vegetable
 stew, 239
 stir-fried garden, with marinated tofu, 248
 see also individual vegetables
vegetarian dishes, 235–66
 tips for quick, 236
vichyssoise, 52
Vidalia onions crostini, goat cheese and, 31
vinaigrettes
 balsamic, 128
 Cobb salad, 126
 lemon-parsley, 126
 lime-cilantro, 127
  black bean salad with, 282
 making a basic, 88
 port wine, 128
 tangerine-pineapple, 127
  warm salad of hearty greens with blood oranges with, 102
vol au vents with fresh berries and whipped cream, 339

Waldorf salad, 103
walnuts
 baklava, 349

chicken, 186
 salad:
  frisée with apples, grapes, blue cheese and, 105
  mixed green, with pears, blue cheese, and, 103
  romaine and grapefruit, with Stilton and, 110
  Waldorf, 103
whipped cream, vol au vents with fresh berries and, 339
wild rice pilaf, 320
wine
 artichokes and mushrooms in white, sauce, 296
 Madeira-glazed portobello sandwiches, 263
 mussels in saffron and white wine broth, 218
 Pinot Noir sauce, sautéed duck breast with, 195
 port, vinaigrette, 128
wonton chips with Asian-style dipping sauce, 20

yellow and red roasted pepper salad, grilled halibut and, 226
yellow squash
 noodles, pan-steamed zucchini and, 281
 ratatouille, 277
 summer squash sauté, 280
yogurt
 avocado, chilled cream of, 57
 cucumber raita, 23

zabaglione, see sabayon
zucchini
 chickpeas with tomato, cilantro, and, stewed, 294
 fettuccine with corn, chiles, crème fraîche, cilantro and, 266
 pan-steamed, and yellow squash noodles, 281
 ratatouille, 277
 summer squash sauté, 280